D0801348

THE PAPACY AND THE MIDDLE EAST

The Papacy and the Middle East

The Role of the Holy See in the
Arab-Israeli Conflict, 1962-1984

George Emile Irani

UNIVERSITY OF NOTRE DAME PRESS
NOTRE DAME, INDIANA 46556

Copyright © 1986 by
University of Notre Dame Press
Notre Dame, Indiana 46556
All Rights Reserved

Manufactured in the United States of America

Library of Congress Cataloging-in-Publication Data

Irani, George Emile.
   The Papacy and the Middle East.

   Bibliography: p.
   Includes index.
   1. Catholic Church—Relations (diplomatic)—
Arab countries.   2. Arab countries—Foreign
relations—Catholic Church.   3. Catholic Church—
Relations (diplomatic)—Israel.   4. Israel—Foreign
relations—Catholic Church.   5. Jewish-Arab rela-
tions—1949-   .   I. Title.
BX1617.I73 1986   327.45'634'056   85-41013
ISBN 0-268-01560-0

TO MY LATE FATHER, EMILE, WHOSE
ENCOURAGEMENT AND SUPPORT MADE
THE COMPLETION OF THIS BOOK POSSIBLE

Contents

Foreword

A THOROUGH EXAMINATION of the role of the Vatican in the Near East is of fundamental importance to the expert in Middle Eastern affairs, to the analyst of Church activities and behavior, and to all those concerned with finding a satisfactory and lasting solution to the Arab-Israeli predicament.

The value of this book resides in its uniqueness. George Irani has succeeded in pulling together and giving cohesiveness to a wealth of widely dispersed materials. Twenty years ago Vatican II opened wide the doors to ecumenism and interfaith relations. The interactions of Jews, Christians, and Muslims in the Jerusalem issue, the Lebanese War, and the Israeli-Palestinian dispute, illustrate the advantages and shortcomings of the movement that was the fruit of Pope John XXIII's initiative.

Another value of this book stems from the objectivity that the author has tried to maintain in his analysis. Well aware of the difficulty in remaining neutral in such a highly passionate and partisan conflict, Irani has accomplished a kind of tour de force in bringing together the Jewish, Christian, and Islamic perspectives. Thus, it is not surprising that a Lebanese scholar has attempted to show the common denominators that unite the three monotheistic religions. Behind this work is a hope that the day will soon come when Lebanon and the Middle East will once again be a living example of peaceful coexistence and dialogue.

Another major contribution that this book brings to the literature on the Holy See is the use of case studies to extricate and explicate complex situations. The author has attempted to demonstrate the interrelations of the three issue-areas he has selected for his analysis. In a more figurative

sense these three issues—Lebanon, Jerusalem, and the Israeli-
Palestinian dispute—constitute, each on its own, a separate
and distinct microcosm of local, regional, and global conflicts. The Lebanese War by itself—the fifth Arab-Israeli war
since 1948—has challenged the Papacy to channel its resources and diplomatic capabilities into the effort to put an
end to the bloodshed. The attention that has been given to
Lebanon is rare in the annals of contemporary Vatican diplomacy. If Lebanon were to wither away, the whole concept of ecumenism and interfaith dialogue would be dis-
credited. Jerusalem is another microcosm. It also contains
all the tensions and contradictions of the Arab-Israeli conflict, but in addition the Holy City has within its walls centuries of religious rivalries. Any resolution to the question
of Jerusalem would therefore require a better understanding
and closer cooperation between the followers of the three
monotheistic faiths. Finally, the Israeli-Palestinian dispute
is the macro-conflict that contains all the elements of the
other two issue-areas.

Irani makes thorough use of sources in four languages—
Arabic, French, English, and Italian—with attention to the
nuances of the original language of a speech or statement.
This is of crucial importance since an understanding of papal
activities and the way policies are conceived by the Holy
See requires close scrutiny of verbal and written statements.
Also, the author has personally visited Lebanon, Israel, and
Vatican City. His commendable efforts serve to remind re-
searchers, particularly those involved in Middle Eastern
issues, that scholarship still has as one of its main aims
educare—to teach, lead, and enlighten.

Finally, this book provides a reference for those interested
in Church affairs in the Levant. I strongly believe that this
work will become a benchmark for future studies on papal
diplomacy in the Middle East.

Rev. Theodore M. Hesburgh, C.S.C.
President,
University of Notre Dame

Acknowledgments

I WISH TO EXPRESS my deepest gratitude to many persons whose assistance and knowledge have contributed to the writing of this book. Special thanks are due to Professor Michael G. Fry, director of the School of International Relations at the University of Southern California, who suggested the topic of this endeavor. My lasting gratitude goes to Professor Gunnar P. Nielsson, who assiduously and attentively followed my steps since I began my academic career at the University of Southern California in 1978. Special thanks are due to Father Joseph L. Ryan, S.J., of the Pontifical Mission for Palestine, whose guidance and help were invaluable. Many thanks go to Dr. Cesar G. Nasr of the House of the Future, Beirut, and Dr. Edy Kaufman of the H. S. Truman Research Institute for the Advancement of Peace, Jerusalem. Thanks also to Robert Vaillancourt and the USC Santa Barbara Circle, Joan Palevsky, Dr. Jo-Ann Ratcliff, and Sharon Carpenter whose help and generosity have been sincerely appreciated. Special thanks are due to Maxine Pennington who carefully undertook the typing of this manuscript. To my wife Sarah who courageously and patiently supported this undertaking I will be forever grateful.

Introduction

THIS BOOK EXPLORES THE diplomatic, religious, and humanitarian roles of the Holy See in the Arab-Israeli conflict.[1] Chronologically, the period covered begins with the inauguration of the Second Vatican Council in 1962 and concludes with Pope John Paul II's pastoral letters on Jerusalem and Lebanon in the spring of 1984.

The book was born of a necessity created by the absence of any comprehensive scholarly work on the overall role and attitude of the Holy See in the contemporary Middle East. The role of the Papacy in this part of the world has not been given the attention it deserves. Church historians and political scientists have found themselves separated by the political divide that inevitably mars research on the Arab-Israeli conflict. Because of the conflictual presence of three religions, the Middle East is a classic case study of the interaction of faith and politics.

Papal involvement in the Middle East has come to occupy a place of importance on the Holy See's scale of priorities which is essentially motivated by a concern to protect the welfare of Catholic minorities, to promote peaceful coexistence, and to win respect for the human rights of Jews, Christians, and Muslims.

The Arab-Israeli conflict that came to the fore with the clash between Palestinian and Israeli claims over Palestine has placed the Holy See in a difficult situation by forcing the Papacy and the Church to reassess their attitudes and long-held prejudices with respect to both Jews and Muslims. This change in policy, however, was not without its own inherent ambiguities. The Holy See has had to maintain an

1

attitude of impartiality, sometimes to the detriment of Eastern Christian, mostly Catholic, communities. The Papacy's
predicament is further complicated by the fact that the three
monotheistic religions—Jewish, Christian, and Muslim—
are interlocked in a battle for survival, a battle entailing
ethno-nationalist implications in the yearning for nationhood
harbored by persecuted minorities.

The presence of the Catholic Church in the Levant goes
far back in history, when its fate was linked to that of European imperial and colonial powers. At a later stage the
Papacy's approach to the Middle East was largely guided
by the geopolitical and cultural interests that Protestant and
Catholic temporal rulers deemed of high priority in the area.
Following World War II and the process of decolonization,
the Holy See has had to rethink its policy in light of the
changes elaborated in the Second Vatican Council.

The impact of Vatican II on papal diplomacy is defined
in the encyclicals of Pope John XXIII (*Mater et Magistra*,
1971; *Pacem in Terris*, 1963) and Pope Paul VI (*Populorum
Progressio*, 1967). The fundamental aims of Vatican diplomacy evolved around the preservation of the faith, the fostering of peace with the consolidation of justice, and the
Church's aim to act as a moral guide on issues of social
justice, hunger, and the arms race. In order to attain these
objectives the Catholic Church's transnational network was
mobilized and more freedom was given to the bishops in
formulating their decisions. In addition the Pope's moral and
spiritual prestige became fundamental to the carrying out
of the Holy See's pastoral and humanitarian activities.

In contrast to its interaction with European and Latin
American states, the Holy See, as a diplomatic and religious
agent in the Arab-Israeli conflict, is dealing with a majority
of non-Catholics and non-Christians. In the Middle East the
Holy See must always draw a clear distinction between the
religious and political realms—*homo religiosus* and *homo
laicus*. Nevertheless, given the pervasive importance of religion in the daily lives of Middle Easterners, matters of faith

and politics cannot be easily dissociated. In the Levant, the Papacy represents a faith, the Catholic faith, whereas Judaism and Islam embody both religion and nationalism. This difference is at the root of misunderstandings that hinder the Holy See in its activities in the area.

An important innovation that came in the wake of Vatican II was the creation and fostering of interfaith and ecumenical dialogues with non-Christian and other Christian denominations. The Papacy felt that the only way it could get its message through and, at the same time, protect the welfare of Catholics was to establish relations based on mutual respect and trust—that is, dialogue. But since then, religious and political factors have been such that the dialogue in its two aspects—ecumenical and interfaith—is still a matter of intellectual debate, especially in the Arab-Israeli conflict where interaction at the grassroot level is one of hostility and confrontation.

Related to the difficulties inherent in this dialogue is the issue of the fate of Christian communities in the Middle East. Depending on the societies in which they live, Middle Eastern Christians differ in their relations and attitudes towards both Judaism and Islam. What characterizes these communities is their status of being "minorities three times over—as Arabs among Jews, Christian Arabs among Arab Muslims, and minorities within the larger Christian society."[2] This situation results in conflicting Christian attitudes toward political problems emerging from the war between Arabs and Israelis. An illustration is given by the hostile attitude towards Arabism and Islam—partly provoked by Palestinian activism in Lebanese politics—among some elements in the Christian community in Lebanon. On the other hand, Palestinian Christians, because of their minority status and their opposition to Israeli authorities, have been reinforced in their identification as Arabs and thus feel more deeply rooted in Arab and Islamic nationalism.

Another important problem facing the Papacy is the ever increasing migration of Christians from the Holy Land. This migratory trend is caused by the scarcity of jobs for Palestinians with graduate school degrees and by the difficulties of their crossing the border to enter Jordan. The implication for the Holy See is that, with the decrease in the number of Christians, Rome has less claim to a say in matters related to the fate of Catholic communities and institutions in the Holy Land. Consequently, a reduced presence of the Church in the Levant would be a symbolic blow to the prestige of the Papacy. The birthplace of Christ would be devoid of the active and proselytic presence of Catholics and Christians.

In this book, the Holy See is conceptualized as a transnational actor. According to Ivan Vallier, an important observer of the Catholic Church:

A nation-state that is closely linked with extranational systems and that holds key positions of power and prestige in those international systems is, in fact, no longer a nation-state but a transnational actor.[3]

The Holy See as a transnational actor does not have significant industrial capabilities or a military presence to wield power and influence. In the case of the Holy See, power and influence rest fundamentally on the moral prestige of the Pope as the head of the Catholic Church and on the importance of Catholic communities in a given society. In conflict situations, the Holy See tries to mediate between warring groups and utilizes the transnational network of the Church for two main purposes: (1) to provide humanitarian relief and (2) to request the help of external powers to stop bloodshed.

The major element that differentiates the Catholic Church from other Christian groups is that it can rely on a juridically recognized and a hierarchally organized city-state, the Vatican, as a platform for its various activities. Furthermore, the figure of the Pope as the "global apex of sacred authority and religious symbolism"[4] distinguishes the Catholic Church from other Christian and non-Christian denominations. In somewhat of an overstatement, a Vatican official suggested to me that the Holy See is to Christendom what the United States is to NATO or the Soviet Union to members of the Warsaw Pact.[5]

The uniqueness of the Holy See as a transnational actor stems from the prestige enjoyed by the sovereign pontiff and the symbolism surrounding papal statements and actions. The prestige of the Pope as a participant in global affairs differs from the concrete power wielded by temporal rulers, who rely on their military and economic resources to attain their goals. In the final analysis, the Pope cannot threaten and this fact gives to his words and actions a weight that is mainly based on the universal and religious character of his mission.

Related to the uniqueness of the Papacy as an institution is its power as a symbol. A papal statement or editorial published by *L'Osservatore Romano* is important because of the message it carries. The Holy See has no means of enforcing what it says, but its word, in its symbolic value, has great weight.

Finally, the issues and the participants in Middle East conflicts offer an opportunity for the Holy See to advocate peace through justice. For instance, both in Lebanon and Jerusalem we find followers of Judaism, Christianity, and Islam interacting peacefully or aggressively. This situation prods the Papacy to demonstrate its skills in developing interfaith relations and encouraging antagonistic parties to settle their disputes in full respect of religious and human rights.

In this book "role" is defined as the pattern of routinized participation and interaction. The extent and nature of the Holy See's involvement is analyzed in terms of the events and circumstances to which it chooses to respond or react. The nature of the role is scrutinized in order to assess whether the Holy See limits itself to the gathering of information and the expressing of opinions or whether it opts for a more active and direct role, such as the sending of mediation missions. In addition, reactions to any statement or action undertaken by the Holy See are examined in order to evaluate the impact of papal diplomacy. These reactions are gleaned from declarations of approval or disapproval issued by governmental figures, members of nonstate groups such as guerrilla movements or militias, and members of the clergy.

The role of the Holy See is analyzed by an examination of the following issue-areas: (1) the Israeli-Palestinian dispute, (2) the status of Jerusalem and the Holy Places, and (3) the Lebanese War that erupted in 1975. In all three issue-areas, the Papacy has major stakes in terms of principles and interests. These three historical issue-areas were selected because of their relevance to and significance in papal teachings and diplomacy.

The main assumption underlying this book is that two fundamental interests guide papal involvement in the Middle East: (1) protection of the welfare of Catholics and (2) the fostering of coexistence and dialogue between the followers of the three monotheistic faiths — Judaism, Christianity, and Islam. In some instances one of these two interests dominates papal concerns and the other is downgraded, a fluctuation that stems from the readiness of third parties to dialogue and from the degree of threat facing Catholic and Christian minorities. A corollary to this assumption would be that the role of the Holy See in the Arab-Israeli conflict is also shaped by papal teachings that advocate the consolidation of peace through justice.

The Papacy's commitment to the right of peoples to self-determination guides the humanitarian aspects of the Holy See's intervention in the Israeli-Palestinian dispute. Diplomatically, the Holy See has in essence made a preferential choice between the Palestinians and the Israelis, but conducts its affairs in ways that demonstrate that it seeks to retain an influential role. Finally, in a conflict opposing the Israeli government to local Catholic groups, the Holy See is bound to seek to protect the interests of the local church, to the detriment of improving its relations with the Jewish state.

Regarding Jerusalem and the Holy Places, the Holy See's policy is based on the universal and spiritual significance of the city to Jews, Christians, and Muslims and on the protection of the civil and religious rights of Christian and Muslim communities. The Holy See is opposed to any political control or religious exclusivity in regard to the Holy Places.

In Lebanon the approach of the Holy See is fundamentally guided by the goal of fostering peaceful coexistence between Christians and Muslims as a way of saving the Christian community. Nevertheless, some Catholics in Lebanon do not totally share the Papacy's advocacy of ecumenism and interfaith relations; these Catholics constitute an obstacle to Rome's objectives in Lebanon. The Maronite leadership sees itself victimized by Rome's hope to play a role in the much larger Islamic world, for whom the Lebanese conflict is an embarrassment. More recently, however, with the increasing strength of Islamic revivalism, some non-Christian Lebanese leaders have come out against Pope John Paul II and his policies vis-à-vis other parts of the world and Lebanon, while dissidents in the Maronite community have expressed renewed faith in the Holy See's capabilities in helping resolve their predicament as a minority.

Given the relative unavailability of Vatican documents related to the period under scrutiny, I undertook a four-month intensive field research trip to Beirut, Jerusalem, and Rome (March to July 1983). Overall, I conducted sixty interviews with, among others, former ambassadors to the Holy See, scholars involved in Christian-Islamic and Christian-Jewish dialogue, and members of the clergy. Moreover, in Beirut, Jerusalem, and Rome some Vatican officials were interviewed. Their information and guidance were of great help in organizing the research material for this book.

The archives of the House of the Future, Beirut, and those of the Harry S. Truman Research Institute at the Hebrew University, Jerusalem, were invaluable and yielded several documents that would have been otherwise unavailable for

research. Furthermore, the files of *L'Osservatore Romano*
and those of the Middle East Council of Churches in Beirut
were examined. Secondary sources included *Proche-Orient
Chrétien*, an important journal published by the White
Fathers in Jerusalem and considered to be one of the most
reliable sources on Eastern Christian Churches. In addition to Lebanese and Israeli newspapers and magazines, the
general literature (in Arabic, French, English, and Italian)
relating to Church involvement in international affairs was
also researched.

This book has as its fundamental objective that of opening new perspectives for research on papal diplomacy. For
example, How does the interplay of religion and politics affect interstate and transnational relations? What does the
figure of the Pope represent at the end of the twentieth century, especially to the followers of non-Christian but monotheistic religions? What is the importance of symbolism,
especially in the case of papal diplomacy?

It is certainly time that the significance of religions and
ethics be included so as to widen the scope of our understanding of interstate and transnational relations. This is
true all the more now that religion has come increasingly
to the fore, especially in the Middle East, as illustrated by
the resurgence of Jewish, Christian, and Islamic revivalisms.

1. The Holy See and the Israeli-Palestinian Dispute

THE ISRAELI-PALESTINIAN DISPUTE, which began early in this century, constitutes a fundamental challenge to the interests of the Holy See. This challenge stems from the long-held misperceptions that exist between Catholics and Jews and from the Church's attitude toward Zionism.

The key problem faced by the Holy See is that Judaism is a "religion with a national basis and a nation with a religious mission."[1] This factor and the creation of the state of Israel as a "national home for the Jewish people"[2] present the Holy See with a dilemma of major proportions. This dilemma stems essentially from the theocratic nature of the Jewish state, which is in diametric opposition to the Papacy's objective of drawing a clear distinction between affairs that are temporal in nature and affairs that are spiritual in nature.

The other facet of the dilemma is that the interests of the Holy See in the Israeli-Palestinian dispute include the fate and welfare of Catholic minorities living in the Holy Land—especially West Bank minorities—and in Arab-Islamic countries, as well as the status of Jerusalem and the Holy Places. In fact, and in light of these interests, the Holy See has opted to pursue its interfaith relations with Islam, thereby protecting the Catholic community. The commonality of interests between the Holy See and the Arab-Islamic states is more pronounced and less controversial than are the Holy See's interests with the Jewish state.

The purpose of this chapter is to assess the role of the Holy See in the Israeli-Palestinian dispute, an involvement rooted in the Church's advocacy of social justice and its own mandate to care for endangered Catholic minorities. Therefore, involvement is executed on two interrelated levels: the humanitarian-religious level and the diplomatic level. Three propositions have directed my analysis:

1. The humanitarian aspects of the Holy See's involvement in the Israeli-Palestinian dispute are guided by the Papacy's commitment to the right of peoples to self-determination and the fostering of peace through justice.
2. The Holy See has in essence made a preferential choice between the Palestinians and the Israelis, but conducts its affairs in ways that demonstrate that it seeks to retain an influential and mediatory role.
3. In a conflict between the Israeli government and Catholic groups, the Holy See is bound to seek to protect the interests of the local Church.

Essentially, the propositions argue that when Catholics are threatened, the Holy See will move to protect them. I have selected five test cases to illustrate the humanitarian and religious aspects of papal involvement, as well as the use of diplomatic efforts to complement the Holy See's humanitarian and religious activities. Bethlehem University and the Pontifical Mission for Palestine are examples of Catholic institutions created to help the Palestinians, and the case involving Bishop Hilarion Capucci is an example of how the Holy See considers interfaith relations of lower priority than saving the Catholic minority in the Holy Land. The other cases center on the diplomatic role of the Holy See in the conflict between Israelis and Palestinians: the 1968 Israeli raid in Beirut, and a comparative test case involving the meeting between Pope Paul VI and Israeli Prime Minister Golda Meir and Pope John Paul II's meeting with PLO Chairman Yasser Arafat.

The Israeli-Palestinian dispute has political, socio-economic, and psychological dimensions. At the core of this conflict lie the disjunctive claims of two peoples—the Israelis and the Palestinians—who, for their own historical reasons, found themselves entangled in a series of tragic events. This tension led to military conflicts between Arab and Israeli armies in 1948, 1956, 1967, and 1973.[3]

The political causes of the dispute are based on the Zionists' determination to establish a state for the Jews in Palestine and on the rejection of Zionist schemes by the local Palestinian population — a rejection later evolving into militant and military opposition. The arrival of Jewish settlers in Palestine coincided with the colonial trend that characterized the policies of some West European countries (Britain, France, Germany, Italy) and the increased struggle for self-determination by the Arabs under Ottoman rule.

The question of Palestine had other roots as well: (1) Britain did not honor its promises for independence made to the Arab leadership in the First World War; (2) the Palestinians perceived that the arrival of a nonindigenous population was bent on tilting the local equilibrium in its favor, given substantial external support by Jewish and Zionist groups; and (3) Jewish settlements in Palestine were viewed as a continuation of the *mission civilisatrice* that had justified most of the European colonial endeavor.[4] In fact, the Zionists convinced the British that Palestine, "a land without people," was there for the Jews to settle, serving both Zionist aims and British imperial policies.[5]

At the socio-economic level, the Israeli-Palestinian dispute is a microcosm of the ongoing struggle between the developed industrialized North and the developing countries of the South. Jewish settlers who had fought in European wars and who had contributed significantly to Western cultural values clashed with the Palestinian and Arab populations trying to liberate themselves from the yoke of centuries of Turkish domination. One of the key factors in the struggle was the organizational gap between a deeply committed Jewish community in diaspora and the still disorganized and embryonic nature of Arab politics.

Moreover, the Israeli-Palestinian dispute has psychological dimensions involving the importance of land, and a sense of insecurity. Being both victims and victimizers, Israelis and Palestinians are the mirror image of each other. Both peoples are continually trying to secure some kind of firm identity for themselves. For example, it is a complicated matter for Arab Christians who are also Israeli citizens to define their identity. The same applies to Israelis who came from very different societies, such as the United States or North Africa. They all share the same citizenship but their different cultural background renders difficult their total assimilation into the Israeli body politic.

The murkiness in the identity of Palestinians and Israelis creates a problem of constant insecurity and fear one of the other. This sense of insecurity is reflected in the claims and attachment that both groups have to the land of Palestine. The legitimacy of the Israeli claim is challenged by the historical roots of the Palestinian presence in the Holy Land.

In the Israeli-Palestinian dispute, the Holy See has elected to follow a policy that establishes its role as one of mediator, moderator, and conciliator between Arabs and Israelis, Muslims and Jews, Muslims and Christians, and Jews and Christians. This policy is not substantially different from the one followed by the Holy See in the Lebanese War that erupted in 1975. The nature of the Holy See's intervention in the Holy Land was defined by Monsignor William F. Murphy, under secretary of the Pontifical Justice and Peace Commission, in an address delivered in Boston in May 1983:

> [the Holy See intends] to offer its services and good offices, such as by arbitration and mediation, in any and every way that is consistent with its spiritual mission. It does not seek to offer technical solutions outside its competence, but rather wishes to be at the service of all in finding the ways to a just and lasting peace that will guarantee the legitimate rights of all involved.[6]

In this cautiously worded statement, the Holy See elucidated a policy that evolves around three key principles: (1) the Papacy intends to act as a mediator between Arabs and

Israelis; (2) the Holy See, given its nature as a religious institution, does not seek to advance practical solutions to the dispute, but will act as a facilitator; and (3) the Holy See recognizes the legitimate rights of both Israelis and Palestinians. However, a close reading of the text indicates the narrow path available for intervention by the Holy See. The rights of Palestinians and Israelis are in radical and apparently irreconcilable opposition. The Israelis deny the existence of Palestinian rights, and the Palestinians assert that their national claims are more justified by historical facts and societal realities. Therefore, the Papacy confronts, in addition to the religious dimensions of the conflict, the task of narrowing the gap between these two peoples. Furthermore, the Holy See is not an impartial actor in the dispute. It has temporal and spiritual interests to defend in the Holy Land, which in some instances reduce its margin of maneuverability and its credibility as a disinterested mediator.

THE HOLY SEE VIS-À-VIS JUDAISM, ISRAEL, AND THE PALESTINIANS

A major turning point in the Catholic Church's attitude toward Judaism occurred in the Second Vatican Council (1962–1965). The debates during Vatican II envisaged, among other issues, clearing Christian teachings of all anti-Semitic remnants and establishing a frank dialogue between the Catholic Church and Judaism.[7]

The basic attitude of the Church toward Judaism has been expressed in the conciliar Declaration on the Relationship of the Church to Non-Christian Religions (*Nostra Aetate*) issued on October 28, 1965.[8] The declaration stated that responsibility for the death of Christ cannot be "blamed upon all Jews then living, without distinction, nor upon the Jews of today." Deploring "the hatred, persecutions, and displays of anti-Semitism directed against the Jews at any time and from any source," *Nostra Aetate* stated that "although the Church is the New People of God, the Jews should not be presented as repudiated or cursed by God, as if such views followed from the Holy Scriptures."[9] The conciliar declaration, recognizing and stressing the common spiritual heritage of Christians and Jews, wished "to foster and recommend that mutual understanding and respect which is the fruit above all of biblical and theological studies, and of brotherly dialogues."[10]

In light of the conciliar recommendations, Catholics initiated a campaign to eliminate from their liturgy all statements unfavorable to Jews. Moreover, Catholic-Jewish dialogue was institutionalized with the creation in 1970 of the International Catholic-Jewish Liaison Committee, which brought together five Vatican representatives and delegates from the five most important Jewish organizations in the world (the Jewish Council in Israel for Interreligious Consultation, the World Jewish Congress, the Anti-Defamation League of B'nai B'rith, the American Jewish Committee, and the Synagogue Council of America). In addition to this committee, whose purpose was to foster reciprocal understanding between the followers of the two faiths, the Holy See established in 1974 the Pontifical Commission for Religious Relations with Judaism, which is linked to the Secretariat for Christian Unity. Father Marcel Dubois described this decision of the Holy See as "a sign of the Catholic Church's growing awareness of its bond with the people of the Bible."[11]

The initiative taken by some conciliar fathers to oppose the conciliar statements on Judaism generated ardent internal debate and elicited highly emotional reactions from individuals and organizations directly involved in the Israeli-Palestinian dispute. This occurred despite the incessant statements from the Holy See on the purely religious significance of *Nostra Aetate*.

From the Jewish standpoint, the main contention was that the Catholic Church's declaration had been considerably watered down to please conservative prelates in the Roman Curia and as a result of pressures from Arab bishops and politicians.[12] Another point raised by Jewish and other observers was that Vatican II, in speaking of the Jews (*Nostra Aetate*, no. 4), had to take into consideration other important facts pertinent to its presence and interests in Arab countries. Writing under a pseudonym, Malachi Martin observed:

> The Vatican is sensitive to Arab pressure for a variety of reasons. First of all, most of the Catholics in the Middle East live in Arab lands, speak Arabic as their daily language, are drawn from Moslem stock. The major Catholic Holy Places are in Jordan [this article was written in 1965]. The vast majority of Church possessions in the Middle East — lands, monasteries, schools, churches — are in Arab lands. And the vast majority of Christian communities not yet in communion with Rome live in Arab lands and partake of Arabic culture. . . . Finally, Vatican foreign policy is tied to the foreign policy of Italy, which means, among other things, that the Church's financial interests are involved with those of Italian capital — and the natural markets of Italy lie along the southern and eastern shores of the Mediterranean, the lands of the Maghreb and the Levant, whose Arab rulers must be kept as friendly as possible.[13]

The importance of economic interests as one of the crucial factors guiding Holy See policy in the Middle East was also raised by other Jewish and non-Jewish observers. For instance, Dr. Geofrey Wigoder stated that he would not dismiss Martin's thesis lightly.[14] Moreover, in his study on the Vatican and Judaism, Rabbi Rose wrote:

> Assuming that it is true that there are some Italian economic interests in North Africa and in the Arab states, aware also of the very real Arab boycott against businesses all over the world which deal with Israel, it is most logical to conclude that Arab threats extended to these Italian financial circles and to the Vatican itself.[15]

Edmond Rabbath, a Lebanese scholar, does not exclude the importance of economic factors, but cautions:

This is a nebulous subject and it would be very difficult
to find documents on this subject. The Papacy has always
acted with an impenetrable and absolute discretion.[16]

On the Arab and Palestinian side, the main fear was that
Zionists would use the Vatican II declaration on Judaism
to obtain official diplomatic recognition of the state of Israel.
During the conciliar debates, the Israeli ambassador to Italy
and some Jewish groups were very active in mustering support for *Nostra Aetate*.

In a book entitled *We, the Vatican, and Israel*, published
by the PLO Research Center in Beirut, the PLO claimed that
the Zionists were playing on the guilt feelings of the Church
in the aftermath of the Holocaust.[17] The PLO document referred to the publication in the early 1960s of Rolf Hochhuth's
play *The Deputy*. In it the German Protestant writer accused
Pope Pius XII of having remained silent during the Nazi extermination of Jews.[18]

The Palestinian document alleged that, before and during Vatican II, the Zionist movement had three main objectives. The first objective was to provoke an uproar against
Pius XII. The second objective was to force the Church to
recognize Zionist aims and gain the sympathy of Catholics
worldwide. The third objective was to press on the conciliar
fathers a major reinterpretation of the Scriptures regarding
Jewish persecutions of early Christian communities and
Jewish responsibility in the death of Jesus Christ.[19]

Most interestingly, the Palestinian publication[20] blamed
the members of the Arab clergy in the council, Arab diplomats accredited to the Holy See, and Arab news agencies
for not having acted at an earlier stage to counter the resolution on Judaism.[21] Nevertheless, Arab governments were
very active in apprising the Holy See of the fact that the adoption of the statement on Judaism would jeopardize Catholic
and Christian presence in the Middle East and could lead
to the separation of the Eastern Churches from Rome. Arab
bishops tried to play down the allegations that *Nostra Aetate*

had any political meaning. As a result of the prolonged discussion of the issue, it became clearer to Arabs that the Holy See was motivated by strictly religious, not political, considerations. During the final session of the council most prelates from Arab countries voted in favor of the declaration.

The PLO document also raised the issue of the Islamic attitude toward Vatican II. The author of the document referred to the fear of Arab Muslims that would stem from a decision to declare Jews innocent of the crime of deicide. Such a decision would be a blow to Christian-Islamic dialogue and would create another obstacle to the dialogue between the two religions.

The Palestinian document also expressed the complaint of the Palestinians against the lack of solidarity shown by Western Christians toward the Palestinian issue:

> It is true that some Western Christian institutions have sent aid and relief to the refugees; but this humanitarian aid is not an expression of support by these relief agencies towards the Palestinians. . . . Muslims in the Arab world have refrained from making of the Palestinian issue an exclusive Arab-Islamic cause. This was because they did not want to be accused of discrimination by their Christian counterparts. Despite all this, the West, with its temporal and spiritual leaders, has demonstrated its willingness to dialogue with Zionists . . . while the majority of Muslims and Islamic countries have stood firmly by our rights both as Christians and Muslims.[22]

Thus, a very important point regarding the gap between Western Christianity and the Eastern Christian Churches was raised by the Palestinian document. Christian and Catholic churchmen in the West, having lived and shared the plight of the Jews in their societies, felt that because of the terrible effects of anti-Semitism among Christians in Europe, a fundamental change was long overdue in the Church's attitude towards Judaism. This call for change was not shared by prominent Arab clergymen. For them the resolution of the Jewish question was in large part a factor in the tragic plight of the Palestinians. In brief, Judaism and Israel occupy a higher place in the scale of priorities of Western Christendom, whereas the Eastern Church is generally in symbiosis with the Palestinian issue and Christian-Islamic dialogue.

Furthermore, the Israeli-Palestinian dispute created divisions inside the Catholic Church; in fact, a dichotomy developed between conservatives in the Curia and liberal clergymen in Western Europe and the United States. The former were still reluctant to recognize a link between the Jewish people and Palestine. The latter, at least some among them, while paying lip service to the rights of the Palestinians, initiated a favorable dialogue with Jews and Israelis.

The opposition by some prelates and clergymen to the acknowledgment of the reality of the Jewish state stemmed from the fact that "to recognize Israel is to admit a long historical, theological, and religious process which is not always in harmony with what is thought of Israel in some Vatican circles."[23] The key to understanding this reluctance is that the Catholic Church has for centuries considered the Jews as a people that had played out its role on the stage of history by rejecting Jesus Christ as the Messiah.[24]

The Holy See in its official statements had refused to recognize a temporal link between the Jewish people and the land of Israel. However, this link was acknowledged in controversial statements issued by certain Catholic groups in Europe and the United States. In its declaration on "the Christian attitude towards Judaism" (April 16, 1973), the French Episcopal Committee for Relations with Judaism wrote:

> Beyond the legitimate divergence of political options, the conscience of the world community cannot refuse the Jewish people, who had to submit to so many vicissitudes in the course of its history, the right and means for a political existence among the nations. At the same time, this right and the opportunities for existence cannot be

refused to those who, in the course of local conflicts resulting from this return, are now victims of grave injustice.[25]

The French document was favorably welcomed in Jewish and Israeli circles. Zwi Werblowski wrote:

The French bishops, with remarkable fairness and integrity, have drawn attention to the need to respect the Jewish "self-understanding," and to the fact that, in the context of the Jewish tradition, the relations between religion, societal order and political life were conceived differently from their conception in Christianity.[26]

In Israel, the French document on Judaism was called a "Catholic Balfour Declaration."[27] Catholics in France, or at least their hierarchy, had finally decided to come to grips with the political significance of the Jewish state.

Although the French episcopal statement balanced its recognition of the link between the Jews and Palestine with the right of the Palestinians to a "political existence among the nations," it provoked outrage in the Arab countries. Yasser Arafat, chairman of the PLO, said:

The document is based on ambiguities and unfortunate confusion between the religious and political domain. It adopts the concept of "Jewish people" as interpreted by the Zionist ideology. The French statement did not adopt the meaning of Jewish people as a universal religious community whose members belong to their respective national groups.[28]

Among the several declarations and articles issued in reaction to the French bishops' statement, there was a declaration issued in the form of protest by forty-two Jesuits living in Lebanon (May 2, 1973). The Jesuits accused the French Episcopal Committee of avoiding mention of the term Palestinian, "thus confirming the Zionist thesis that there is no Palestinian people." Moreover, the clergymen blamed Israel for having "caused the exodus of hundreds of thousands of refugees." Their letter of protest went further:

> If we condemn the persecutions which Jews underwent in Europe, we ought also to denounce the constant use today of the reminder of those deaths, a use which aims at making people forget the oppression that a powerful state—and how powerful it is—inflicts on others today.[29]

Another important issue is illustrated by the Holy See's reluctance to get involved in the internal affairs of Judaism. Yehoshua Rash explained this hesitation when he wrote that "by establishing diplomatic contacts with Jerusalem, would not the Vatican commit the sin of fostering the Zionist option to the detriment of other, non-Zionist movements?"[30]

The fundamental question here is that Zionism is not considered as the sole expression of Jewish feelings. Liberal Jews accused Zionists of deforming the messianic and cosmopolitan character of Judaism by adopting racial and reactionary positions to justify their goals. Some liberal Jews had found in socialism an answer to the Jewish question. The other criticism was that with their attempt to establish a homeland for the Jews, Zionists were bound to unleash anti-Semitic feelings among non-Jews.

In a sense, the struggle was between Jews who believed in the universal and religious character of Judaism and those who, fearing further pogroms and anti-Semitism, advocated a state for the Jews in Palestine. In an important article on the debate regarding Jewish attitudes toward Zionism, Walter Laqueur summed up the problem:

> The case against Zionism was, very briefly, that as a secularist movement it was incompatible with the religious character of Judaism; as a political movement it was inconsistent with the spiritual emphasis in Judaism; as a nationalist movement it was out of keeping with the universalist character of Judaism; and it was a threat to the welfare of Jews as it confused gentiles in their thinking about Jews and thus imperilled their status.[31]

The cautious stand adopted by the Holy See toward Zionism and its aims reflected the highly controversial nature
of the question. In this context, a well-known debate ensued in the early 1970s between Father Joseph L. Ryan, a
Jesuit scholar known for his sympathy to the Palestinian
cause, and Father Edward H. Flannery, then executive secretary for Catholic-Jewish relations for the United States,
famous for his pro-Zionist stands. The nature of the polemic
between the two clergymen evolved around the issue of
whether or not a Christian who adopts an anti-Zionist viewpoint would automatically be anti-Semitic. In an article entitled "Anti-Zionism and the Christian Psyche," Father Flannery wrote that "it is especially the Christian who is expected
to rejoice at the upturn of the fortune of Jews that Zionism,
or any other agency, has brought about in our time."[32] In
reply to Flannery's statement, Father Ryan wrote:

> Freedom to criticize Zionism and Israel is required for
> both Christians and Jews to cultivate mutual good rela-
> tions. This freedom is also required by our concern for
> justice in the Middle East, for the development of under-
> standing between Muslims and Christians, and for the
> very welfare of the Jews in Israel.[33]

Since the early days of the Zionist movement and its stated
aim to establish a homeland for the Jews in Palestine, reaction by the Holy See has been mostly negative.[34] The central concern of the Papacy was the fate of the Holy Places
and the Catholic presence and interests in the Holy Land.
Following the proclamation of the state of Israel (May 14,
1948), *L'Osservatore Romano*, the Holy See's daily newspaper, stated:

> Zionism is not the embodiment of Israel as it is described
> in the Bible. Zionism is a contemporary phenomenon
> which undergirds the modern state [of Israel], which is
> philosophically and politically secular. The Holy Land
> and the Holy Places as they are form part and parcel of
> Christendom.[35]

Since then, there has been an evolution in the attitude of the Holy See toward Israel. This evolution can be characterized as having a mixture of theological prejudice and political pragmatism. Following the 1967 Middle East War, when the Holy Places of Christianity fell under Israeli control, the Holy See opted for informal talks with the Israeli government in order to work out a modus vivendi regarding the status of Catholic interests in Palestine.

Nevertheless, despite its readiness to acknowledge the Jewish state as a political entity, the Holy See has not yet established diplomatic ties with Israel. Its position was expressed by Monsignor William Murphy, under secretary of the Pontifical Commission on Justice and Peace at the National Workshop on Christian-Jewish Relations, held in Boston in May 1983:

> The Holy See recognizes the factual existence of Israel, its right to exist, its right to secure borders and to all other rights that a sovereign nation possesses. The Holy See would have no problem in principle with establishing diplomatic relations. However, there are certain difficulties and problems that the Holy See would first want to have resolved. I might add that it is the common custom of the Holy See not to be the initiator of diplomatic relations with any country, although it welcomes and appreciates diplomatic relations.[36]

More recent reasons used by the Holy See to explain the absence of diplomatic relations with the Jewish state are: (1) the Israeli invasion of Lebanon in the summer of 1982, (2) the Jewish settlements on the Israeli-occupied territories of the West Bank and the Gaza Strip, (3) the fate of the Palestinians, and (4) the status of Jerusalem and the Holy Places. Father Marcel Dubois said that these reasons were expressed in a meeting in Rome between Cardinal Achille Silvestrini, secretary of the Council for the Public Affairs of the Church, and representatives of six Jewish organizations.[37]

Other motives can be divided into formal and substantial issues. The former include the fact that the Holy See avoids establishing diplomatic relations with a state that lacks definitive and recognized borders. An example is illustrated by the Holy See's position regarding the Oder-Neisse border between Germany and Poland.[38]

The substantial issues can be divided into two categories: (1) the reluctance of the Holy See to recognize states in controversial and changing situations, which is the case of Israel today; and (2) the substantial loss (from the Middle Ages) of the Pope's exclusive authority over all matters of consequence. Today the Pope has to take into account "the global view and undoubtedly the views of the Christian Churches in the Arab countries [Greek Catholic, Maronite, Coptic, etc.]."[39]

Finally, yet another problem would arise from the establishment of official diplomatic relations between the Holy See and Israel. As in the case of all other countries with which it has diplomatic ties, the Holy See would require guarantees regarding the regulation of Catholic teaching and presence in Israel proper. The Christian presence in Israel is not viewed favorably by some Orthodox Jews, who are concerned about the threat of possible Christian missionary activities.[40]

Notwithstanding all the problems and obstacles facing normal Holy See–Israeli relations, the Papacy adopted a pragmatic stance toward the Jewish state, especially after 1967 and the Israeli occupation of Jerusalem. The apostolic delegate has frequent contacts with the Israeli Foreign Ministry and the Ministry of Religious Affairs. In Rome, Israeli diplomats accredited to the Italian government are often received in Vatican City. After the 1967 Arab-Israeli War Pope Paul VI received in audience Israeli Foreign Minister Aba Ebban (1969), Prime Minister Golda Meir (1973), and Moshe Dayan (1978). Former Prime Minister Yitzhak Shamir visited the Vatican in 1982, and Prime Minister Shimon Peres was welcomed in 1985.

If the Holy See is handicapped by its historical stand toward Judaism and by the absence of diplomatic relations with Israel, it nevertheless has a major advantage: that of being in permanent contact with all the parties involved in the Israeli-Palestinian dispute. Moreover, the prestige and influence enjoyed by the Holy See in international institutions such as the United Nations clearly motivate Israeli leaders to pay close attention to the positions adopted by it.

In criticizing the official Israeli attitude toward the Eastern Christian Churches in the Holy Land, and the Israeli government's lack of attention toward them, Zwi Werblowski commented that "after all, when it comes to a vote at the United Nations, the Armenian and Greek Orthodox Churches do not have the weight that the Vatican has as a political factor."[41]

Three important elements regarding Holy See–Israeli relations should be pointed out. The first is that Vatican City is legally recognized by the international community as the territorial base for the Holy See, but the legitimacy of Israel as a homeland for Judaism is still in doubt in the minds of dissenting Jews and some gentiles. The second factor that works in favor of the Holy See is that Israel does not want to alienate its relationship with the Holy See, because the Jewish state has diplomatic ties with many countries that have large Catholic communities. Finally, the whole issue of the status of Israeli–Holy See relations gained a new dimension with the intervention of US Catholic and Jewish members of Congress (November 26, 1984) urging Pope John Paul II to initiate the necessary steps that would lead to the establishment of diplomatic relations with Israel.[42]

For the twenty-six American legislators, "the exchange of ambassadors between Israel and the Vatican would be a watershed in the history of Jewish-Catholic relations equivalent only to the Second Vatican Council."[43] In their overstatement the members of Congress probably were not aware that the declaration on the Jews issued during Vatican II had a purely religious significance. The establishment of diplomatic ties between Rome and the Jewish state is more a matter of temporal politics that would place the Holy See in an awkward and untenable position in the Arab-Israeli dispute.

The call by the members of the House of Representatives came at a time when disagreements were reported inside the Roman Curia between prelates favoring the creation of a Palestinian homeland and those favoring closer ties with Israel.[44] This whole affair was the result of a leak to the US media by someone in the State Department. In fact the US ambassador to the Holy See, William A. Wilson, had had a meeting with a personal associate of Pope John Paul II, and the outcome of the meeting was not to be revealed.

In a letter to me, Ambassador Wilson, reacting to the events mentioned just above, wrote:

> Unfortunately this matter is receiving far too much publicity and, in my personal opinion, the publicity which it is receiving and which was recently augmented by a letter to the Holy Father signed by a group of Congressmen may have the unfortunate effect of even postponing such a decision [to establish relations with Israel].[45]

At this point, it is important to point out another major background component: the Holy See's relationship with the Palestinian people.

Similar to the relationship between Judaism and the state of Israel, a close link exists between Christianity, Islam, and the question of Palestine. Acknowledging this important factor, the Holy See tried to improve its relations with the Muslim world with a frank and open dialogue. In fact, the history of past relationships between the Catholic Church and Islam was troublesome.

In the first centuries of its expansion, Islam spread rapidly into the heart of Christendom. Following this was the European invasion of the Middle East under the pretext of religion (the Crusades). Finally, in the nineteenth century, the activity of Catholic missionaries was closely tied to the colonial enterprise. It was not until after World War II that a tradition of respect for other religions became generalized little by little in Catholic theology.

This change in perspective was officially sanctioned by Vatican II, through which Pope John XXIII wished to generalize for all Catholics the renewal that some had already experienced. After dealing with internal questions of the Catholic Church and those of its relations with the world, the conciliar fathers dealt with the problem of the relations between Catholics and believers of other religions.[46] With regard to Islam, the council declaration *Nostra Aetate* stated:

> Although in the course of the centuries many quarrels and hostilities have arisen between Christians and Muslims, this most sacred Synod urges all to forget the past and to strive sincerely for mutual understanding. On behalf of all mankind, let them make common cause of safeguarding and fostering social justice, moral values, peace, and freedom.[47]

Both Arab and non-Arab Islamic countries and the Holy See find themselves allied against common challenges: atheism and materialism. Another common interest is the fate of Jerusalem. Furthermore, Christian-Islamic dialogue has been institutionalized in several meetings and it has provided the Holy See with formal channels through which it can express its views regarding the fate of Catholics in Arab and Islamic countries. In October 1974 the Holy See established a Commission for Religious Relations with Islam, within the Secretariat for Non-Christians. Finally, the Holy See has normal diplomatic relations with a number of Arab and Islamic countries—Sudan, Iran, Kuwait, Morocco, Pakistan, Syria, Tunisia, Iraq, Egypt, Lebanon, and Turkey.

Since the beginning of the Israeli-Palestinian dispute, the Holy See had adopted a stand sympathetic to the plight of the Palestinian people. This attitude was mainly motivated by the Papacy's concern for the fate of Catholics in Palestine and the humanitarian needs of Palestinian refugees following the various wars between Arab and Israeli armies. Moreover, the role of the Holy See was faithful to the policy adopted following Vatican II and especially after the publication of Pope Paul VI's encyclical *Populorum Progressio*, which called for the consolidation of peace through justice.

Since the mid-1960s, the Popes have condemned acts of terrorism from all sides and have called for a just and equitable solution to the Arab-Israeli quarrel in the framework of the resolutions adopted at the United Nations.[48]

Diplomatically, while recognizing the rights of the Palestinians to a homeland, the Holy See believes that "this cannot happen in isolation, but a solution must be constructed with the agreement and cooperation of all the countries involved."[49] By the end of the 1960s, and following the defeat of Arab armies, the Palestinians reasserted their yearning for nationhood by resorting to guerrilla warfare.[50] A Vatican official drew a parallel between the Palestine Liberation Organization and the Zionist movement. Father Dubois stated that "it is Jewish Zionism which has awakened Palestinian Zionism."[51] Palestinian guerrilla actions and ensuing military retaliation became the typical pattern of response that still characterizes the relationship between Palestinians and Israelis.

Important changes took place in the leadership, policies, and actions of the PLO after the 1967 Arab-Israeli war. The PLO backed armed struggle and the acquisition of all of Palestine—a program not acceptable to the world community or to the Holy See. After the 1973 war, however, the mainline leadership under Yasser Arafat reassessed the situation and concluded that the elimination of Israel and the setting up of a single secular state of Palestine was no longer practical and would continue to stand in the way of the PLO becoming acceptable to most nations of the world. Therefore, moderate leaders under Arafat began to tone down their call for armed struggle and a single state of Palestine and indicated a readiness to accept a smaller Palestinian state to be established on the West Bank of the Jordan River and the Gaza Strip, and they began to stress diplomatic and political means to attain their aim. Because of these changes in PLO policies and actions, and because most members of the world community were convinced that the Palestinian problem was the key issue for an overall settlement of the Arab-Israeli dispute and that there could be no true and lasting solution without providing for the political rights of Palestinians, most nations began to back a Palestinian state and acknowledge the PLO as the legitimate representative of the Palestinian people. These developments also made it easier for the Vatican to publicly acknowledge Palestinian rights and to establish contacts with PLO leaders.

The resurgence of Palestinian nationalism was reflected in Paul VI's speeches. By the end of 1975, he had declared that both peoples, Palestinians and Israelis, had to recognize each other's right to self-determination and nationhood. His feelings were dramatized in an often-quoted address he gave on December 22, 1975. In it the Pope said:

> Even if we are well aware of the tragedies not so long ago which have compelled the Jewish people to seek a secure and protected garrison in a sovereign and independent state of their own, and because we are aware of this, we would like to invite the children of this people to recognize the rights and legitimate aspirations of another people which also have suffered for a long time, the people of Palestine.[52]

Given Pope John Paul II's personal background in Poland, which was directed mainly toward the struggle for justice and human dignity, he adopted a more active and outspoken posture toward the Israeli-Palestinian dispute.[53] The Pope's attitude toward the conflict was highlighted in a controversial speech he delivered on October 5, 1980, in Otranto. John Paul II said that the situation in the Middle East had reached an explosive stage. He then explained his perception of the origins of the dispute between Israelis and Palestinians:

> The Jewish people, after tragic experience linked to the extermination of so many sons and daughters, gave life

to the State of Israel. At the same time a sad condition
was created for the Palestinian people who were in large
part excluded from their homeland.[54]

This address was stunning in its frankness. No previous
Pope had ventured to go so far, publicly linking Israeli responsibility in part for the plight of the Palestinians.

The controversial character of the papal speech elicited
the anger of Jewish and Israeli leaders. They basically disagreed with John Paul II's illustration of historical facts related to the Palestinian issue. In reply to the Pope's address,
Rabbi Joseph Sternstein, president of the American Zionist
Federation, expressed his group's point of view:

> The Arabs living within the borders of the newly-
> established State of Israel fled their homes at the insistence
> and admonition of their Arab leaders and despite assur-
> ances of safety from the Israeli army. Moreover, the Vat-
> ican statement ignored the fact that at the same time as
> Arabs fled their houses in Haifa and Jaffa, Jews were forc-
> ibly driven from their homes in cities throughout the Arab
> world.[55]

Pope John Paul II's address can be considered as the most
explicit papal statement regarding the Palestinians. It was
also symbolic of the stand that the Holy See had decided
to adopt in light of the increasing militance and expansionist
policies of the Israeli government vis-à-vis the Occupied Territories after 1967. In fact, on November 10, 1977, *L'Osservatore Romano* published an article critical of the Israeli settlement policy on Palestinian-occupied lands. In this article,
the Vatican daily stated:

> It is clear to everyone that a massive Jewish presence in
> the occupied territories would make it impossible to re-
> alize their return to the Arabs. As regards the West Bank
> the introduction of Jewish population radically upsets the
> plans that are being made to set up there a "Palestinian
> homeland" whatever form this "homeland" may take—

in order to solve the Palestinian problem, which has now become the most complex and at the same time fundamental difficulty in the whole tangle of the Middle East crisis.[56]

The plans mentioned by *L'Osservatore Romano* were those agreed upon in the Camp David Agreements (1978) between Egypt and Israel under the supervision of the United States. In fact, the Holy See adopted a position not too different from that of the Carter administration with regard to the future status of the West Bank and Gaza. Even if the Papacy remains faithful to its stated policy of not offering "technical solutions" to the conflict between Palestinians and Israelis, it nevertheless keeps the door open to support a possible involvement of Jordan in deciding the fate of the Occupied Territories.

Having set the background for the attitude of the Holy See toward Judaism, Israel and the Palestinians, my analysis will now delve into the humanitarian aspects of the Holy See's intervention in the Israeli-Palestinian dispute. In fact, the intervention of the Holy See is guided by its commitment to the right of peoples to self-determination and the fostering of peace through justice.

THE PONTIFICAL MISSION FOR PALESTINE

One of the central interests of the Holy See in the Middle East is the welfare of Catholic minorities living in the area. This concern is directly linked to the plight of the Palestinian refugees, which, since the start of the Israeli-Palestinian dispute, has elicited the Papacy's constant solicitude. For this purpose, and in light of papal teachings, two major institutions were established by the Holy See to supervise relief and educational initiatives in the Holy Land: Bethlehem University and the Pontifical Mission for Palestine.

The Pontifical Mission for Palestine was founded in 1949 by Pope Pius XII. Its purpose was to assist Palestinian refugees through the provision of goods and services for educational, cultural, religious, and humanitarian needs. It predated the United Nations Relief Work Agency (UNRWA), established for similar purposes.

The main offices of the Pontifical Mission are in New York, but it has regional offices in Beirut, Jerusalem, Amman, and a liaison office in Rome. The pontifical agency is closely associated with the United States–based sister organization, the Catholic Near East Welfare Association (CNEWA), the papal mission aid agency for the Eastern Churches.[57] CNEWA, which was established in 1924, was to be "the sole instrumentality authorized to solicit funds for Catholic interests in these regions [Near East] and shall be so recommended to the entire Catholic population in the United States."[58]

To highlight the importance of the pontifical mission in its humanitarian work in the Middle East, Pope Paul VI sent to its president, Monsignor John G. Nolan, a letter (July 16, 1974) in which he wrote:

> The work of the Mission for Palestine has been one of the clearest signs of the Holy See's concern for the welfare of the Palestinians, who are particularly dear to us because they are people of the Holy Land, because they include followers of Christ, and because they have been and are still being so tragically tried. We express again our heartfelt sharing in their sufferings and our support for their legitimate aspirations. May our paternal solicitude bring comfort and encouragement, especially to the refugees, who for years have been living under inhuman conditions. Unfortunately, such a state of affairs has produced in many Palestinians a sense of frustration and, in some, violent protest which with sorrow we have been constrained strenuously to deplore.[59]

The papal message dramatized the importance attached by the Holy See to the plight of the Palestinian people. First, it is "the people of the Holy Land," entitled to the same rights to self-determination as any indigenous population. There is here an implicit rebuttal to the Zionist claim that Palestine was a land without a people. Secondly, some Palestinians are Christians, a fundamental reason for papal attention. Finally, the Palestinians are considered a beloved people by the Pope because they have been and are still "being so tragically tried." This concern of Paul VI echoed his oft-repeated theme of fostering peace through justice.

Two other very important points emerged from the Pontiff's letter. First, he expressed his "support for [the Palestinians'] legitimate aspirations," which in a sense means that the Holy See, though not stating it explicitly, backs efforts for the establishment of a Palestinian homeland. Secondly, Pope Paul VI gave an explanation as to why the Papacy had to condemn "acts of violent protest" perpetrated by Palestinian commandos. The Holy See's condemnation was done in full awareness of the causes that led to such acts of violence.

BETHLEHEM UNIVERSITY

In 1964, following Pope Paul VI's pilgrimage to the Holy Land, the Holy See became aware that immediate action should be taken to stem the decline of Christian communities and to improve the quality of education. As a concrete step, the Sacred Congregation for the Oriental Churches signed a contract with the Brothers of the Christian Schools (Christian Brothers) to administer Bethlehem University, which opened its doors on October 1, 1973.[60]

In a memorandum prepared for Monsignor Nolan, then apostolic delegate in Jerusalem, Archbishop Pio Laghi, later the apostolic pro-nuncio in Washington, wrote about the necessity and urgency of establishing Bethlehem University:

[It was] necessary to keep the elite here, otherwise there will be no leadership in any field of public or private life, religious life included. It is necessary to consolidate the Christian presence in the Holy Land and to show by example that we care not only for stones and shrines but also for people and, in particular, the youth.[61]

Together with a few other academic institutions on the West Bank, Bethlehem University has become a center for training the leadership of a possible future Palestinian state. This situation has caused tension with the Israeli military authorities.

For Brother Scanlan, vice-chancellor of Bethlehem University, the Israeli government is worried about the success of educational establishments in stabilizing the population and increasing its level of education. "As we stabilize the population, we are running against the policies of the present [Israeli] government, which would like to increase emigration and make annexation easier."[62] Moreover, the universities are the only substantial institutions left on the West Bank. In emphasizing this factor, Brother Scanlan stated that if "the universities were terminated, the next focus of pressure would be on the churches because they are providing many social services, committing the same 'sin' that we are."[63]

The Israeli government's suspicion of Bethlehem University and of other Palestinian educational institutions reflects how history can repeat itself in reverse. In 1922, almost twenty years prior to the establishment of the Jewish state, Chaim Weizmann, the most prominent Zionist diplomat, met with Cardinal Gasparri, then secretary of state of the Holy See. Weizmann explained to the cardinal the purposes and aims of the Jewish national home in Palestine. After having detailed what the Zionist settlers were doing (drainage, afforestation, education, etc.), Gasparri looked at his guest and exclaimed in French: "C'est votre université que je crains."[64]

My first proposition (p. 10, above) has been confirmed by the selected test cases. The Holy See has in fact demonstrated through concrete actions its humanitarian concerns for the Palestinians. The Pontifical Mission for Palestine has furnished aid and relief, and has provided for the religious needs of refugees. It was an institution created in view of the Church's mission to help the oppressed and the down-trodden. Bethlehem University is an expression of the urgency that the Holy See feels toward the Holy Land. The Papacy seems to have a sense of "time running out" and a sense of anxiety about the younger generation. Indeed, the Holy See knows that if the exodus of young persons from the Holy Land is not stopped, then the only role left for the Church will be that of a caretaker and curator of museums and stones. So education is an effective answer to the need for maintaining and training leaders, and for giving them reasons not to emigrate. What is interesting to note here is that, indirectly, the Holy See is contributing actively to establishing the seeds of a Palestinian homeland. Moreover, given that Bethlehem University is directly supervised by the Holy See, the Israeli military authority in the West Bank has to be very careful about deciding to restrict or shut it down, even temporarily. Any harm to the Vatican-sponsored university could endanger the modus vivendi that exists between Rome and Jerusalem.

Given that the conflict between Palestinians and Israelis is directly linked to the fate of Catholics in the Holy Land, the Holy See could not adopt a policy of being a neutral bystander in the dispute. However, in order to be able to defend its interests and preserve the credibility of its intervention, the Holy See had to adopt a public stance based on impartiality.

THE ISRAELI RAID ON BEIRUT AIRPORT (1968)

On December 28, 1968, following a Palestinian attack on an Israeli airplane in Athens, an Israeli commando force landed at the Beirut International Airport and destroyed the entire Lebanese civil air fleet. Two days later, Pope Paul VI sent a telegram to Lebanese President Charles Hélou in which he expressed his commiseration:

> We wish to express to your Excellency our sorrow at the grave event which took place in Beirut. We strongly deplore violent acts from wherever they come and which cannot but aggravate a situation already tense.[65]

The Pope urged the Lebanese not to be drawn into the path of violence by retaliating against Israel.

In Israel, where the text of the papal message was not published in its entirety, reactions flowed from a feeling of anger against the inequity in Paul VI's treatment of Israel. The *Jerusalem Post* wrote in an editorial:

> The strange silence of Rome at the time of the Nazi Holocaust would seem to be maintained whenever Jewish lives are at stake, whether in the Arab states, or behind the Iron Curtain or when Israelis are killed in their own country or on foreign soil. It is only natural that we should react to such a one-sided position.[66]

In this context, it is important to mention that Paul VI did not enjoy the same popularity that his predecessor Pope John XXIII had had in Israel. During his brief stop in Israel in 1964, Paul VI defended the actions of Pius XII during the Holocaust.[67] Furthermore, the Israeli frustration with the Pontiff's cable stemmed from the "silence" that the Holy See observed when bombs, placed earlier by Palestinian commandos, exploded in Israeli targets such as the Tomb of the Patriarchs in Hebron and the Mahane Yehuda Market in Jerusalem.

The emotional uproar that the Pope's message provoked in Israel climaxed in a harsh diatribe delivered by (Sefardi) Chief Rabbi Nissim.[68] The rabbi accused Paul VI of waging "a total war against the country that God had given to His People."[69] Israel's chief rabbi, already fuming at the papal cable to the Lebanese president, found in an editorial pub-

lished in *L'Osservatore Romano* another reason to vent his
frustration with the Holy See.[70]

The Israeli govenment, however, felt that Nissim had
overreacted and that his statement, made without prior consultation, could jeopardize rapprochement between the Jewish people and the Catholic Church.[71]

The incident provoked a public hue and cry in Israel. It
originated in the feeling that Paul VI had sent his condolences
to Lebanon without condemning Palestinian attacks against
Israeli targets. Nevertheless, some Israeli observers understood the balanced nature of the Pontiff's message. *Haaretz*,
a major Israeli newspaper, took on itself the task of put-
ting things in perspective. Criticizing Rabbi Nissim's blunt
words, the article stated that, after all, Paul VI was the Pope
of Catholics

> and not of all peoples. . . . It is certainly understandable
> that the Pope has a scale of preferences. He did not send
> a letter of condolences when we blew up bridges and killed
> Egyptian and Jordanian civilians and soldiers. But when
> it comes to a State [Lebanon] whose population is more
> than 50% Christian . . . when we consider the dangerous
> situation facing this community, what is more natural
> than the Pope sharing their pain? In the final instance,
> he is their Pope.[72]

The Israeli newspaper underlined also the fact that Paul
VI's message had expressed his disapproval of any act of
aggression whatever its origin. "Is this not a true condem-
nation of Arab terrorism, especially when we recall that the
letter was addressed to an Arab head of state? Should the
Pope not be praised instead of being condemned?"[73] The
Haaretz editorial showed that despite the acrimony provoked
in Israel by the papal cable to the Lebanese president, some
Israelis could maintain a sense of balance when judging Paul
VI's action.

The whole Beirut raid affair ended following a private
audience that the Pope granted to the late Dr. Nahum Gold-

mann, president of the World Jewish Congress (January 6, 1969). The Holy See's move was an attempt to correct the impression that Paul VI was biased against Israel.

Finally, it should be remembered that the Israeli raid occurred in Lebanon, which had adopted, until the end of the 1960s, a neutral stand in the Arab-Israeli quarrel. Furthermore, the importance of Lebanon stems from the fact that the Holy See gives a high priority to the preservation of the pluralistic formula of coexistence between Christians and Muslims. In fact, the day after the Israeli raid, Paul VI told an Italian journalist that for him it was a "black Sunday."[74] The Pope had a premonition that Lebanon was on the verge of being dragged into the Israeli-Palestinian conflict. Paul VI's feeling were further confirmed by a Lebanese diplomat when he wrote that "the Lebanese did not give much heed to the Pope's words, whose prophetic character events would reveal."[75]

The case of the papal reaction to the Israeli raid against Beirut airport exemplifies the fact that it is almost impossible for the Holy See to adopt an impartial stand without being criticized. The fundamental source of misperception between some Israelis and the Holy See centered on religious and historical factors. Religious factors are epitomized by the still deep chasm that exists between some segments of Judaism and the Catholic Church. For instance, Rabbi Nissim has been a staunch opponent to any dialogue with Catholics. Israel's chief rabbi considered that the ideal for Judaism was to be "in splendid isolation."[76] Historical factors are dramatized by the vivid memory of the Holocaust and the attitude of the Holy See toward the Jews at that time.

GOLDA MEIR AND POPE PAUL VI (1973)

Despite the absence of diplomatic relations between the Holy See and the Jewish state, Golda Meir's audience in

Rome was hailed as a historic event. In fact it was the first time that an Israeli prime minister was welcomed by a Sovereign Pontiff. Furthermore, and in light of the Israeli occupation of the eastern sector of Jerusalem following the 1967 war, the Holy See was trying to find accommodation with Israeli authorities regarding the status of the Holy Places and the fate of the Catholic community living in the Holy Land. The visit of Golda Meir was considered an auspicious occasion and one that would illustrate papal concerns. Another factor favoring the meeting was a thaw in Israeli–Holy See relations following the 1967 Middle East War.

Following the one-hour audience, on January 15, 1973, the Holy See issued a communiqué in which it was stated:

> Pope Paul VI, after having recalled the history and the suffering of the Jewish people, explained the viewpoint of the Holy See on questions that touch most closely its humanitarian mission, such as the problem of the refugees and the situation of the various communities living in the Holy Land, as well as questions regarding its more specific religious mission, concerning the Holy Places and the sacred and universal character of the city of Jerusalem. [77]

According to the Vatican communiqué, Golda Meir spoke of "the phenomenon of terrorism and of the unique situation of Jewish communities in various parts of the world." [78] In her own memoirs, the Israeli prime minister mentioned that she had asked Paul VI "to use his influence to try to bring about a settlement in the Middle East and to do whatever he could to secure the return to Israel of the Israeli prisoners who had been in Egyptian and Syrian jails ever since the War of Attrition [1970] and whom the Arab states had refused to release." [79]

Well aware of Arab reactions to the papal decision to meet with the Israeli prime minister, and before distributing the Holy See's official communiqué to the press, Professor Federico Alessandrini, the director of the Vatican press office, issued a verbal statement in which he said of the meeting between Paul VI and Golda Meir:

> [It] does not mean or imply the least change—in fact no such change has taken place nor is there any reason for change—in the attitude of the Holy See concerning the problems of the Holy Land. . . . The attitude of the Holy See with regard to Israel remains equally unchanged. The Pope had accepted the request of Mrs. Golda Meir because he considers it his duty not to miss any opportunity to act in favor of peace, for the defense of human rights and those of the communities, for the defense of the religious interests of all, and in order to aid especially those who are the weakest and those who are defenseless, in the first place the Palestinian refugees.[80]

Alessandrini's verbal statement was an unusual one by Vatican diplomatic standards. The Holy See wanted to put things in their right perspective and preempt any propagandistic speculations from both the Arab and the Israeli sides. Moreover, the frankness of the Holy See's spokesman left no doubt as to where the Holy See stood on the Israeli-Palestinian dispute.

The verbal note explicitly emphasized the consistent pattern of papal diplomacy. The intervention of the Papacy in the Israeli-Palestinian dispute is motivated by (1) concern for peace; (2) defense of human rights and the rights of the communities living in the Holy Land; (3) defense of the religious interests of the followers of Judaism, Christianity, and Islam; and (4) humanitarian aid to the Palestinians whose plight is very important in the Pontiff's eyes.

Given the intractability of the conflict between Arabs and Israelis, the Pope's receiving Golda Meir in audience constituted a skillful act of diplomacy by the Holy See. The mere fact that the meeting took place was, according to the Lebanese newspaper *Al-Anuar*, "unfortunately an achievement for Israeli diplomacy, which was able to get the Vatican to receive its first official at the level of Prime Minister since 1948."[81] Nevertheless, several Arab leaders praised the firm stand adopted by the Pope in the course of his talks with Golda Meir.

The Vatican spokesman's verbal note was viewed in the Israeli media as "an insult to Israel and to the Jewish people."[82] As an answer to the verbal statement, Golda Meir, breaking the rule of discretion that usually surrounds papal audiences, revealed the tone of her meeting with Paul VI, in an interview to *Maariv*, an Israeli evening newspaper.

In that interview, the prime minister touched on the controversial nature of her audience with the Pope. Meir stated that she "did not like the opening of the conversation at all. The Pope said to me at the outset that he found it hard to understand how the Jewish people, which should be merciful, behaves so fiercely in its own country."[83] Paul VI's statement was an extraordinary indication of the Pontiff's concern for the Palestinians. It also underscored the restraint that the Holy See adopts in its public dealings.

Later on in the interview, speculating on whether her meeting in the Vatican would lead to official diplomatic relations between her country and the Holy See, Golda Meir said:

> At this stage, I'm satisfied that the Pope said thank you, three times, for our conduct in respect to the Holy Places in Jerusalem and to the Christians.[84]

The meeting between Pope Paul VI and Golda Meir epitomized the contentious nature of the relationship between the Holy See and Israel. However, the controversial aspect of the audience was overshadowed by the willingness of both sides to reach a minimum of pragmatic understanding, now that the Jewish state had taken under its control the Holy Places of Christianity.

If pragmatism was a major motivation in the Pontiff's decision to meet with the Israeli premier, the same realpolitik was behind Pope John Paul II's decision to grant an audience to PLO Chairman Yasser Arafat.

YASSER ARAFAT AND POPE JOHN PAUL II (1982)

To set this audience in its context, mention should be made of the fact that the Pope was helped in his decision by several events related to the Arab-Israeli conflict. In their 1982 summit in Fez (Morocco), Arab heads of state, together with Arafat, approved a resolution that inter alia implicitly recognized the existence of Israel. This was the first time that an Arab gathering had accepted the reality of the Jewish state. The Fez Declaration was in a sense an answer to diplomatic initiatives taken at the international level, such as the European Community's Venice Declaration (June 13, 1980), which stressed the importance of PLO participation in any settlement of the Israeli-Palestinian dispute.[85] Moreover, the audience granted to the Palestinian leader was justified on the grounds that Arafat was a prominent personality and could say yes or no to any decision related to his people's fate.[86] The meeting between John Paul II and Arafat also allowed the Holy See to express emphatically its stand on the conflict in the Middle East.

For some Israelis directly involved in Catholic-Jewish dialogue, the announcement of the meeting came as a shock. Dr. Geofrey Wigoder expressed the belief that the audience granted to Arafat was a personal decision by the Pope.[87] The Israeli scholar explained that Vatican sources gave to their Jewish counterparts the following reasons for John Paul II's decision. First, the Pope wanted to get a message through to the Palestinians. Secondly, in light of a traditional policy established by the Holy See, the Pope would meet both sides involved in a conflict in which he is interested; in no way should the meeting with Arafat be interpreted as implying recognition of the PLO.[88]

In expressing the feelings of Jews and Israelis, Wigoder replied:

We for our part felt that if the Pope wanted to deliver a message to the Palestinians, there are other ways of doing it than through Arafat who symbolizes so much for us.[89]

Furthermore, in his criticism of the announced meeting, an unnamed Israeli official, believed by some to be Prime Minister Begin himself, expressed his government's outrage in these words:

> The Church, which did not say a word about the massacre of the Jews for six years in Europe and has not had much to say about the killing of Christians for seven years in Lebanon, is now ready to meet a man who committed the killings in Lebanon and who wants the destruction of Israel in order to complete the work carried out by the Nazis in Germany. . . . If [John Paul II] meets with Arafat it is indicative of a certain moral standard.[90]

This statement synthesized the contentious nature of the relationship between the Holy See, Judaism, and the state of Israel. In the eyes of the Israeli government, the legitimation of the Palestinian leader was total anathema—more so now that the meeting in Vatican City was held in the aftermath of the Israeli invasion of Lebanon (summer 1982) to destroy what was left of PLO forces operating from that country.

Furthermore, the Israeli statement contained a two-pronged accusation. First, there was the contention that the Catholic Church did not take necessary steps to save Jews from the Holocaust. Secondly, the Israelis blamed the Holy See for not speaking out forcefully in defense of Lebanese Christians attacked by PLO forces and their leftist and Muslim allies.

The issue of Lebanon has been a point of contention in the relationship between the Holy See, Israel, and the Christian militias in Lebanon. (This is discussed in further detail in chapter 3, below.) What is important to stress here is that the Pope's initiative was also heavily influenced by the Israeli decision to invade Lebanon. In weighing the pros and cons of a meeting with the PLO chairman, the Pontiff must have calculated that the massive invasion of Lebanon by the Israeli army outweighed any accusations that the Palestinians were bent on the destruction of the Jewish state.

Finally, the harsh words used by the Israeli government against the person of Pope John Paul II did not serve Israeli purposes. Rabbi Marc H. Tannenbaum, the national inter-religious affairs director of the American Jewish Committee, said that the Israeli official's "angry language created the impression that the sole issue is that of Begin versus the Pope, when the real issue is the immorality of Arafat having access to the Pope."[91]

In commenting on the contemptuous words referred to the Pontiff, the Vatican communiqué revealed that the Israeli official's statement showed "little regard for the person of a pope in regard to whom one cannot overlook what he has said on numerous occasions, and particularly during his visit to Auschwitz, to condemn and denounce the genocide of the Nazis against the Jewish people [and not only against them]."[92]

The last sentence is a clear demonstration of how John Paul II's Polish background affects his views of world affairs. In this specific case, the Vatican statement wanted to emphasize that together with the Jews, who were the massive target of Nazi genocidal plans, there were other populations, Gypsies and Poles, for example, who were not spared from Hitler's onslaught.

The meeting between John Paul II and Arafat, on September 15, 1982, lasted more than twenty minutes. A press communiqué released by the Holy See after the audience reported:

> The Holy Father—moved by his constant preoccupation to foster the difficult process of peace in the Middle East—received Mr. Yassar Arafat. . . . During the conversation

the Supreme Pontiff manifested his good will for the Palestinian people and his participation in their long suffering, expressing the hope that a just and lasting solution
might be reached as soon as possible for the Middle East
conflict, a solution which, excluding recourse to arms and
to all violence — in any form, and especially terrorism and
reprisals — may lead to the recognition of the right of all
peoples and in particular the right of the Palestinian people
to a homeland of their own, and the right of Israel to its
security.[93]

In light of this communiqué it appears that there are three
major principles guiding the papal attitude toward the Israeli-
Palestinian dispute. The first principle is unambiguous opposition to acts of terrorism and the use of reprisals. This
assertion is in line with the policy followed by the Holy See
since the beginning of the conflict.

The second principle is that the Palestinians are entitled
to a homeland of their own. This was also the expression
of a new approach adopted by the Polish-born Pope to grap-
ple courageously with the political implications of the Israeli-
Palestinian dispute. Furthermore, it was consistent with
papal statements that, since 1973, have stressed the necessity
of recognizing the Palestinians as being more than refugees —
that is, as a people with a definite and legitimate right to
self-determination.

The third principle is the acknowledgment of the de facto
existence of the Jewish state and its right to secure and defined borders. However, John Paul II's call to Arafat to recognize the right of Israel to be secure did not have the desired
impact. Some Israeli observers argued that as long as the
Holy See did not officially establish diplomatic links with
Israel, it could not impart any credible advice in that direction to anybody. In defending its stand, the Holy See has
always said that by not establishing diplomatic ties with the
Jewish state it could contribute to a great extent to the settlement of the conflict in the Middle East.

The same day that the meeting took place in Rome, Pope John Paul II addressed the Middle East crisis. Papal concern was heightened by the assassination the day before of the newly elected Lebanese president, Bashir Gemayel. In his speech, the Pope restated in unequivocal terms the Holy See's position regarding a resolution to the conflict between Palestinians and Israelis:

> The Holy See is convinced above all that there will not be able to be *true peace without justice*; and that there will not be able to be justice if the rights of all the people involved are not recognized and accepted, in a stable mode, fair and equal. Among these rights, primordial and irrenounceable, is that of *existence* and *security* on one's own territory, in *safeguarding the proper identity* of each one. It is a dilemma which is debated in a bitter manner between two peoples, the Israelis and the Palestinians, who have seen simultaneously or alternately their rights assaulted or denied.[94]

The Pope's speech could not have been more explicit and balanced. Without any overstatement, the papal address constituted the ultimate and clearest statement available on the Holy See's perception regarding a solution to the Israeli-Palestinian dispute. The fact that the Pontiff mentioned the necessity to reach peace through justice was a consistent reminder of papal teachings since Paul VI issued his famous encyclical on the "development of peoples" (1967).

Moreover, the Pope defined what he meant by legitimate rights for both Palestinians and Israelis. These rights include that of "existence," "security," and the preservation of "the proper identity of each one." In light of John Paul II's background and the impact of his experience in Poland, it is not surprising to see the Pope speaking in such clear and lucid terms. In fact, in January 1982, in an address to the diplomats accredited to the Holy See, the Pontiff, referring to martial law in his native Poland, stated that "every people must be able to act freely in what regards the free determination of its own destiny. The Church cannot fail to give her support to such a conviction."[95]

The political impact of the meeting between John Paul II and Yasser Arafat can be assessed through the reactions of Western diplomats in Rome, Palestinians on the West Bank, and some independent observers interviewed in Jerusalem.

The reactions of Western diplomats residing in Rome were reported in a confidential dispatch sent by a Lebanese diplomat in Rome to the Foreign Ministry in Beirut, immediately following the papal audience.[96]

The French and United States chargés d'affaires thought that the meeting was "symbolically a victory for Mr. Arafat." The French chargé is reported to have said that Arafat had for a long time planned for this visit. Moreover, the same diplomat added that "French officials did not understand the haste with which the Pope agreed to grant an audience to Arafat. These officials suspect that the Italian foreign minister had to a great extent influenced the Holy See's decision."[97]

The same Lebanese diplomatic message, referring to the German ambassador's impression of the Arafat visit, quoted him as saying that the Pope in his desire "to enhance his relations with the Islamic world, had provoked a row with the Jewish world."

For the Palestinians, the meeting between John Paul II and Arafat was the clearest sign yet of papal solicitude toward them. Gaby Baramki, vice-president of Bir-Zeit University in the occupied West Bank, expressed his people's feelings when he said:

> We would have been surprised if the Pope had refused to meet with Arafat. As the representative of the Palestinian people, Arafat symbolized the PLO. Since John Paul II had taken certain stands vis-à-vis the rights of the Palestinians to self-determination, it would have been a contradiction had he reneged on that.[98]

If the Pope's political decision had an impact viewed positively by the Palestinians, it was not so for observers watching the evolution of Vatican-Israeli relations.

An important assessment of these relations, in light of the Arafat visit, came from the rector of the Holy See–sponsored Ecumenical Institute in Tantur, Jerusalem. Donald Nicholl criticized the Holy See for not considering in sufficient depth the psychological roots of the Israeli-Palestinian dispute: diplomacy alone is not enough to go about spreading the message of the gospel and gaining the good will of other religions. As a concrete step, the rector of the Jerusalem-based institute suggested that the Vatican should recognize that, over the course of centuries, the Catholic Church "has done terrible things towards the Jews." This is why the "Church has got to stand somewhere where Jews can release their anger upon it."[99]

Finally, Father Bruno Hussar wondered "why the Pope put himself with those who do not like Israel." He was referring to the former Austrian chancellor Bruno Kreisky and to the Greek government, which had decided to grant official diplomatic status to PLO representatives in Athens. Alluding to the Pope's humanitarian and pastoral aims, and his willingness to meet with anybody, Hussar stated that Arafat and John Paul II did not speak the same language. The Palestinian leader had a political aim and used his audience in the Vatican to enhance his status. The Pontiff hoped to convince Arafat to renounce the use of violence in achieving his people's objectives.[100]

The meeting between the Pope and the Palestinian leader epitomized the nature of the role of the Holy See in the Israeli-Palestinian dispute. John Paul II chose to risk the wrath of Jews and Israelis in order to express his concern for a just and peaceful solution to the conflict in the Middle East. In some ways, the Pontiff felt that any damage done to interfaith relations between the Catholic Church and Judaism could always be repaired and enhanced.

The meetings between Paul VI and Golda Meir in 1973, and John Paul II and Yasser Arafat in 1982, showed similarities and noticeable differences. One similarity was the fact that the Holy See had no diplomatic ties with Israel or the PLO. There is, however, an underlying de facto recogni-

tion of the two entities, given the role they play in the dispute
that separates them. Another similarity was the consistent
defense by the Papacy of the legitimate rights of the Palestinians. Finally, there is the ever present memory of the Holocaust, raised in both 1973 and 1982. This demonstrates the
fact that after almost twenty years the resolution on Judaism
adopted by Vatican II and the generous outpouring of good
will invested in Catholic-Jewish dialogue were not enough
to erase past suspicions between the Holy See and the Jewish
state.

As far as differences are concerned, they were evidenced
in the contrast of the personalities and approach of Paul
VI and John Paul II. As a cautious diplomat, Paul VI
took advantage of the visit of Golda Meir to lay stress
on issues directly related to Vatican interests: its humanitarian mission, the issue of Christian communities in the
Holy Land, and the problem related to Jerusalem and the
Holy Places.

Unlike the 1973 meeting, the audience granted to Arafat
occurred in an atmosphere of grave tension between Palestinians and Israelis. It took place against the background of
the Lebanese War and the dangers that that war created for
both the integrity of Lebanon and the fate of the Palestinian movement. In fact, it was the first time since the beginning of the conflict that Palestinians and Israelis fought bat-
tles for a protracted period, climaxing in the seige of Beirut
in the summer of 1982. For these reasons, the Pope focused
on general issues related to the use of terrorism and reprisals,
and the reciprocal recognition of Palestinians and Israelis
of their respective rights to existence and security.

At the circumstantial level, it should be noted that unlike
the controversial verbal note issued after the visit of Golda
Meir to Pope Paul VI in which the Holy See defended the
papal action to the Arab side, John Paul II's decision to meet
with Arafat was defended by some prelates in the Curia and
by Archbishop John Roach, then president of the United
States National Conference of Catholic Bishops. The dra-

matic situation in Lebanon and the tragic impact of the Palestinian issue required the mobilization of the transnational network of the Church. The fact that the American hierarchy had to enter into the fray was an expression of the necessity to keep channels open to the influential Jewish community in the United States while reaffirming the soundness of the papal decision.

The cases analyzed here—the Israeli raid in 1968, the meeting between Golda Meir and Paul VI, and the audience granted by John Paul II to Yasser Arafat—solidly support my proposition related to the diplomatic nature of the Holy See's intervention in the Israeli-Palestinian dispute (see p. 10, above). There is an underlying theme to this intervention emphasized by the Holy See's concern for the welfare of the Catholic minority living in the Levant and the defense of Church principles such as the fostering of peace through justice illustrated by the papal emphasis on the right of both Israelis and Palestinians to self-determination.

Furthermore, there is the fundamental fact that given its nature as a religious institution any action taken by the Holy See or by other actors toward the Holy See can be given a symbolic meaning. In international affairs, the personality of the Pope is highlighted by his role as a moral and spiritual guide to world leaders. In addition, the fact that the Papacy is not impartial in the Israeli-Palestinian dispute is compensated by the prestige enjoyed by the Pope and the fact that he does not have "divisions" to command in case of threats to the Church's interests. Both Palestinians and Israelis understood the importance of the Papacy as a symbol in order to enhance their own cause and interests.

The last test case selected for this chapter deals with another facet of papal intervention in the Israeli-Palestinian dispute. Fundamentally, the Capucci affair demonstrates that in a conflict between the Israeli government and Catholic groups, the Holy See is bound to seek to protect the interests of the local Church.

THE HOLY SEE, ISRAEL, AND ARCHBISHOP
HILARION CAPUCCI

On August 8, 1974, the Israeli police arrested the Greek Catholic Patriarchal Vicar of Jerusalem, Archbishop Hilarion Capucci. In December, the Syrian-born vicar was put on trial and convicted of gunrunning in behalf of the PLO. The prelate was sentenced to twelve years in jail.

Bishop Capucci's lawyer defended his client's innocence and challenged the legitimacy of the Israeli court. Aziz Shehadeh, a Palestinian lawyer from Ramallah, argued that the prelate could not be sentenced, because of his diplomatic immunity and because of the fact that as long as the status of Jerusalem has not been settled at the international level, no Israeli court could have jurisdiction in the eastern part of Jerusalem.[101]

The Greek Catholic community strongly reacted to the Israeli decision. In expressing his community's outrage, the Melchite[102] Patriarch, Maximos V Hakim, said:

> Is this Bishop reprehensible if he thought it was his duty to bear arms or help the fedayeen or take actions that Israel does not approve? If we go back in history, we find the case of other bishops who have smuggled weapons, gave their lives, and committed other illegal actions, in order to save Jews from Nazi occupation. I do not see why a man who is ready to save Arabs should be condemned. The Jews are in East Jerusalem against UN decisions. This Bishop could have thought that their presence was illegal.[103]

The tenor of this reaction was reflected by several other statements that were echoed in the Arab media. Melchite Monsignor Lutfi Laham, Bishop Capucci's successor as Patriarchal Vicar of Jerusalem, stated that "Bishop Capucci liked politics. He believed that a clergyman should be active politically in his society."[104] Monsignor Laham said also that Greek Catholics in Jerusalem have had a history of political engagement in Jerusalem and the Holy Land. "We can say that the Greek Catholics in the Holy Land are like the Greek Orthodox in Syria and Lebanon for their pro-Arab feelings."[105]

Bishop Capucci expressed his own political philosophy in an interview:

> When your country is occupied, it is your duty to resist. Of course, if there are ways to do something without harm, like Gandhi, it would be best. But when your adversary — I never use the word enemy — does not want to understand you, to understand your legal or just point of view, what will you do?[106]

Another kind of reaction came from a group of eight Catholic clergymen living in Israel and actively involved in Christian-Jewish dialogue. A member of the group, Father Bruno Hussar, criticized Capucci's activism as being against "a passage in the gospel where Jesus says to render to Caesar what is Caesar's and to God what is God's."[107] The Dominican priest meant that Bishop Capucci should have forsaken his political engagement in order to be faithful to his pastoral duties. However, Hussar's advice would have had more of an impact had he not himself been involved in Israeli politics.

Given the Melchite ties to Rome, some observers in Israel thought that Capucci's imprisonment would inevitably lead to a confrontation between Israel and the Holy See.[108] At the beginning of the Capucci affair, the Holy See took a wait-and-see attitude to clarify the veracity of Israeli allegations. For this purpose, Pope Paul VI had a long meeting on September 7, 1974, with the apostolic nuncio in Lebanon, Monsignor Alfredo Bruniera, who had previously met with a PLO delegation.[109]

In reaction to the Israeli court's verdict, the Holy See issued a communiqué in which it expressed its deep regret about the conviction of Capucci:

> This episode is a painful blow to one of the glorious Eastern Catholic communities, the Greek Catholic Church,

where Monsignor Capucci has exercised for many years
the episcopal function. . . . He is the pastor of the faithful
who live in Jerusalem and the Holy Land, places dear to
the veneration of believers and where the presence of
Catholics is the object of the Holy Father's great interest.
This verdict, unfortunately, cannot but aggravate tension
in the complex situation of this territory where, notwithstanding laudable efforts, just peace is still far from being established, and where populations live in a climate
of anguish, conflict, and uncertainty.[110]

This statement, which has been characterized as a "master-
piece of prudence and ambiguity,"[111] did not satisfy the
Israelis who were looking for an explicit condemnation by
the Holy See of the bishop's alleged offense. It also illustrated
where priorities lie when it comes to the Middle East: the
fate of Catholic communities is of paramount importance
to the Holy See.

During his captivity, pressures mounted from several Muslim quarters in Israel, the Arab countries, and from the UN
Commission for Human Rights in Geneva, asking for prompt
release of the Melchite bishop. The Israeli government refused these requests. The minister of justice stated that the
Capucci affair "is part of the fight that Israel is waging
against terror. It has nothing to do with Israel's relations
with the Catholic Church and Christian communities."[112]

The case of Archbishop Capucci presented the Holy See
with yet another dilemma. On the one hand, it did not want
to alienate the Arab and Palestinian communities, but it did
have to respond to the mounting pressures to take concrete
steps to free the Melchite prelate. On the other hand, the
Holy See had to keep its channels open with the Israeli government to find a way out for Capucci.

On November 3, 1977, Paul VI sent a letter to the Israeli
president in Jerusalem. In it the pontiff called on the Israeli
leader "to make use of your clemency as President of the
State of Israel in favor of Archbishop Hilarion Capucci and

to have him released from prison. And we are confident that his release will not be detrimental to the state of Israel."[113] In reply to the Pope's request, the Israeli president, Efraim Katzir, stated that he was freeing Capucci, "fully recognizing the significance and the importance of your request and the weight which attaches to your expression of confidence that the matter will not be detrimental to the state of Israel."[114] In addition, the two sides agreed that the archbishop would thenceforth dedicate himself to purely pastoral duties and never again be involved in Middle East politics.

The Israeli government thought that giving in to the Pope's request would "create a fund of goodwill in the Catholic world. It expects the phrasing of the papal missive to put relations between Jerusalem and the Catholic world on a more normal footing of mutual recognition."[115] The archbishop's sentence was commuted and on November 6, 1977, Capucci was escorted to Ben Gurion Airport and put on a commercial flight to Rome.

The Capucci affair did not end with the prelate's liberation. Given his total commitment to the Palestinian cause, Capucci decided to continue to be actively involved in the Middle East political arena. In January 1979 he attended in Damascus a gathering of the Palestine National Council (the Palestinian parliament in exile) and played a key role in organizing the meeting of the Holy See's secretary of state, Cardinal Agostino Casaroli, with the PLO "foreign minister," Farouk Kaddoumi (March 1981), and the meeting of Pope John Paul II with Yasser Arafat (September 1982).

For obvious reasons, the Israelis, following the liberation of Capucci, felt betrayed by his political activism. They accused the Holy See of having violated its pledge to the Israeli head of state. *The Jerusalem Post* printed in an editorial:

> The PLO is evidently viewed in the Vatican as a significant channel of communication to the Islamic world, and under the circumstances — and however absurdly — as a hedge against the worst befalling the Christians of Leba-

non. Closer ties to the PLO may also be seen as a means of expressing the Holy See's dissatisfaction with the Knesset's passage of Geula Cohen's Jerusalem Law.[116]

This Israeli interpretation of Holy See policy toward the Palestinians was further confirmed when Pope John Paul II dispatched Bishop Capucci to Teheran. His mission was to solve problems that some Catholic institutions were having with Iranian authorities. In addressing the papal emissary, Ayatollah Khomeini, in a violent speech, accused the Catholic schools of being "spy dens" in Iran.[117]

The case of Archbishop Capucci eloquently demonstrates the Papacy's predisposition to side with one of its local churchmen to the possible detriment of its relations with Israel. The Holy See, even if convinced that the prelate had by-passed his pastoral duties, could not acquiesce in the Israeli decision to jail Capucci. In some ways, given the vulnerability of the Eastern Churches, the Papacy had to take action, even at the cost of sacrificing improved relations with the Jewish state.

There are parallels here with the consequences resulting from the meeting between John Paul II and Arafat. The fate of the Catholic community in the Arab-Islamic world, and the importance to the Church of the Palestinian issue, moved the Holy See to take bold actions, well aware of the harm these actions could do to Catholic-Jewish relations, the essential point being that most Catholics in the Middle East are of Arab descent. Non-Arab Catholics who have chosen Israeli citizenship are not so numerous as to be a prime concern.

The Papacy finds itself in a dilemma: how to protect the Catholic minority in the Levant and yet improve Jewish and Israeli attitudes toward the Church. The two concerns in some instances seem compatible, but in reality they are contradictory in light of the unyielding antagonism between the Palestinian and the Israeli conception regarding the settlement of their dispute.

CONCLUSIONS

This chapter has dealt with the nature and implementation of the Holy See's intervention in the Israeli-Palestinian dispute. An assessment has been made of the Holy See's attitude toward Judaism and Israel, and toward the Palestinians.

One conclusion is that there are fundamental objectives for the Holy See in the Israeli-Palestinian dispute. The first objective is to preserve and maintain a Catholic presence in Israel. The Papacy dreads the thought that, as a result of intense emigration, the birthplace of Christ might some day be bereft of Catholics. To stem the tide of exile, the Holy See created two important institutions—Bethlehem University and the Pontifical Mission for Palestine—through which it hoped to keep local Catholic communities in place. The Catholic Church cannot afford to lose its credibility on a global scale through the loss of the Holy Land.

Tied to the welfare of Catholic communities is the question of the Palestinians. It is a question that relates closely to papal teachings and most importantly to the implementation of peace through justice. One cannot be achieved without the other, and the Holy See's second objective—that of advocating the right to self-determination for the Palestinians—is consequently rendered more difficult, given the intractable nature of the Arab-Israeli quarrel.

Furthermore, the close relationship between temporal and religious matters in both Islam and Judaism is a serious obstacle to the Holy See in the attainment of its objectives. Some Jews and Israelis have a deep mistrust of the Papacy because of its alleged attitude during the Holocaust. Even though the Holy See has tried to set the record straight regarding its involvement during World War II, it will take several generations and much good will to fill the gap between the Holy See and the Jewish community.

The Holy See is eager to arrive at a final settlement of the Palestinian problem in the form of a national homeland where Palestinians could exert their full right to nationhood. But the road toward this goal is fraught with obstacles and traps. Moreover, the Palestinian issue is linked to the outcome of the Lebanese War, in which the Holy See intervened to maintain the integrity of the country.

In the final analysis, the Holy See's policy is derived from both long- and short-term perspectives. In the long-term perspective, the Holy See strives always to maintain and support the Catholic presence. In the short-term perspective, the Holy See continues to prod both Palestinians and Israelis to arrive at a peaceful settlement. This policy is translated by a pragmatic attitude that motivates the intervention of the Holy See with both Palestinians and Israelis. The Papacy is aware that the Jewish state is here to stay and the best way for the Holy See to defend its interests is to accommodate Catholic interests with Israel's whenever compromise is possible.

For Israel, the Holy See represents a powerful symbol, even if partisan, and any concession that the Israeli authorities would like to get from Rome has to be balanced against the limited means of the Papacy. Israeli–Holy See relations are thus rendered hostage to the ebb and flow of the conflicts between Arabs and Israelis. They are also dependent on the Jewish state's decisions regarding the city of Jerusalem and especially the fate of the Christian communities in the Holy Land.

Regarding the Palestinians, the best course for the Holy See would seem to be that of stressing common interests with the Arab and Islamic world, and fostering moderation toward the reality of Israel.

The Holy See is a mediator in the Israeli-Palestinian dispute, but a mediator whose involvement is unlike that of other powers. The Papacy has no strategic sea lanes to defend or oil fields to protect. It has the fate of the Catholic community in the Levant and the weight of its prestige and moral teachings with which to negotiate.

2. The Holy See, the Holy Places, and Jerusalem

AN ANALYSIS OF THE Holy See's role in the Middle East must include an assessment of the Jerusalem issue. The question of Jerusalem is replete with political, historical, and religious elements—all of which make its resolution extremely difficult.[1] Unlike the Lebanese War and the Israeli-Palestinian conflict, in which the Holy See has acted as mediator, moderator, and conciliator, in the specific instance of Jerusalem the Papacy is a party to the dispute. The Holy See is trying to salvage Christian interests and presence in the Holy Land.

Essentially, Jerusalem presents a fundamental challenge to the Holy See's two paramount priorities in the Middle East: ecumenical concerns and the welfare of Catholic minorities. This challenge stems from the highly religious and historical importance of Jerusalem to the followers of the three monotheistic religions—Jews, Christians, and Muslims. In the other two problematic Middle East situations—the Israeli-Palestinian dispute and the Lebanese War—the Holy See's course of action is determined by the intensity of the threat facing the Christian community and the readiness for ecumenical and interfaith relations.

In Lebanon, the Holy See is actively fostering coexistence and has made its ecumenical concerns of primary importance. In the Israeli-Palestinian dispute, the Holy See rates its interfaith objectives secondary to the protection of Christian communities. But in Jerusalem the two priorities are so intricately linked that neither priority dominates policy.

Under Ottoman and British rules, the Popes usually stressed the prominence of Catholic privileges over those of other religious groups. This position was altered following the Second Vatican Council. In fact, both Paul VI and John Paul II have stressed the universal character of Jerusalem, and expressed their opposition to any exclusive religious and political control. Nevertheless, behind the calls to safeguard the peculiar character of Jerusalem, the Holy See is primarily concerned with maintaining its voice in the fate of the birthplace of Christianity. The Holy See makes its presence and impact felt through this policy, which is based on pragmatism and its need to act as a spiritual guide. Finally, the status of Jerusalem and the Holy Places constitutes a major stumbling block for the establishment of formal diplomatic relations between the Holy See and Israel.

This chapter will first deal with the religious significance of Jerusalem to Jews, Christians, and Muslims. Subsequently, a short account will be given of the changing juridical status of Jerusalem from Ottoman and British domination through the United Nations resolution calling for the partition of Palestine and the internationalization of the Holy City. Then a section will deal with the local, regional, and global attitudes and interests in Jerusalem. Finally, the involvement of the Holy See in the Jerusalem dispute will be analyzed. The fundamental premise of this chapter is that the Holy See is totally opposed to any political control and religious exclusivity over Jerusalem. Moreover, there is a direct and clear relationship between the extent of papal intervention and the severity of the threats to the civil and religious rights of the communities in the Holy Land.

The test cases selected to support the premise are: (1) the "judaization" of Jerusalem, (2) the 1973 joint memorandum issued subsequent to the audience of Pope Paul VI with African leaders, (3) the papal exhortation *Nobis in Animo*, (4) the Tripoli Seminar, (5) the statement on Jerusalem published by *L'Osservatore Romano* in 1980, (6) John Paul II's apostolic letter *Redemptionis Anno* (1984), and (7) the Notre Dame affair (1970–1973).

RELIGIOUS SIGNIFICANCE OF JERUSALEM
TO JEWS, CHRISTIANS, AND MUSLIMS

The religious importance of the city is unquestionably rooted in the presence of holy shrines highly revered by all three monotheist religions. Throughout its troubled history, Jerusalem has been a sacred place for the followers of the Jewish faith. According to Jewish law, when a Jew prays he must face in the direction of the "City of Eternity," as it is specified in the Bible.[2] This is an integral part of the Jewish religion. Following the destruction of the first Temple (587 B.C.), and the dispersal of the Jewish people, the Jews took a sacred oath that, according to Psalm 137, stated:

> If I forget Thee, O Jerusalem
> Let my right hand forget its cunning.
> Let my tongue cleave to the roof of my mouth
> If I remember Thee not
> If I set not Jerusalem above my chiefest joy.

This attachment that Jews feel for Jerusalem is one of the main reasons why there exists such an intimate link between the temporal and the spiritual in Judaism. In clarifying the preeminence of Jerusalem, Rabbi Marc Tannenbaum has said:

> Christianity has become indigenous in many parts of the world; it is represented by strong Christian states. There is nowhere a desire of homeless Christians to return to the original land of their religion. Jewry has nowhere established another independent natural center, and as is natural, Jerusalem and the land of Israel are intertwined far more intimately with the religious and historic memoirs of the Jewish people.[3]

Still, there is not among Jews complete agreement about Zionism and the temporal importance of Jerusalem. The fundamental question remains whether Israel is a secular or a theocratic state. The Israelis refuse to consider their state a religious entity. But a closer look at several rules and laws adopted since the establishment of Israel leads the observer to conclude that the Jewish state is not significantly different from neighboring Arab-Islamic countries. As Joelle Le Morzellec put it:

> When one resides in Israel one notices immediately that because of the Law of Return which grants citizenship to any Jew who wishes to settle in the Jewish state, while every non-Jew has to follow the normal procedure of civic integration; or also, because of the importance of the Sabbath as the weekly day of rest, Israel is a confessional state like the Arab countries where laws are dictated by the Koran.[4]

The lack of agreement about Israel is further illustrated by the controversy surrounding the rebuilding of the Temple of Solomon in Jerusalem. Twice destroyed during its history, the Temple survives only in a remnant of the Western Wall, which is very sacred in the Jewish faith. For some Orthodox Jews, the Temple will be rebuilt only when the Messiah comes. According to halakah (Rabbinic law), the site where the Temple was built cannot be walked upon until all the rituals for purification have been performed. However, together with some Western fundamentalist Christian groups, other Jews believe that the third Temple must be built before the coming of the Messiah.[5]

The major Jewish holy places include the Tomb of Absalom, the Cemetery on the Mount of Olives, the Tomb of David, the Wailing Wall, Rachel's Tomb, as well as a number of ancient and modern synagogues. It is essential to note here that there is an overlap between Jewish holy sites and highly revered Muslim shrines. For example, the Haram al-Sharif compound, which includes the Dome of the Rock and the Aqsa Mosque, is built on the site of the second Jewish Temple, located near the Wailing Wall.

For Christians, Jerusalem is the place where Jesus preached

his message and where he was crucified and died. Moreover, in the New Testament Jerusalem symbolizes the new people of God redeemed by the Messiah. This Christian expectation is founded in the New Testament, as revealed to the Apostle John:

> Then I saw a new heaven and a new earth; for the first heaven and the first earth had passed away, and the sea was no more. And I saw the holy city, new Jerusalem coming down out of heaven from God, prepared as a bride adorned for her husband . . . and death shall be no more, neither shall there be mourning nor crying nor pain anymore, for the former things have passed away [Revelation 21:1–4].

The holy shrines of Christendom in Jerusalem are the Basilica of the Holy Sepulchre, the Cenacle, the Church of Saint Anne, the Tomb of the Virgin, the Garden of Gethsemani, the Sanctuary of the Ascension, and the Mount of Olives.

As in the Jewish faith, so too among Christians there are several positions regarding the importance of the Holy City. Father Youakim Moubarac writes that currently there are two Christian positions regarding Jerusalem. Some Western Christians consider "the struggle for Jerusalem as theirs because of the Jews and the sacred character of the city to Israel."[6] For Catholics and especially the Popes, "the problem of Jerusalem is important because it is a question of justice and not of Holy Places."[7] Consequently, for these Christians there is "a Palestinian problem, not a problem of Jerusalem."[8] Jerusalem is a symbol of redressing the rights of the oppressed and the fostering of peace through justice.

For Muslims, Jerusalem is sacred because of its association first with Abraham and his descendants and then with the Prophet Muhammad and his followers.[9] Jerusalem is never mentioned in the Qur'ān, but Muslims believe that the Prophet made a miraculous journey by night to Jerusalem. He rode on a winged steed (Buraq) from Mecca to the

Aqsa Mosque in Jerusalem. There the Prophet ascended into heaven until he reached the seventh heaven. This night journey is described in the Qur'ān:

> Glory be to Him, who carried His servant by night from the Holy Mosque [Mecca] to the Farthest Mosque [Jerusalem] the precincts of which We [God] have blessed, that We might show him [Muhammad] some of our signs [Surah 17:1].

From then on, the site of the Jerusalem temple, referred to in the Qur'ān as the Farthest Mosque, has been a sacred place of worship for Muslims, after Mecca and Medina (Saudi Arabia).

Religious feelings run very deep and are very strong. The emotional attachment of so many religious believers to a particular place is unparalleled in the world today. No other site holds as much symbolic value as Jerusalem for millions of Jews, Christians, and Muslims. This historical phenomenon gives to the holy city its unique and universal character.

JURIDICAL STATUS OF JERUSALEM

Since the inception of Christianity, Jerusalem has been subjected to more than ten foreign dominations. These occupations were the results of conquests or rivalries between regional or great powers vying for control in that part of the Levant. From 1517 to 1917, Jerusalem and the Holy Places came under the control of the Turkish Ottoman Empire. Under the Turks, Palestine was divided between the province of Beirut and the Sanjak (district) of Jerusalem. According to Peter Mansfield, "the Sanjak comprised about two-thirds of Palestine and more than three-quarters of its population. . . . Some 16 percent were Christian—mainly Greek Orthodox, Latin, and Greek Catholics—and about 5 percent were Jews."[10]

In 1453, after the conquest of Constantinople, the Ottomans adopted a policy favoring the Greek Orthodox hierarchies. This decision provoked tensions between the Greek and Latin communities living in the holy city. Rivalries between these two groups led to increased intervention by external powers—France, Imperial Russia, and others. After the Crusades, France unofficially played the role of protector of Catholics in the Levant and of the followers of the Latin rite in Jerusalem. Then, at the beginning of the eighteenth century, Russia's Peter the Great defended the interests of the Greek Orthodox community in Jerusalem.[11]

The Latins accused the Greek Orthodox in Jerusalem of having violated the capitulations of 1604 and 1740 between the French and the Turks, which granted the Latins the right to possess the Holy Sepulchre, the Church of the Nativity, and the Church of the Virgin.[12] This deplorable situation of confrontation between Christian communities ended with a statute (*Status Quo*) enacted by the Ottoman Sultan. In 1852 it became the legal instrument regulating the rights of ownership and administration of the Holy Places by the various Christian groups present in the Holy Land.[13]

Following World War I and the defeat of the Ottoman empire, the League of Nations approved the British mandate for Palestine on terms embodied in the Balfour Declaration (November 2, 1917), providing for the facilitation of Jewish immigration, land purchase, and implementation of public works, services, and utilities. The status of Jerusalem and the Holy Places became the focus of a power struggle between France and Italy—the two Catholic powers most interested in Jerusalem—and, later on, between Palestinians and Israelis.

Following the failure of the League of Nations to form a commission to deal with the rights of the religious communities in Jerusalem, the mandatory power (Great Britain) became the arbitrator between the Christian communities living in Jerusalem and between the major religions having interests in the Holy Places.[14] The *Status Quo* agreed upon in 1852 was maintained and adhered to by all the parties present in Jerusalem.

In 1937, the Palestine Royal Commission (Peel) recommended the partition of Palestine into Jewish and Arab states, and a British mandated area including Jerusalem, Bethlehem, and Jaffa.[15] The tensions between Arabs and Jews and the issue of Jerusalem were also the major concern of the Anglo-American Committee which was appointed in July 1945. The committee asked Morrison and Grady to come up with a plan to implement its recommendations. The Anglo-American Committee called for the creation in Palestine of a cantonal state with autonomous Arab and Jewish provinces, and two areas—including a Jerusalem enclave—under the control of the British government.[16]

At the end of World War II and following increased tensions between Palestinians and Israelis in the Holy Land, the United Nations decided to formulate an overall solution to the question of Palestine and Jerusalem. In its meeting held on November 29, 1947, the UN General Assembly approved a plan for the partition of Palestine into Jewish and Arab states. Regarding Jerusalem, the Palestine Partition Resolution 181 stated:

> The City of Jerusalem shall be established as a *corpus separatum* under a special international regime and shall be administered by the United Nations. The Trusteeship Council shall be designated to discharge the responsibilities of the Administering Authority on behalf of the United Nations.[17]

In February 1948 the Trusteeship Council drew up a statute for an internationalized Jerusalem but did not act upon it because a special session of the General Assembly had been called to review the entire Arab-Israeli problem. When the draft statute for the city of Jerusalem was taken up by the Trusteeship Council, the delegate from Iraq stated the Arab position that Jerusalem was an integral part of

Palestine and that the partition plan was illegal and so was the statute for a separate Jerusalem. Israel, whose admission at the UN was contingent upon its reassurance to Arab and Catholic delegations of its intentions regarding Jerusalem, reluctantly accepted the internationalization proposal. Israel reversed its stand immediately after having been voted in as a member of the United Nations.

In the meanwhile, following the outbreak of the Palestine War in mid-May 1948, Jerusalem was divided between Jordanians and Israelis. The old city with its Holy Places came under Jordanian control and the western part of the city fell under Israeli hegemony. In light of these changes, and the opposition of both Jordanians and Israelis to the internationalization plan, the UN Trusteeship Council adopted in April 1950 an amended proposal prepared by its president, Roger Garreau. The original proposal suggested by Garreau stated that only a small part of Jerusalem, including major Holy Places, should be internationalized under UN control.[18] This latest UN proposal and other plans advanced by Sweden and Bolivia were rejected by the Fourth and Fifth Assembly of the United Nations.[19] While the UN shelved the Jerusalem issue after 1950, prior resolutions providing for a *corpus separatum* remained alive but unimplemented.

The Papacy supported the internationalization plan and continued to call for an international control over Jerusalem. Moreover, the Holy See opposed the idea that any one government should have exclusive control in the city. From 1967 onwards, following the Israeli annexation, the Holy See's position shifted to one that is spiritual in nature and proposes that Jerusalem be safeguarded by a special statute internationally guaranteed.[20]

CHRISTIAN COMMUNITIES IN JERUSALEM

Having set the background surrounding the evolution in the legal status of Jerusalem, my analysis will now take up the situation of the Christian communities in Jerusalem. In the Lebanese War, one of the basic guidelines of Holy See diplomacy was to save Lebanon as a living example of Christian-Islamic coexistence and thus save Lebanese Christians. This policy led to a deep misunderstanding between the Holy See and the Christian militias, who thought that they could count on Rome's backing in their fight against the Palestinian-Islamic-Leftist coalition.

For Jerusalem, the Holy See's main concern was to save the Christian communities and have a say in the future status of the Holy Places of Christianity. The Papacy's feelings toward the fate of local Christians was dramatically emphasized by the apostolic delegate in Jerusalem, Archbishop Pio Laghi. Addressing local Christian tourist guides, the papal representatives said:

> You could move New York to another site, but you can't move Jerusalem: elsewhere it would be nothing. . . . The Church, through history, lives in the Arab Christians. The Church here is in a way wedded to the Palestinian Arab culture. If the Arab Christians move out, Christianity will disappear, as 96% of the believers are of Arab extraction, language, and culture.[21]

There are currently in the diocese of Jerusalem, which includes Israel, the West Bank, the Gaza Strip, and Jordan, some 182,000 Christians of different confessions. There are also 3 million Muslims and 2.9 million Jews.[22] One of the problems facing the Holy See is that of demographic changes in Jerusalem. According to a census taken in the wake of the June 1967 war and the annexation of Jerusalem to Israel, the population of Jerusalem included 199,000 Jews and 66,000 Arabs, of whom 11,000 were Christian (4,000 Greek Orthodox, 3,600 Roman Catholic, and 1,200 Greek Catholic), plus some 3,000 non-Arab Armenian Christians. The number of Christians as of 1979 was estimated to be less than 15,000.[23] The Christian portion of the Arab population has declined from 48.9% in 1949 to only 9.8% in

1978.[24] The decline is not in absolute numbers but in proportionality, in the context of rapid increases in the size of other ethnic-religious groups. The fact remains, however, that Christians are leaving the Holy Land, even though the exodus is less than it was in 1980 or 1975. Two major causes of the exodus are the Christian status as a minority and the westernized background of some Arab Christians.

Other important problems affect Christian minorities in the Holy Land. The presence of several religious communities in Jerusalem has led some observers to define this situation as a mosaic. This mosaic is not unlike that of the pseudo federation of ethno-religious communities in Lebanon. This mosaic is comprised of a large number of Christian communities in the Holy Land. According to a study by S. P. Colbi, there are thirty-five Christian Churches, which can be divided into four categories: Catholic, Orthodox, Monophysite, and Protestant.[25]

The oldest among the Christian Churches is the Greek Orthodox, which has about forty-four thousand followers. In the nineteenth century, other Christian groups—Catholic and Protestant—settled in Palestine. Until then, Catholic interests in Jerusalem were protected by the Franciscans present in Palestine since the fourteenth century. In 1847 Pope Pius XI established the Latin Patriarchate. The Greek Catholic (Melchite) Church is the most important among the Uniate Churches in Jerusalem, including the Armenian, Maronite, Syrian, and Coptic Churches.

These Christian communities have faced the same problems encountered by other minorities in the Levant—that is, an identity issue and the interreligious rivalries and squabbles peculiar to the Holy Land and Jerusalem. The fundamental issue for the Christian minority in the Holy Land has been that of acceptance on an equal footing. The same has applied to other non-Muslims under Islamic rule.

In fact, throughout history, under Arab and Turkish dominations, non-Muslims (Christians and Jews) were treated as *dhimmis*—tolerated minority—by the Muslim majority.

In the Ottoman empire, Islamic tolerance of Christians was defined by the millet system. "Under the system local communities of a particular sect were autonomous in the conduct of their spiritual affairs and civil affairs relating closely to religion and community, such as church administration, marriage, inheritance, property, and education."[26]

The millet system estranged Christians from political life and deepened suspicions between them and Muslims. Christians were treated as foreigners and suspected of being agents of foreign powers. Their loyalty was often put in doubt. After the fall of the Ottoman empire and in reaction to their plight, Middle Eastern Christians were at the forefront of the movement of Arab nationalism, the secular movement in the Arab world, and some among them founded socialist parties, such as the Baath (resurrection) Party now in power in Syria and Iraq.

The activism by Arab Christians was justified by the need to get out from the ghetto in which they had been forced to live.[27] Furthermore, for Christians living in the Holy Land, the dilemma relating to their identity was compounded by their status as a minority in Israel after the establishment of the Jewish state. In a sense, it was the second time in the history of Christianity that a Christian minority found itself living in the midst of a Jewish majority.[28]

Unlike some Christian groups in Lebanon that opted to follow a policy of total opposition to their Muslim counterparts, especially because of PLO presence in the country, Christians in the Holy Land have found themselves on the same side as Muslims regarding the Israeli-Palestinian dispute. For Rafiq Khoury there are several factors that explain the low level of antagonism between Palestinian Christians and Muslims. These factors are illustrated by:

- The fact that the Palestinian people as a whole have suffered from the drama that has affected Palestine since the beginning of this century.
- The fact that Christians and Muslims have struggled together to defend their legitimate rights.

- The fact that Christians in Palestine . . . have always had an acute sense of Arab nationalism, unlike what has occurred in other Arab countries.
- The fact that Christians have always played an active part in national life in all its aspects since the awakening of nationalist feelings at the end of the nineteenth century.[29]

In addition to the problems posed by the definition of their identity, Christian communities in Jerusalem have had to overcome centuries of mutual distrust and ill feeling. This situation is highlighted by rivalries — for example, between the Greek Orthodox Church, which is the oldest in the Holy Land, and the other Christian denominations (Catholic, Protestant, etc.). In fact, the Greek Orthodox Church, regarding itself as the "Church of the origins," considers "the Latins as intruders, the Greek Catholics as traitors, and the Protestants as proselytizers."[30] Moreover, the Orthodox community in the Holy Land cannot accept the fact that sometimes the Holy See talks about Jerusalem and the Holy Places as if it had an exclusive mandate to speak in behalf of all Christians. The Greek Orthodox Church considers itself one of the parties interested in the status of Jerusalem and has its own opinion to express on the matter.[31] Finally, the Greek Orthodox Church is reluctant to participate in any ecumenical efforts because it does not want to lose more of its faithful to the Latin and Greek Catholic communities. Historically, these two denominations have received the majority of their followers from the Greek Orthodox community.

Another problem facing the Christian communities in Jerusalem and of direct concern to the Holy See is the fact that the hierarchies — with the clear exception of the Greek Catholic — usually represent external interests (Greek, French, Russian, Italian, etc.) rather than the interests of indigenous Christian minorities. The Greek Orthodox hierarchy is Greek, the Latin is Italian, the Anglican is British, and so forth. Monsignor Laham, the Greek Catholic Patriarchal Vicar, pointed out that "it is only in Jerusalem that Arabic cannot be used as a language of communication in the intercommu-nitarian meetings of the heads of Christian communities."[32]

Finally, ownership of the Holy Places is another conten-tious issue in relations between Christian communities. Sev-eral Holy Places are shared by more than one denomina-tion and sometimes this situation leads to awkward disputes. For example, the Church of the Holy Sepulchre is shared by the Greek Orthodox, the Roman Catholics, the Arme-nians, the Copts, the Syrians, and the Ethiopians. The keys to this sacred Christian shrine have been, since Ottoman domination, in the hands of a Muslim family. However, in recent years a modus vivendi was reached between the vari-ous Christian communities in Jerusalem regarding the res-toration of the edifice.[33]

Besides the problems facing them internally Christian communities have to contend with the Israeli authorities. Ever since the Israeli government made the decision to ex-tend its law to Jerusalem, tensions have risen with some Christian denominations. The fundamental reason is that, besides the status quo based on customary law, Christian Churches in Jerusalem have no other guarantees protecting them. Other sources of friction with the Israeli government are the antimissionary law and the attacks mounted by Jewish extremist groups against Christian institutions in Jerusalem.

In reaction to the wave of anti-Christian activities, rep-resentatives of the Catholic and Protestant communities in Jerusalem issued a joint statement demanding "an interna-tionally guaranteed special statute concerning the rights and liberties of the great monotheistic faiths in Jerusalem."[34] The clergymen were expressing their fears of being continually victimized by the arbitrary decisions taken by the dominant power in the holy city. This has also been the position taken by the Holy See.

In summary, there are four major sources of tension vex-ing the Christian presence in Jerusalem, to which the Papacy must be permanently alert and responsive. The first is the problem of emigration affecting the Christian minority. The second is the long-held historical prejudices and misperceptions between Christians and Muslims in the Levant. The third is the absence of harmonious relations and unity among the various Christian Churches, which makes them vulnerable to each other and to outside divisive forces. The fourth is the precarious nature of the status of non-Jewish communities living in Jerusalem and the impact of this status on relations between the Israeli government and Christian hierarchies.

It is important to point out how the tensions plaguing the relations between the various communities in Jerusalem constitute an obstacle to the Holy See's ecumenical and interfaith concerns. In order to have a clearer understanding of these tensions, I now set my analysis in the broader perspective of the problems facing the Holy See in the Middle East.

In the Lebanese War obstacles to ecumenism and interfaith relations emerged from inter-Christian feuds and from tensions between some Christian and Muslim communities. The prejudices and fears commonly found in minority-majority relationships are an overriding factor in both Lebanon and Jerusalem. However, in the Holy Land, Palestinians—Christians and Muslims—share the same plight. Moreover, there is a difference in the tensions between Christian communities in Lebanon and Jerusalem.

In Lebanon misunderstanding between Christian communities and inside some of them is caused primarily by political considerations. The question of the Palestinian presence and nationalism in Lebanon is the fundamental source of differences. Although some in the Maronite community accuse the PLO of abusing Lebanese hospitality, the Greek Orthodox, for instance, are opposed to the links between some Christian militias and Israel.

In the Holy Land the obstacles to ecumenism are: (1) intercommunitarian feuds, (2) the dichotomy between the hierarchies representing international religious interests and the local Christian population, and (3) the question of the ownership of the Holy Places. If in Lebanon there are problems with inter-Christian and Christian-Islamic dialogue, in the Holy Land it is the presence and control of the Jewish state that causes tension. Additionally, most Christians in Jerusalem are Arabs, and therefore frank and sincere dialogue between Christians and Jews becomes more problematic.

Finally there is the problem of the attitude of local Christian communities regarding the internationalization of Jerusalem. Some Christians and Muslims are against the UN-sponsored plan on the grounds that "it might stengthen the influence of Western Christendom and generally give too much emphasis to the Christians abroad."[35] Christian communities in the Holy Land fear that the question of shrines and places of worship in Jerusalem may be considered more important than the fate of its inhabitants. These feelings were eloquently expressed by an Arab Christian when he wrote:

> Christianity, because of the number of its European adherents and its European culture, appears to many as European. . . . The idea of the internationalization of Jerusalem is a fruit of this European influence and an implicit affirmation that what matters in Jerusalem is the ancientness of its sacred places—its stones and not its people. . . . To give a special statute to the city of Jerusalem independent from Palestine means, in fact, to affirm that the city of Jerusalem is more important than Palestine.[36]

INVOLVEMENT OF REGIONAL AND GLOBAL POWERS IN JERUSALEM

In addition to the problems facing the Christian communities, the Holy See has also to contend with the irreconcilable stands of Arab and non-Arab Islamic governments and Israel toward Jerusalem and the Holy Places.

Since 1949, the Israeli position toward Jerusalem has been one of increased and unilateral control of the city. The first

Israeli position was illustrated in a memorandum submitted on November 16, 1949, to the Ad Hoc Political Committee of the UN General Assembly. In that document Abba Eban proposed an agreement with the UN regarding the functional internationalization of the Holy Places. In May 1950 Israel adopted a second position, calling for a partial internationalization of Jerusalem limited to the Holy Places. Except for the Cenacle, most of the Holy Places were under Jordanian control.[37]

In the aftermath of the June 1967 Arab-Israeli War, and the occupation of the eastern sector of Jerusalem by Israeli troops, the Israeli government adopted a law that considered the city annexed territory.[38] Unlike the West Bank of the Jordan and Gaza, which were considered Occupied Territories, Israel considered its stand on Jerusalem "irreversible and nonnegotiable."[39] A new situation emerged for the Holy Places: for the first time since 1948, Jewish, Christian, and Muslim shrines were under the control of one government. Moreover, for the followers of the Islamic faith, such an outcome could only result in grave consequences: their third most important place of worship was totally under Jewish control.

In order to calm the fears of local communities, the Israeli government enacted a law stipulating that "the Holy Places shall be protected from desecration and any other violation and from anything likely to violate the freedom of access of the members of the different religions to the places sacred to them or their feelings with regard to these places."[40]

In 1980, the Israeli Knesset adopted a "basic law" whereby Jerusalem was unilaterally declared "the eternal capital of Israel."[41] This decision epitomized the Israeli ruling coalition's desire to control Jerusalem. It set off a wave of protests and angry opposition, especially from Arab and non-Arab Islamic governments, that still find vehement expression today. The Holy See also objected to the Israeli decision to annex Jerusalem.

To complicate the situation even more, the Israeli government has been acquiring and even confiscating land in and around Jerusalem. Since 1967, the actions of Israeli authorities have provoked a controversy centered on the attempts to "Judaize" the city of Jerusalem. Christian and Muslim groups accused the Israelis of using housing projects and urban planning "to reinforce the Jewish character of the city,"[42] and forcing the exodus of the non-Jewish population.[43] The United Nations adopted several resolutions condemning Israeli actions and declaring them invalid.

In reply to the international body's disapproval, the Israeli government made it clear that it had no intention of "exerting a unilateral jurisdiction or exclusive responsibility on the Holy Places of Christianity and Islam."[44] Jerusalem as a city had come under Israeli control, but the government was willing to encourage and foster negotiations with local religious communities in order to guarantee the right of each in the Holy Places. In commenting on Israel's attitude toward the Holy Places, Monsignor Bernardin Collin, a renowned scholar on the Jerusalem issue, wrote:

> It does not matter whether the Holy Places are in Israel or elsewhere. Most of all, they must be safeguarded from political vicissitudes in relation to either local or general politics. This is the substance of the problem. From this comes the necessity for a special status for the Holy Places.[45]

Following the 1947 UN resolution on Jerusalem, Arab and non-Arab Islamic governments have expressed their opposition to the internationalization scheme. Arabs have feared that, under the cover of an international regime, Jewish agencies would spare no efforts to control Jerusalem. Nevertheless, when it became apparent that Jerusalem was going to be partitioned under Israeli and Jordanian rules, some Arab governments backed the idea of placing Jerusalem under international control.[46]

The clearest statements available on Arab and Islamic stands toward Jerusalem can be found in the resolutions adopted at several international conferences, such as the meetings in Rabat (Morocco, September 22–25, 1969), the Islamic summit of Lahore (Pakistan, February 22–24, 1974), and the Islamic summit of Taef (Saudi Arabia, January 25–29, 1981).

In all these gatherings, Arab and non-Arab Muslim leaders expressed their total opposition to the internationalization of Jerusalem and its control by a non-Arab entity. Moreover, "for Arabs and Muslims of the world, Jerusalem is part and parcel of Palestine and its fate cannot be dissociated from that of the Palestinian problem."[47]

In this context, mention should be made of the important role played by Saudi Arabia. As guardians of Mecca and Medina, the House of Saud has tried to persuade Arab and Islamic countries that the liberation of Palestine should include that of the Holy Places of Islam in Jerusalem. The prominence of the Saudi role was underlined in the peace plan proposed by Prince Fahd (August 7, 1981).

Among the seven principles of the plan, one called for the "Israeli evacuation of all Arab territories seized during the 1967 Middle East War, including the Arab sector of Jerusalem." Another called for guarantees of "freedom of religious practices for all religions in the Jerusalem holy shrines." Finally, another called for the setting up of a "Palestinian state *with East Jerusalem as its capital.*"[48]

In summary, the Arabs see the Jerusalem issue as an integral part of the Israeli-Palestinian conflict. Their major concerns are access to their Holy Places and recognition of the rights of the Palestinians. On the other hand, the Israeli perspective is one of sovereignty over the city. The Holy See essentially acknowledges the claims of both sides with its proposal for an internationally guaranteed special status for Jerusalem. The Holy See through this proposal has addressed the fundamental aspect of the Jerusalem question — the spiritual character of the issue, free access to the Holy Places, and preservation of the rights of the religious communities. Furthermore, the Papacy's proposal serves to define the issue of sovereignty by providing the framework for the establishment of an international body that would oversee Jerusalem.

INTERNATIONAL ATTITUDES:
THE UNITED STATES AND THE SOVIET UNION

Since 1948, the international community has not accepted the domination of either Arabs or Israelis over the Holy City. D. Jaeger wrote:

> The international position . . . is, or ought to be, motivated by a reasonable hope that continued refusal to recognize any nation's sovereignty in Jerusalem may induce those nations concerned to establish such claims to agree to a realistic, just international arrangement whereby freedom of access to the shrines and the liberty and legitimate rights of the religious communities to which these are sacred would be firmly and effectively guaranteed.[49]

Following the Israeli government's decision to move its foreign ministry to Jerusalem (1953), the United States refused to transfer its embassy from Tel Aviv. The American government, however, has continued to maintain a consulate in Jerusalem, independent of the embassy in Tel Aviv. By 1967 nearly 40 percent of the fifty-four foreign diplomatic establishments in Israel were in Jerusalem. Most of these legations belonged to African and Latin American countries.

In 1960 the United States opposed Jordanian plans to build offices for the king, the cabinet, and the parliament in Jerusalem. Then in 1967, following the Israeli occupation of the old city, the United States expressed its opposition to the Israeli decision to place all Jerusalem under its jurisdiction and administration. In 1980, following the Knesset's vote making Jerusalem the eternal capital of Israel, most of the countries having diplomatic relations with the Jewish state transferred their diplomatic establishments back to Tel

Aviv. Only Costa Rica and El Salvador have embassies in Jerusalem.

The United States position toward Jerusalem was expressed by President Reagan in his September 1, 1982, Middle East peace initiative. He stated that "Jerusalem must remain undivided, but its final status should be decided through negotiations."[50]

In 1948, during the debates on the internationalization of Jerusalem, the Soviet Union adopted a stand favorable to the UN plan provided that it would guarantee the interests of the population and religious groups, and ensure peace and security for the city. Behind the Soviet support there was "the hope that it could somehow increase its influence in the Middle East through participation as a major power in UN supervisory activities over an internationalized Holy City."[51] The Soviet Union dropped its backing for *corpus separatum* in 1950.

Following the 1967 war, the Soviet Union broke its diplomatic relations with Israel, and together with its East European allies backed a Pakistani resolution at the UN considering the Israeli annexation of Jerusalem invalid.

In conclusion, the global powers disagree with Israel's exclusive control of Jerusalem. The United States advocates that the city remain undivided. The Soviet Union aligned itself with the Arab-Islamic position.

THE HOLY SEE, THE HOLY PLACES, AND JERUSALEM

The Holy See's policy toward Jerusalem has, over the past century, evolved from one of supremacy to one of fostering ecumenism and interfaith relations. Throughout history, the Holy See has never wavered in asserting its rights in Jerusalem and the Holy Places. These rights have been recognized by international organizations such as the United Nations, other Christian churches, Arab and non-Arab Islamic countries, and even Israel.[52]

Until 1947, the Papacy defended the preeminence of Catholic rights and privileges in the Holy Land over those of other religious denominations. The Balfour Declaration, with its promise of a Jewish homeland in Palestine, became a major concern for the Holy See. Pope Benedict XV was worried about the impact of such an eventuality on Catholic influence in Palestine. In an address on March 10, 1919, he stated:

It would be a terrible grief for us and for all the Christian faithful if infidels were placed in a privileged and prominent position. Much more if those most holy sanctuaries of the Christian religion were given to the charge of non-Christians.[53]

The paramount importance of preserving Catholic interests and claims in Jerusalem was again emphasized in a short address — Vehementer Gratum — by Pope Pius XI (December 11, 1922). In that statement the Pope declared:

It is our apostolic duty to ask that the rights of the Catholic Church in Palestine — in cases where they are evidently superior to the rights of other interested parties — be respected and safeguarded and given priority not only over the rights of Jews and infidels, but also over those of members of non-Catholic confessions.[54]

From 1922 to 1948 the thrust of Pius XI's address guided the position of the Papacy and became the underpinning of the Church's ethnocentric attitude prior to Vatican II. In the aftermath of the UN resolutions and debates related to the status of Jerusalem (1948–1950), the Holy See came out in favor of the internationalization of the city. This position was elucidated in two subsequent encyclicals issued by Pope Pius XII. In the first encyclical, In Multiplicibus Curis (October 24, 1948), the Pontiff, without explicitly mentioning internationalization, called for international guarantees to assure "both free access to Holy Places scattered throughout Palestine, and the freedom of worship and the respect of customs and religious traditions."[55] One year later, in his encyclical *Redemptoris Nostri Cruciatus* (April 15, 1949), Pius XII wrote that it was of the "utmost importance that due immunity and protection be guaranteed to all the Holy Places of Palestine not only in Jerusalem but also in other cities and villages as well."[56]

This second papal document came in the aftermath of plans, discussed at the UN, that would have permanently divided Jerusalem between Israel and Jordan. According to Eugene Bovis, "under such an arrangement, there would be little prospect for concentrating a Christian population in Jerusalem in sufficient numbers to have much say in the conduct of the affairs of the city or to provide a base for promotion of Vatican interests in the Near East."[57] Furthermore, the Holy See's support for internationalization was due to the increased alarm that the Pope felt for the shrines and Catholic institutions that had suffered damages in the course of the 1948 Arab-Israeli war. The other major reason had political overtones. A recent Italian study based on thorough research of British and American diplomatic archives suggests that France had urged its ambassador to the Holy See, Wladimir d'Ormesson, "to ask the Holy Father to take an official stand favoring the internationalization of Jerusalem and the Holy Places. . . . Pope Pius XII welcomed this suggestion."[58] There was no doubt that the Pope had chosen to please "the eldest daughter of the Church," France.

From 1967 onwards, reflecting the changes that had occurred at the United Nations where the majority of members were from the non-Catholic Third World and the changes brought about by the Israeli occupation of the old city, the Holy See reassessed its policy toward Jerusalem and the Holy Places. In fact, the Papacy dropped its call for an international regime for Jerusalem and opted instead to call for a special status with international guarantees. Nevertheless, the fact that no single nation should control the city remained the fundamental principle guiding Vatican policy toward Jerusalem. It was the application that was modified.

The evolution in the Holy See's approach toward Jerusalem was reflected in several of Pope Paul VI's speeches, but most of all in his allocution to the Sacred College of Cardinals on December 22, 1967. In his address the Pontiff elaborated on his views regarding a solution to the Jerusalem question:

> There are two essential aspects that are impossible to evade. The first concerns the Holy Places properly so called and considered as such by the three great monotheistic religions, Judaism, Christianity, and Islam. It is a matter of guaranteeing freedom of worship, respect for preservation of and access to the Holy Places, protected by special immunities thanks to a special status, whose observation would be guaranteed by an institution international in character, taking particular account of the historic and religious personality of Jerusalem. The second aspect of the question refers to the free enjoyment of the legitimate civil and religious rights of persons, residences, and activities of all communities present on the territory of Palestine.[59]

The attitude of Paul VI was that internationalization was a political stand, rendered ineffective by the United Nations' failure to implement its resolutions. Therefore, the Holy See opted to call for international guarantees for the Holy Places and the unrestricted enjoyment of civil and religious rights for the communities living in Jerusalem. In some way, the Church, in light of the ecumenical spirit fostered by Vatican II, regained its true position as a spiritual guide advancing proposals for a solution to the question of Jerusalem and the Holy Places. It left to the international community the task of setting the modalities by which the guarantees of these rights ought to be implemented. Moreover, it is important to point out that unlike the addresses of Benedict XV and Pius XI, Pope Paul VI in his address placed the three religious communities present in Jerusalem—Jewish, Christian, and Muslim—on an equal footing. There was no reference to the Holy See's fear that Palestine come under the control of infidels, "*in potestate infidelium.*"

Finally, reference should be made to the fact that papal solicitude was no longer limited to churches and institutions alone, but included the civil and religious rights of the "communities" present in "Palestine," which were of equal if not greater importance. The Pontiff's stand toward Jerusalem was supported by other Christian groups such as the World Council of Churches. Following a meeting of its Central Committee in West Berlin (August 1974), the World Council of Churches affirmed in a statement on the Middle East that "the question of Jerusalem is not only a matter of protection of Holy Places, it is organically linked with living faiths and communities of people in the Holy City."[60]

The approach adopted by the Pope toward Jerusalem was bound to clash with that formulated by the Israeli government. In a sense, the Holy See's suggestion for Jerusalem and the Holy Places constituted a check by the international community on total Israeli sovereignty. Consequently, the differences between the two sides led to frictions and misunderstandings.

The "Judaization" of Jerusalem

Following the 1967 war, a controversy erupted regarding Israeli plans to "Judaize" urban Jerusalem. The Holy See did not stay out of the fray but expressed its displeasure in a polemical article in *L'Osservatore Romano*. In its March 22, 1971, issue, the Vatican newspaper stated:

A very grave state of affairs is being created against legality, on the basis of the logic of "accomplished facts." The measures of expropriation suffice to give an idea of the radical manner in which a character not conforming to its historical and religious nature and to its universal vocation is being imposed on the City. In January 1968, 300 acres of land were confiscated in the Mount Scopus area and are already largely built up with Jewish residential quarters. In August 1970, another 1,200 acres have been confiscated in the Arab zone of Jerusalem and around the city, in order to implement the "Greater Jerusalem" plans. Another project is under study for the Old City of Jerusalem, according to which about 6,000 Arabs will be displaced and several buildings confiscated. It is impossible to avoid experiencing a profound apprehension towards such grave changes. Even in Israel itself these plans have provoked motivated criticisms and not just from an urbanistic point of view.[61]

L'Osservatore Romano concluded its article by stressing the need for "an international body that would truly guarantee the particular character of Jerusalem and the right of its minority communities."[62] The question here was how to accommodate the position of the Israeli government in its intent to extend its sovereignty over the city and at the same time protect the right of non-Jewish communities living in Jerusalem.

The Joint Memorandum (1973)

The concern of the Papacy to maintain and preserve the "unique" and "universal" character of Jerusalem led to other controversies with the Israelis. In December 1973, Paul VI granted an audience to a delegation of African heads of state. Following the meeting a joint communiqué was issued and published by an independent news agency (KIPA). The agency reported that the African leaders came to the Vatican to share with the Pope their concern regarding the city of Jerusalem.

For the African delegation, "Jerusalem should not fall under the exclusive control of one religion. The solution for the city must be found on the basis of UN resolutions."[63] In referring to the Pope, the joint memorandum stated that the "Holy Father has confirmed the position of the Holy See regarding the Holy Places and the city of Jerusalem in particular."[64]

In Israel, the news of the Rome meeting reached the news-papers without making a distinction between the African leaders' statement and the Pontiff's. It looked as if Paul VI had himself stated his opposition to any exclusive control by one religious group over Jerusalem. Some Israeli politi-cians, such as Dr. Joseph Burg, minister of the interior, and Dr. Z. Warhaftig, minister for religious affairs, publically reproved Paul VI. Some influential Italian newspapers re-ported that Israeli attacks against the Pope had provoked deep discontent in the Vatican.[65]

Davar, the organ of the Israeli Labor Party, wrote that the Pope's "words . . . are at the same time a false descrip-tion of the situation as it exists and a false illustration of Israel's declared intentions regarding the future. . . . The [Pope's] call for a 'special status' for Jerusalem expresses the intention to change its status as the 'capital of Israel.' "[66]

The incident demonstrates the degree of apprehension and distrust between the Holy See and the Jewish state. Since 1967 the flexibility that the Holy See had decided to adopt in its relations with Israel had become hostage to the linger-ing disagreements regarding the status of Jerusalem and the Holy Places.

The opposition expressed by the Holy See to any exclu-sive control—religious and political—over Jerusalem was the source of further friction between the Papacy and the Israelis.

Nobis in Animo (1974)

The preoccupation of the Holy See with Jerusalem and the fate of Christians living in the Holy Land was evidenced in the underlying theme of an important document issued by Paul VI on March 25, 1974. In his apostolic exhorta-tion, *Nobis in Animo*, "To the Bishops, Clergy, and Faithful on the Needs of the Church in the Holy Land," the Pope spoke of the intimate link between the Holy Land and Chris-tians everywhere:

The Church in Jerusalem . . . has a privileged place among the cares of the Holy See and the whole Christian world. . . . The continuation of the state of tension in the Middle East . . . constitutes a serious and constant danger. . . . In addition, the continuing existence of situations lacking a clear juridical basis internationally recognized and guaranteed, far from constituting a fair and acceptable solution that takes account of everyone's rights, can only make such an achievement more difficult. We are thinking especially of Jerusalem . . . towards which turn more intensely in these days the thoughts of Christ's followers, and of which, on a par with Jews and Muslims, they ought to feel fully "citizens." . . . Were the presence of Christians in Jerusalem to cease, the shrines would be without the warmth of a living witness and the Christian Holy Places of Jerusalem and the Holy Land would become like museums.[67]

Paul VI called for peaceful coexistence between the various communities and groups living in the Middle East:

In fact, everybody knows that the various civilizations . . . in the course of the centuries in the Holy Land have to converge [with others] in order to allow different groups, even if they are different for several reasons, to cooperate among themselves and "march together," to give to the Greek expression syn-hodos [i.e., "synod"] its deep meaning. In this process of convergence, the Christian presence in the Holy Land, together with that of Jews and Muslims, can be a coefficient of harmony and peace.[68]

The Pope's statement could not be more explicit in illustrating the Holy See's vision for a peaceful settlement of the question of Jerusalem and the Israeli-Palestinian dispute. A fundamental issue raised by Paul VI was his contention that Jews, Christians, and Muslims should enjoy the rights and privileges that "citizens" enjoy without any hindrance. It was in a way a rebuke to the Israeli thesis advocating an exclusive political control over Jerusalem, while allowing some kind of narrow autonomy limited to spiritual matters to the Christian and Muslim communities in Jerusalem.[69] Moreover, the Pope's concern was increased by the fear that the permanent situation of tension and conflict in the Middle East would lead to an exodus of Christians from the Holy Places, rendering them mere "museums."

Israel's chief rabbi, Shlomo Goren, vehemently attacked Paul VI's statement and declared:

> The Vatican's request for a juridical status for the Holy Places is of a purely political nature not based on justice, religious integrity, or historical right. We are astonished by the fact that the Vatican never issued the slightest protest when the Holy Places in Jerusalem were in Jordanian hands. [The Jordanians] refused access to Jews and profanated the most sacred cemetery on the Mount of Olives. The world must know that Jerusalem is the capital of Israel, that it is the soul of the Jewish people, and that it is our duty to defend the city with our lives.[70]

Rabbi Goren's statement dramatized the gap that existed between the head of the Roman Catholic Church and Israeli religious leaders. Israel's chief rabbi pointed to the fact that the Holy See did not come out strongly against the Kingdom of Jordan when Jerusalem and the Holy Places were under its control. During Jordanian rule, the Jewish cemetery on the Mount of Olives was desecrated and Jews were denied access to the Wailing Wall. However, the status of Jerusalem at that time was significantly different from what it is today. King Hussein had in fact refused to declare Jerusalem an "Arab city," despite mounting pressures from the PLO to do so.[71] Furthermore, unlike the Israeli government, the Hashemite rulers never intended to transfer their capital from Amman to Jerusalem.

The Tripoli Seminar (1976)

The position adopted by the Holy See toward Jerusalem was also the source of an embarrassing incident that occurred in a meeting where a Vatican delegation was present together with Arab religious and political leaders in February 1976. A seminar on Islamic-Christian dialogue was held in Tripoli, Libya, under the joint sponsorship of the Libyan government and the Holy See.[72] The Vatican was represented by Cardinal Sergio Pignedoli, president of the Secretariat for Relations with Non-Christians, Monsignor Pietro Rossano, and Father François Abu Mokh of the same secretariat.

The seminar issued a 24-paragraph statement dealing with religious freedom, religion and science, religious cooperation, Lebanon, and other issues. Two controversial paragraphs (20 and 21) dealing with the Israeli-Palestinian dispute were inserted. In fact, the Vatican representatives did not approve of paragraphs 20 and 21.

Paragraph 20 stated that "the two parties . . . distinguish between Zionism and Judaism, considering Zionism an aggressive, racist movement, alien to Palestine and the whole Levant."[73] Paragraph 21 dealt with the status of Jerusalem. It said that the two parties "affirm the national rights of the Palestinian people and its right to return to its land, assert that *Jerusalem is an Arab city*, and call for the setting up of a permanent commission to investigate attempts to change the character of Islamic and Christian Holy Places."[74]

From the reactions to the Tripoli seminar, it seemed as if the Vatican delegation might have fallen into a trap whereby, from a religious encounter, a political stand was elicited.[75] The Holy See did not approve the assertion that "Jerusalem is an Arab city" without making a distinction between the western sector, which has been Israeli since 1948, and the old city, conquered in the aftermath of the June 1967 war. Cardinal Pignedoli restated the Holy See's well-known position toward Jerusalem—an internationally guaranteed special status.

L'Osservatore Romano was quick to point out that, after a close examination of paragraphs 20 and 21, "the Holy See has declared that it cannot accept them, because their content does not correspond, on essential points, to the already known stand of the Holy See."[76] In essence, what Rome wanted to demonstrate by its rejection of the two paragraphs in the Tripoli statement was that (1) the Papacy refused to be dragged into the Arab-Israeli quarrel in order to champion the cause of either party, and (2) the Holy See considers the holy city as the common heritage of the three monotheistic religions on an equal basis without differentiation.

The *Osservatore Romano* Statement (1980)

One month before the Israeli government enacted its "basic law" to formalize the annexation of Jerusalem, the Holy See issued the clearest and most detailed statement regarding its stand on the question of Jerusalem. In an article published by *L'Osservatore Romano* (June 30-July 1, 1980), the Holy See requested:

1. that the overall character of Jerusalem as a sacred heritage shared by all three monotheistic religions be guaranteed by appropriate measures;
2. that religious freedom in all its aspects be safeguarded for them;
3. that the complex of rights acquired by the various communities over the shrines and the centers for spirituality, study, and welfare be protected;
4. that the continuance and development of religious, educational, and social activity by each community be ensured;
5. that this be actuated with equality of treatment for all three religions;
6. that this be achieved through an "appropriate juridical safeguard" that does not derive from the will of only one of the parties interested.[77]

The article explained that this "juridical safeguard" was similar to the "special statute" that the Holy See would like to see implemented for Jerusalem. Having stressed that the "significance and value of Jerusalem are such as to surpass the interest of any single state or bilateral agreements between one state and others," the article recalled the 1947, 1948, and 1949 UN resolutions and the 1950 "special statute" approved by the Trusteeship Council.[78] Finally, *L'Osservatore Romano* elucidated what is in a sense a conditional acceptance of Israeli or possibly Jordanian sovereignty over the city:

> The Holy See considers the safeguarding of the sacred and universal character of Jerusalem to be of such primary importance as to require any power that comes to exercise sovereignty over the Holy City to assume the obligation, before the three religious confessions spread throughout the world, to protect not only the special character of the city but also the rights connected with the holy places and the religious communities concerned, on the basis of an appropriate international body.[79]

From this article, some important points emerge. The Holy See, while reaffirming its opposition to any exclusive control of the city by any "single state," was willing to accept the sovereignty of whatever "power," in this case Israel, provided that an international body guarantee the special status of the holy city. In this context one must underline the fact that the Vatican newspaper does not mention the United Nations as a guarantor of the special character of Jerusalem. Furthermore, as a Vatican official explained:

> The idea was in all probability that a group of sovereign states with a traditional interest in safeguarding and promoting the Christian presence in the Holy Land should come together to draw up the form of the special statute, which they would also guarantee. The names of Italy, France, Spain, Britain, Greece, and the United States were mentioned.[80]

This viewpoint adopted by the Holy See toward Jerusalem and the Holy Places represents the fourth stage in the evolution of the papal position. Stage one of the evolution was characterized by the championing of the supremacy of Catholic rights and privileges (Benedict XV, Pius XI). Stage two had at its core both the UN plan for the internationalization of Jerusalem and free access to the Holy Places for pilgrims (Pius XII). Stage three was distinguished by its spiritual emphasis on three basic points: (1) a special status for both Jerusalem and the Holy Places, to be guaranteed by an international body, (2) maintenance of the civil and religious rights of all religious communities, and (3) recognition of the equality of all three major monotheistic religions (Paul VI and John Paul II). Stage four is marked by the Holy See's willingness to accept national sovereignty subject to international supervision.

This policy evolution may be conceptualized as a shift in emphasis from *places* to *people*, from *political* to *spiritual* matters, and from *exclusivity* to *ecumenism*, but with a central principle—no nation should exercise exclusive control over Jerusalem—that has not fundamentally changed.

There were three factors that influenced the evolution of the Holy See's policy: (1) an international regime for Jerusalem was rendered obsolete by the Arab-Israeli conflict and by international disinterest; (2) the Israeli government's annexation and "Judaization" of Jerusalem was deemed to be unacceptable; and (3) the Holy See's need to find a compromise between external religious interests in the Holy Places such as the rights for pilgrimage, and those interests more crucially related to the full enjoyment of civil and religious rights by the communities living in the Holy Land.

The fourth stand adopted by the Holy See predictably generated a response from members of the Jewish faith. In reaction to the article published by *L'Osservatore Romano*, two American rabbis, Rabbi Martin A. Cohen and Rabbi David H. Panitz, co-chairmen of the Interfaith Affairs Committee of the Anti-Defamation League of B'nai B'rith (ADL), sent a letter to the Holy See's secretary of state, Cardinal Agostino Casaroli (July 2, 1980).[81] In the letter, the two religious leaders expressed their dismay with the Holy See for not acknowledging an Israeli achievement:

. . . Israel's laudable administration of the Holy Places. Israel has clearly demonstrated its concern over the situation of Christians in its own territory as well as in neighboring countries desolated by war and religious persecution, and in its recognition of religious rights, which has been acknowledged by religious leaders of all denominations.[82]

The ADL letter went on to point out the difference between "Israel's constant preoccupation with the preservation of Jerusalem's historical and spiritual heritage," and Jerusalem's situation when it was under Jordanian control.

The two rabbis also expressed their dismay at the timing of the Holy See's article:

. . . when for economic reasons, nations are prepared to dismiss moral standards as the measure for their performance. Their basic aim is the destruction of Israel . . . We are deeply troubled that the Holy See's Document has already become part of their ideological arsenal.[83]

Once again, the differences in perceptions between Rome and Jewish leadership were clearly demonstrated in the American rabbis' letter. The fact of the matter remains, however, that the Holy See does not approve of Israel's taking upon itself the task of defending and protecting Christians and Christian interests in the Middle East. The same theme was resorted to by the Israeli government when reacting to the announced meeting between John Paul II and Arafat in 1982.

Still another fundamental difference between Jewish attitudes toward Israel's behavior and the Holy See's attitude is that the Jewish community feels that Israel has shown sufficient concern for the Christian communities. On the other hand, the Holy See feels that the Israeli concern is limited exclusively to "religious rights." The Holy See is calling for protection and guarantees for both *religious* and *civil rights* of *all* the communities in Jerusalem, not only for the Christians. Then too, the Holy See supports a "special statute" internationally guaranteed and opposes the exclusive rule of any predominant power.

There is an underlying contradiction that characterizes the relationship between the Holy See with both Arabs and Israelis regarding the question of the holy city. Since 1967 Pope Paul VI has shifted the Holy See's stand from a purely political stand based on the call for the internationalization of Jerusalem and the preservation of Catholic rights, to the suggestion of an internationally guaranteed special status. The status of Jerusalem is a matter that should be solved by the three monotheistic religions on an equal basis.

The Papacy's decision to adopt a position more attuned to its spiritual nature clearly challenged the intricate linkages between temporal and religious matters in both Judaism and Islam. This situation was definitively illustrated in the harsh Israeli reactions to any move—diplomatic or other—undertaken by the Holy See toward Jerusalem. Moreover, what occurred in the Tripoli seminar showed the dilemma the Holy See faces. Rome knows that the majority of Christians in the Holy Land are Arabs. It also knows that the future of Jerusalem is directly linked to the outcome of the Palestinian question. Although aware of these realities, which directly affect Christian presence in the Holy Land, the Pope has tried to demonstrate to the Israelis that the doors for cooperation are open as long as the rights of these communities are adequately preserved.

Redemptionis Anno (1984)

A new stage in the Holy See's attitude toward Jerusalem and the Holy Places came to light in Pope John Paul II's apostolic letter Redemptionis Anno (April 20, 1984).[84] The Pontiff's letter reiterated the Holy See's official position on Jerusalem already enunciated in Pope Paul VI's exhortation Nobis in Animo (1974) and the article published by L'Osservatore Romano (1980).

Fundamentally what the Pontiff had done was to take the Catholic position a step further and suggest that Jerusalem, with its various communities, should become the fulcrum

of a possible resolution of the Israeli-Palestinian dispute.[85]
The "city of peace" thus would become the unifying and
pacifying religious element between Arabs and Israelis—
Christians, Muslims, and Jews. John Paul II wrote:

> I also feel it an urgent duty . . . to repeat that the ques-
> tion of Jerusalem is fundamental for a just peace in the
> Middle East. It is my conviction that the religious iden-
> tity of the city and particularly the common tradition of
> monotheistic faith can pave the way to promote harmony
> among all those who in different ways consider the holy
> city their own.[86]

The Pope further expressed his conviction that a lack of
effort in arriving at a satisfactory solution to the status of
Jerusalem would "only compromise further the longed-for
peaceful and just settlement of the crisis of the whole Middle East."[87]

Redemptionis Anno could be considered the most elab-
orate position yet adopted by the Holy See regarding the
question of Jerusalem. To the juridical status of the city
and the stress on the civil and religious rights of the communities living in Jerusalem, John Paul II added the sensitive
political dimension. The Pontiff acknowledged the right of
Israel to have secure borders and the right of the Palestinians to a homeland, and called on "all the peoples of the
Middle East" to discover "again the true sense of their history" in order to be "able to overcome the tragic events in
which they are involved."[88] John Paul II did not miss the
opportunity to recall the tragic plight of Lebanon, which
had evoked mention of his solicitude and special concern
on other occasions.

The Holy See wanted to alert the peoples of the Middle
East to the fact that religion can and should play a positive
and constructive role in resolving the conflicts marring that
part of the world. It is as if the Pope were warning Jews,
Christians, and Muslims that the path of religious fundamentalism and fanaticism would certainly lead to disasters and

that the only solution to their problems resided in their dis-covering the true meaning of "their faith in the one God."

As in the case of other papal statements regarding Jeru-salem, the Israeli authorities did not wait to react. Jerusalem's Mayor Teddy Kollek stated that John Paul II's apostolic let-ter was "not very appropriate" and that "under no regime, not even the British, has the city been so easily accessible, so well taken care of, and so safe as now."[89]

An important point must be made here, related to both the future status of Jerusalem and to Vatican relations with the Jewish state. At the beginning of his letter, John Paul II recalled the joy that his predecessor Paul VI felt when he visited the Holy Land in 1964. Twenty years later, however, the Pontiff acknowledges that he "cannot be there physi-cally." It is my belief that a visit by the Pope to Jerusalem is warranted—not because of the political implications it could generate but for the sake of the Christian communities in the city.

The Notre Dame Center

A concrete example of the Holy See's concern for the Christian communities in Jerusalem can be found in its in-volvement in the controversy surrounding the Notre Dame affair. The Notre Dame Center was built in 1885 and owned by the Assumptionist Fathers to accommodate French pil-grims. The building was heavily damaged during the con-flict between Arab and Israeli forces in 1948. The south wing facing the old city became uninhabitable as a result of bomb explosions, and came to be used as an Israeli bunker and frontier post in no-man's-land.[90]

Deprived of outside help, the Assumptionist Fathers sold the property in 1970 to the *Hamenuta*, a branch of the Jewish National Fund. Later on, the Notre Dame building was do-nated to the Hebrew University for use as a student residence.

The transaction was opposed by the Holy See on the grounds that the Assumptionists could not have proceeded to an important transaction without prior consent from Rome. Moreover, the Arab community loudly expressed its discontent with Israeli seizure of properties belonging to non-Jewish communities living in Jerusalem.

The apostolic delegate hired two lawyers and, for the first time in the history of Holy See–Israeli relations, the Holy See made a claim before an Israeli court. An out-of-court settlement was reached in 1972; the Israeli government rescinded the sale of Notre Dame and resold it to the Holy See. The compromise with the Israeli government was reached following the visit in January 1972 of Monsignor Benelli, a prominent member in the Holy See's secretariat of state.[91]

In 1973, with the help of outside contributions, mostly from the United States, Notre Dame of Jerusalem was resurrected as an international pilgrim center. The direct involvement of the Holy See was meant to cool the fears of local Christian minorities, especially the Palestinians. In a sense, Rome wanted to establish concrete proof that it was not abandoning Arab Christians to their fate by bowing to the Israeli authorities. As Gelin wrote:

> Notre Dame de France is perhaps no longer a guest house, but it remains today a symbol of fidelity, not only in the eyes of Catholics, but in those of indigenous Christians and of some attentive Muslims. In the Levant, symbols hold a significant value, which Westerners generally do not understand.[92]

The case of Notre Dame, a hostel for pilgrims, exemplifies international religious interests in the Holy Land and how these interests are intertwined with the fate of local Christian communities. In order to preserve its rights in Jerusalem and demonstrate its solicitude toward Christian communities, the Holy See is willing to go to great lengths. In some ways the symbolism that pervades the entire issue of Jerusalem creates impressive leverage for the Papacy. The Pope as the head of the Roman Catholic Church can use this leverage in a discreet and skillful way. Israel, well aware of this fact, cannot afford to alienate the Holy See, knowing the good will and sympathy that the cause of Israel elicits in some Western Catholic circles.

CONCLUSIONS

This chapter has dwelt on the religious significance of Jerusalem to Jews, Christians, and Muslims. The three monotheistic religions have, with varying degrees, important stakes in the city's status and its Holy Places. There are very few other issues in contemporary international relations in which religion and politics are so deeply entwined in the minds of so many people.

In fact, for Muslims, from Indonesia to Morocco, Jerusalem symbolizes the life of the Prophet, which began in Mecca, where he spread his message, to Al-Qods, where he ascended to heaven. For Christians, Jerusalem is the symbol, both historical and geographical, of Christ's life on earth. It is also the symbol of the divisions that have marred Christianity, Eastern and Western, Catholic and Protestant. For Jews, Jerusalem represents redemption from centuries of persecution. It is also a source of deep misunderstandings between those Jews who believe in the messianic and universal character of Judaism and those who give purely temporal and political interpretation to their religion.

Regarding its legal status, Jerusalem has known all kinds of occupation and invasion. The long-lasting one was that of the Ottoman Turks. With the Balfour Declaration and the creation of a Jewish homeland, the whole question of Jerusalem and the Holy Places became hostage to the political rivalries between Arabs and Israelis.

The Holy See in its stand and role in the issue of Jerusalem has reflected changes affecting the status of Jerusalem. In brief, the Catholic Church's current position toward Jerusalem can be summarized in three propositions: (1) the Church holds that the city should have an internationally guaranteed special status; (2) the Church insists on full religious and civil rights for Arab inhabitants of Jerusalem; and (3) the Church is alarmed at the exodus of Christians.

The Holy See is against any exclusive control over the city and the Holy Places. It is willing to accept a national sovereignty over Jerusalem provided it is checked by an international body. The Holy See has left the decision regarding the nature and duties of this body to the international community.

The fundamental question that emerges from the preceding analysis is illustrated by the challenges and contradictions facing the Papacy's ecumenical and interfaith concerns. By stressing that Jews, Christians, and Muslims should coexist and cooperate to find a solution to the question of Jerusalem, the Holy See is in some ways prodding the Christian communities in Jerusalem to put aside their rivalries and petty quarrels. If Christians cannot agree on a coherent and unified stand, they cannot expect to gain the respect of the other two religious groups. This situation is not unlike that in Lebanon.

Probably, only time will tell whether there will still be a Christian community living in Jerusalem or whether the Holy City will become a museum of historical stones and shrines to be admired and visited by Western pilgrims. Herein lies one of the fundamental tragedies of Christianity in the Holy Land. Pilgrims from Europe and the United States visit the Holy Land and the Holy Places, typically unaware of the possibility that if local Christian communities were to disappear because of a slow but steady exodus, Jerusalem would become like the Colosseum in Rome.

The other facet of the ecumenical challenge is the difficulty of establishing a dialogue between Christians, Muslims, and Jews. The majority of Christians in the Holy Land are Arabs. Moreover, the majority of Israelis are "more or less identified with Zionism and . . . Muslims would a priori refuse to meet its representatives."[93] Finally, there is the Israeli-Palestinian dispute, the resolution of which has become a

prerequisite for a possible settlement regarding the status
of the "city of peace."

In the final analysis, the situation in Jerusalem offers a
picture of three worldviews locked in a battle of interests,
the significance of which extends far beyond the narrow
ranges of the political realm. For instance, none of the three
monotheistic religions — Judaism, Christianity, and Islam —
can claim full hegemony over the city. The Catholic Church,
with the presence of several religious orders and institutions,
has made sure that its voice in the Holy Land will not be
ignored. For Arabs and non-Arab Muslims, any attempt to
trample on their right of access to their holy shrines would
certainly lead to increasing pressures on world religious and
political leaders to deter such an eventuality. Moreover,
Jerusalem's Muslim community is still active despite the
pressures and vexations stemming from occupation. The
Israelis, given their strong attachment to Jerusalem, will
make the utmost efforts to keep Jerusalem under their permanent control. But this control is checked by the claims
of the followers of the other two faiths.

The controversy surrounding Jerusalem can be considered
a microcosm of the multifaceted conflicts that plague the
Middle East. The importance of the issue emerges from the
spiritual symbolism of the city and its pervasive mosaic of
interests and communities. Finally, it can be said that the
question of Jerusalem is a crucial test of the Holy See's skills
in using its resources to balance its interests with those of
the other two monotheistic religions.

3. The Holy See and the Lebanese War

THIS CHAPTER SETS THE Lebanese War in its local, regional, and global dimensions, with special focus on the actors and their preferences regarding a solution to the conflict. Following this assessment, an analysis is made of the attitude of the Holy See to the actors and the issues involved in the war. The principal focus will be on the activities and impact of the papal delegations dispatched in the course of the strife.

Because of its pluricommunitarian constitution, Lebanon has long been considered an example of coexistence of multiethnic and multireligious groups. Nevertheless, there is an inherent corollary to this pluralism that has led some scholars to characterize Lebanon as "precarious," "improbable," "fragmented."[1] To frame properly the conflict under investigation it is necessary to present a brief overview of the origins and issues involved.

The ecumenical and interfaith movements inspired by Vatican II made the Lebanese formula of Christian-Islamic coexistence of fundamental importance to the Holy See. In fact, in the eyes of the Papacy, Lebanon was supposed to be a living example of how different groups can interact in the same societal context. Moreover, with the exception of the Philippines, Lebanon for the Catholic Church, "is the last citadel of Christianity in the whole Levant, at the crossroads of three continents."[2]

Throughout its history, Lebanon has been a microcosm of changes — socio-political and religious — in the Arab world. As a land of refuge, enjoying a high degree of freedom and tolerance, the Lebanese polity became the testing ground of internecine struggles, opposing Arab regimes, and ideologies.

The war in Lebanon itself became a theater of confrontation for the Arabs and the Israelis. This is one of the major reasons why Lebanon is so important to papal diplomacy. By the end of the 1960s the increasing militancy of Palestinian nationalism trapped Lebanon in the Arab-Israeli struggle: first, passively, Lebanon gave asylum to waves of Palestinian refugees (1948, 1967, 1970, 1971); then actively, following the Jordanian subjugation in 1970 of the PLO. Moreover, with the involvement of regional powers (Syria, Israel, etc.), the Lebanese War escalated to the point where Lebanon became by proxy the center of confrontation between East and West.

The Lebanese War, which erupted in 1975 and had not been resolved by 1985, is a very complex conflict involving several actors and issues (Table 1 lists the various actors involved in the war).[3] The strife—which was not of a religious nature—pitted against each other the Maronite-dominated Phalangist Party and its allies, and a Muslim-Leftist coalition, actively backed by Palestinian guerrilla organizations (Fatah, Saika, and those that rejected any peaceful settlement with Israel).

TABLE 1

Actors Involved in the Lebanese War

Lebanese Front (al-Jubha al-Lubnaniyya, founded in 1976)
The Lebanese Phalange Party—Kataib
National Liberal Party (Camille Chamoun)
Guardian of Cedars
Permanent Congress of the Lebanese Orders of Monks
Al-Tanzeem (Dr. Fuad Shemali)
The Maronite League (Shaker Abu-Suleiman)
The Marada (Suleiman Franjieh)
Dr. Charles Malek

Christian Groups outside the Lebanese Front
National Bloc (Raymond Edde)
Armenian Parties (Tashnaq, Hentshaq, Ramgavar)
Democratic Party (Dr. Emile Bitar)
Destourian Party (Michel al-Khoury)

Lebanese National Movement (al-Haraka al-Wataniyya al-Lubnaniyya)
Progressive Socialist Party
Lebanese Communist Party
Organization of Communist Action in Lebanon
Movement of Independent Nasserites (al-Murabitun)
Syrian National Socialist Party
Socialist Action Party
Arab Socialist Baath Party (Iraqi-sponsored)
Harakat Amal
Syrian Baath Party

Traditional Muslim Leaders
Saeb Salam (Sunni)
Rashid Karame (Sunni)
Kamel al-Assaad (Shiite)

Palestinian Guerrilla Organizations
Al-Fatah
Al-Saika
Popular Front for the Liberation of Palestine (Dr. George Habbash)
Democratic Front for the Liberation of Palestine (Nayef Hawatmeh)

Syrian forces

Israeli forces

United Nations Interim Force in Lebanon (UNIFIL)

Domestically, the developments that led to the Lebanese War included (1) a disruption of the demographic balance in favor of the Muslims who called for a reallocation of government posts, (2) social difficulties caused by soaring prices, housing problems, and student unrest, and (3) an internal crisis inside the Maronite Church where the monastic orders contested the authority of the patriarch, and (4) the controversy within the Greek Catholic community resulting from the demotion of the bishop of Beirut, Monsignor Grégoire Haddad.

At the regional level, the defeat by Israel of the Arab armies in 1967 led to a marked disenchantment with the policies followed by the champion of pan-Arabism, Gamal Abdel-Nasser. The major issue in the Middle East became the Palestinian question and its resolution to the satisfaction of the Arabs. In the mid-1970s, following the fourth Arab-Israeli war (1973) and the United States–sponsored peace process in the Middle East, Lebanon became the battlefield for those in favor of or against negotiations with the Jewish state. To complicate the situation further, Palestinian commando groups were transformed into a symbol of righteous revenge.[4] Furthermore, the resurgence of Islamic fundamentalism had a major impact in realigning alliances and coalitions in the Middle East.

At the global level, the process of détente that characterized superpower relations in the late 1960s did not fully include the Middle East. A case in point was the shelving of the 1977 joint United States–Soviet statement for peace between Arabs and Israelis based on UN Resolutions 242 and 338, and the exclusion of the USSR from the Middle East peace process initiated by the United States. Finally, the oil crisis had an important effect on the policies of both producers and consumers, leading to a major but ineffective involvement of Western Europe and Japan in Middle Eastern affairs.

The major events that led to the Lebanese War began with the signing of the Cairo Agreements (1969) between the Lebanese government and the PLO. Palestinian fighters used the Lebanese south as a launching pad for guerrilla attacks against Israeli settlements in Galilee. The Israelis retaliated after each PLO action, which in turn heightened tensions, first with the Lebanese army, which clashed with the Palestinians, and then with the Christian militias after 1975. The turmoil in Lebanon also provoked a greater Syrian and Israeli involvement in Lebanese politics and resulted in their direct presence on the ground. Moreover, the Camp David Accords (1978) and the Egyptian-Israeli Peace Treaty (1979) destroyed what was left of Arab unity. This situation was reflected dramatically in the Lebanese arena. The Palestinians were left out of bilateral peace negotiations and had to obtain the backing of those Arab regimes that were willing to champion their cause.

In Lebanon itself, the Egyptian-Israeli entente led to polarization of the conflicting parties and increasing fear of the possibility of the permanent settlement of Palestinians in Lebanon and the partition of the country. By 1982, the major events in Lebanon included the emergence of Bashir Gemayel as a powerful Maronite leader; the Israeli invasion of Lebanon; and the massacres of Palestinian civilians in the camps of Sabra and Shatila.

Since the beginning of the Lebanese War, the role of the Holy See was guided by three major principles: (1) no party in Lebanon should jeopardize Christian-Islamic dialogue, (2) the behavior of some elements in the Christian community should not compromise the formula of coexistence sanctioned in the 1943 National Covenant, and (3) the Palestinians, who for years have suffered exile, should not fall victims to a "new injustice in Lebanon."[5] The Lebanese War constituted a threat to these objectives and, in order to thwart serious attempts to disrupt the Lebanese formula, the Holy See dispatched several mediation and fact-finding missions to Lebanon (1975, 1976, 1978, 1980).

ACTORS AND ISSUES IN THE LEBANESE WAR

Because of its formation as a federation of ethno-religious communities, Lebanon cannot be considered a nation-state. Lebanese communities, each jealous of its socio-religious traditions and prerogatives, have never evolved from a confessional, sectarian "mosaic" to form an integrated political system.[6]

Coexistence between Christian and Islamic communities was first sanctioned by the Lebanese Constitution of 1926 and by the unwritten National Covenant of 1943. In Article 95 of the Constitution, which was supposed to be only transitory, it is written that "the communities will be fairly represented in public jobs and the composition of the government."

The National Covenant of 1943 was more of a political act aimed at the "lebanonization" of Muslims and the "arab-

ization" of Christians. It was based on the premise that the
Maronites would renounce their allegiance to French protection and the Muslims would forego their dreams of unity
with Syria. During the discussions on the National Covenant, it was agreed that the president of Lebanon would
be a Christian Maronite, the prime minister a Sunni Muslim,
and the speaker of the parliament a Shiite Muslim.[7]

The National Covenant of 1943 (*Mitha'k al-Watani*) was
the origin of the ongoing misunderstanding between Christians—mostly Maronites—and Muslims in Lebanon. In
1949 a prominent Lebanese journalist, Georges Naccache,
writing about the covenant, said that "two negations will
never make a nation."[8]

One of the major consequences of the modus vivendi
worked out in the 1943 covenant has been that confessionalism thwarted any possibility for the creation of a solid
Lebanese national identity. In fact the unwritten agreement
had institutionalized the heterogeneous aspect of the Lebanese body politic. Unlike Western societies where the primary allegiance is toward the state, in Lebanon citizens have
no bearing on the social system if they do not belong to a
given religious community and pay allegiance to a *zaim*
(leader), whether political or religious.

The communities that constitute Lebanon's basic popula-
tion are, on the Christian side, the Maronites, the Greek
Orthodox, and the Greek Catholics; and on the Muslim side,
Shiite Muslims, Sunni Muslims, and the Druzes.[9]

Since 1932, when the last population survey was undertaken in Lebanon, no formal census has been carried out
to analyze the demographic weight of the Lebanese communities. According to French estimates in 1977, the population of Lebanon was as given in Table 2.

The Maronites, the only group among Eastern Christians
to have remained united, take their name from a hermit,
Maroun, who lived in northern Syria where he died in 410.
Following their persecution, they migrated to Lebanon where
they settled in the mountains. There they have been able

to maintain their identity as a people and develop a high degree of independence and cohesion. Maronite communion with the Holy See dates back to the period of the Crusades. The spiritual head of the Maronite community is the patriarch of Antioch and all the East. Outside Lebanon, Maronite communities are found in Syria, Cyprus, Egypt, and Palestine. Following World War I, Maronites migrated to the United States, Latin America, Africa, and Australia.

The political weight of the Maronite community goes beyond its numerical importance. In fact, the Maronites believe that Lebanon is their last refuge and that any threat to their presence and privileges would transform the country into another Arab-Muslim state. Both religious and political leadership is influential in the Maronite community.

At the religious level, the Maronite patriarch and some monastic orders have played an important role in Lebanese politics. Since the beginning of this century, the patriarch has taken a leadership role in defending the Maronite presence in Lebanon. Since 1958, he has spearheaded efforts to preserve the coexistence formula between Christians and Muslims. Throughout the Lebanese War, Cardinal Antonios Butros Khoreish, the patriarch, kept his distance from the more extreme elements in the community. Khoreish faith-

TABLE 2

Major Communities in Lebanon

	POPULATION	PERCENTAGE
Shiite Muslims	850,000–900,000	28
Maronite Christians	750,000–800,000	25
Sunni Muslims	600,000	19
Greek Orthodox Christians	300,000	9
Druze Muslims	250,000	8
Greek Catholic Christians	200,000	6
Armenian Christians	160,000	5

Source: Helena Cobban, "Lebanon's Chinese Puzzle," *Foreign Policy*, 53 (Winter 1983–84) 35.

fully reflected the Holy See's position of being a moderator
and conciliator between the various Lebanese communities.[10]

Being large landowners, the Maronite monks have been
the most active proponents of Lebanese and Maronite nationalism.[11] During the war, some monks were actively involved in battling Palestinians and their allies in Beirut. One
of the most influential institutions supervised by a Maronite
monastic order is the University of the Holy Spirit in Kaslik.
During the Lebanese War, a research group of the university issued several pamphlets and books dealing with the
origins of the conflict in Lebanon and the monks' stand on
the conflict.

In one of these publications, it is stated that Lebanese
Christians are opposed to "any idea of pacific existence in
an Islamic state like the *dhimmi*s living in Arab countries
[Copts in Egypt, Assyrians in Iraq, etc.]."[12] In the Qur'ān,
"peoples of the book"—Christians and Jews—are treated
as "protected peoples," *dhimmi*s, which literally means those
on the conscience (*dhimma*) of the Islamic community. In
order to be protected, non-Muslims had to pay a *jizya* (tax).[13]
In this same pamphlet, the Maronite monks called on the
"moral forces" of the earth, headed by the Holy See, to do
their utmost not to allow Lebanon, "this unique refuge of
all the Orient, where one lives, breathes, trades, thinks, wor-
ships, sings, and prays in total freedom," to be engulfed in
the flow of Arab and oil politics.[14]

Furthermore, Father Sharbel Kassis,[15] former superior of
the Permanent Congress of the Lebanese Orders of Monks,
stated that the formula agreed upon between Christians and
Muslims in the 1943 Covenant was a case of an "aborted
coexistence." The clergyman went on to say that this has
been unfortunate:

> [If] coexistence truly succeeds in Lebanon, we would have
> contributed as Christians to the creation of a new con-
> cept of society. In fact, societies at the end of the twenti-
> eth century tend to be less and less homogeneous.[16]

As an alternative to the failure of the National Covenant, several Maronite personalities advanced solutions ranging from the creation of a federal or a confederal state in Lebanon to the outright partition of the country.[17]

From the political standpoint, the most important group that embodies and defends Maronite and Christian aspirations in Lebanon is the Phalangist Party.[18] The Lebanese Phalange Party (*Hizb al-Kataib al-Lubnaniyya*) was founded in 1936 by Pierre Gemayel, a leading figure in Maronite and Lebanese politics. From the Phalangist standpoint, the Lebanese entity is a historical fact, having its roots in the trade center of ancient Phoenicia. The pillars of Lebanese nationalism — the 1920 borders, the 1926 Constitution, and the National Covenant of 1943 — are uncontestable facts and cannot be subject to question. Lebanon should cooperate with the Arab countries, provided that political relations are based on the principles of mutual respect and equality.

Since the beginning of the war in 1975, the Phalangists have staunchly opposed the military involvement and political meddling of Palestinian guerrillas in Lebanese politics. In fact, they have called for the abrogation of the 1969 Cairo Agreements and the relocation of the Palestinians to the other Arab countries. Most Phalangist Party members are recruited from the Maronite community.

In 1976 the Phalangists became members of a larger coalition of major Christian conservative parties known as the "Lebanese Front." The front included the National Liberal Party of former President Camille Chamoun, the Guardians of Cedars, the Permanent Congress of the Lebanese Orders of Monks, Al-Tanzeem of Dr. Fuad Shemali, the Maronite League headed by Shaker Abu Suleiman, and other personalities such as Dr. Charles Malek. The Lebanese Front charter stressed "the need to maintain the unity of Lebanon, to reestablish the authority of the law, and to respect private enterprise in the economic sector."[19] The militias controlled by the member parties of the Lebanese Front were unified in 1980 in the "Lebanese Forces" headed by the late Bashir Gemayel.

The other mainly Christian groups that have remained outside the front included Raymond Edde's National Bloc, the Armenian parties (Tashnaq, Hentshaq, and Ramgavar), Emile Bitar's Democratic Party, and Michel al-Khoury's Destourian Party.

In order to preserve their presence and survival during the war, the Phalangists and their allies called first on regional powers, then on global intervention, to defend the integrity of the state of Lebanon. In the summer of 1976, the Syrian regime of Hafez al-Assad was invited to intervene in Lebanon. The Syrian army played a crucial role in boosting the morale of the conservative Christian militias with whom Damascus had sided to forestall victory by the Islamic-Leftist-Palestinian coalition.

Strengthened by Syria's support, the Phalangists and their allies mounted an attack (June-August 1976) against the Palestinian camps situated in the Christian-dominated sector of Beirut. These camps surrounded an important area comprising 30 percent of Lebanon's industrial capacity. The most important and heavily populated of these camps was that of Tall-Zaatar.[20] It included Palestinians and Shiite refugees from southern Lebanon.

The Syrian-Lebanese conservative Christian harmony did not last very long—less than two years. In order to counter the Palestinian and Syrian presence in Lebanon—the Syrian involvement was not favorably viewed by some leaders in the Maronite community—the Christian-dominated militias decided to establish close ties with the Israelis.

The Israelis came to the Lebanese Christians' rescue because of their status as a threatened minority in the Near East. The Israeli-Maronite connection goes as far back as the 1930s when some prominent Maronite leaders, mostly the patriarch, then Monsignor Arida, advocated the creation of a "Christian homeland" similar to the Jewish homeland promised to the Jews in the Balfour Declaration.[21]

Mention should be made of the letters exchanged in the 1950s between Israeli Prime Minister Moshe Sharett, and the former Israeli premier, David Ben-Gurion. The essence of these letters centered around the possibility of fostering the creation of a Maronite entity in Lebanon allied to Israel.[22]

Two major consequences ensued from this close Israeli-Maronite cooperation. First, there was a shift in alliance between the Syrians and the Lebanese Front. Having entered Lebanon to help the Maronites, the Syrians wanted to exact a high price from the Christian militias, given their relationship with Israel. By 1978, the Christian-populated areas of east Beirut were heavily bombarded by Syrian troops. Then a split erupted inside the Maronite camp itself and took the form of bitter clashes between the followers of former President Franjieh in northern Lebanon and the Phalangist militias.

At the beginning of 1978, Franjieh became critical of the negotiations between Israel and Egypt (which were approved by the other members of the Lebanese Front), and accused the Phalangists of various provocations in the areas controlled by his own militia. The whole affair climaxed in the killing of Franjieh's son Tony and his family (June 3, 1978).[23]

Moreover, dissent against Maronite-Israeli contacts was also expressed by other Christian communities in Lebanon. A French observer, writing from southern Lebanon, reported that "in Marjayoun, Greek Catholics and Greek Orthodox, who are numerically superior to the Maronites, have been shocked by the collusion between Christian militias and Israel. . . . They even refused, as the Maronites had requested, the reopening of schools where some Israelis were supposed to teach."[24]

During the war, the Greek Orthodox and Greek Catholic communities tried to distance themselves from the more militant policies of the Maronites. The Greek Orthodox community is headed by the patriarch of Antioch who resides in Damascus. The Greek Orthodox reject the primacy of the pope in matters of faith. Members of this community have played an influential role in the revival of Arab nationalism. In 1942 the Orthodox Youth Movement was founded and had an important impact in reviving the religious values of the community and encouraging political participation among lay Orthodox intellectuals.[25] Greek Orthodox communities are also found in Syria, eastern Turkey, the Arabian Gulf States, and in the diaspora (United States, Canada, etc.).

The position of the Greek Orthodox community during the war was clearly elucidated by Monsignor Elie Corban in an interview given to the Lebanese daily *An-Nahar*. In it the prelate denounced all the schemes for the partition of Lebanon and called for the abolition of "political confessionalism" in the recruitment for public jobs. This meant that candidates' prospects should be based on their professional competence, not on their community's population ratio. Monsignor Corban stressed the close ties that existed between Lebanese and Palestinians: "Lebanon is part and parcel of the Arab world. . . . The cause of Palestine is Lebanon's cause too; likewise, Lebanon's security and unity are the cause of Palestine."[26]

The Greek Catholics or Melchites — which in Arabic means the "king's men" — are linked to Rome and headed by the patriarch who also resides in Damascus. Patriarch Maximos V Hakim adopted controversial stands during the war, especially in the summer of 1978 when Syrian guns were pounding Christian towns. The patriarch praised the Syrian intervention in Lebanon and expressed his opposition to the partition of Lebanon and the creation of a Christian entity:

> We Christians condemn any contact with Israel because we are aware that the Jewish state aims at its expansion to the detriment of neighboring states. . . . We refuse the protection of Israel and its claims to defend Christianity in this part of the world, where for centuries Christians and Muslims have lived side by side.[27]

Despite their small numbers, Greek Catholics have played a prominent role in Lebanon's financial and business sectors. In addition to Lebanon, membership of the Greek Catholic Church is now concentrated in Syria and Palestine.

Together with the Christian communities in Lebanon, Muslim communities have played an ever increasing role in Lebanese politics. Unlike the Sunni community, which follows the mainstream teachings of Islam, the Shiites (derived from the Arabic for "partisans," the Shiites being partisans of Ali, nephew and son-in-law of the Prophet, Muhammad) belong to the sect of the Twelvers, which is predominant in Iran. It was not until the 1970s that the Shiite community began playing an active role in Lebanese politics. The catalyst and leader of this community was Imam Mousa al-Sadr, who disappeared in the mid-1970s on a trip to Libya.[28]

Given their status as an underprivileged and docile community until the end of the 1960s, the Shiites then became more organized and challenged the status quo forced on them by the Sunni-Maronite domination of Lebanese politics. Two major institutions were established to channel Shiite demands: the Supreme Shiite Council, which was founded to advocate the community's case on a national level, and Harakat Amal, a politico-military force that became a significant group to be contended with, especially in west Beirut and southern Lebanon.[29]

The Druze religion is an offshoot of Shiism. Following their persecution in Egypt, the Druzes settled in Syria and Lebanon. There are also Druzes who have settled in Israel and serve in the Israeli army. The Druzes have played an important role in the formation of modern Lebanon.[30] Formed from two clan alliances—the Junblatti and the Yazbaki—the Druzes became unified under the spiritual leadership of the more radical Junblatti Sheikul Aql Muhammad Abu Shaqra. The late Kamal Junblatt was the founder and leader of the Lebanese opposition before and during the war, and in 1977 was replaced by his son, Walid.

During the war, the Muslim communities in Lebanon did not present a unified front. Nevertheless, both conservative and radical elements were in agreement on fundamental issues. Given the demographic changes that occurred in their favor since the formation of the Republic of Lebanon in

1920, Lebanese Muslims claimed that the distribution of power in Lebanon has been to their disadvantage. The other issue that united the Muslim communities was their total opposition to the partition of Lebanon and their stress on the Arab identity of the country. The other objectives that united Lebanese Muslims included (1) the consolidation of relations between Lebanon, the Arab countries, and the Third World; (2) solidarity with the Palestinian people, though rejecting its permanent settlement in Lebanon; (3) the end of all cooperation with Israel; and (4) the dismantlement of the militias.[31] Furthermore, the Muslims in Lebanon advanced two requests: (1) a major role for the prime minister, who until recently was considered a rubber stamp to the president's decisions; and (2) a better distribution of economic wealth.

The key issue that stands in the way of total agreement between Christians and Muslims in Lebanon is that of the deconfessionalization of the system. Until now, the traditional Muslim leadership refused to secularize the laws governing personal status (such as civil marriage) and to admit laicism as a modus operandi in daily life. The separation of religion from civil life is seen as incompatible with the ideals of an Islamic theocratic state.[32] On the other hand, the Maronites believe that the abolition of political confessionalism is not enough if it is not followed by complete secularization. They saw in the Muslim calls for reforms an attempt to dominate Lebanese politics by their sheer numerical superiority. Consequently, for some Christians, Lebanon is considered the last refuge where they could practice their own faith without being subjected to the Islamic majority rule prevalent in most of the Arab and Islamic countries.

From the military standpoint, the Maronite-dominated Lebanese Front was confronted during the war by the Lebanese National Movement (*al-Haraka al-Wataniyya al-Lubnaniyya*). One of the main objectives of the LNM was to be an active and militant advocate for dispossessed Lebanese living in the "misery belt" around Beirut. In its August 1975 "program for the democratic reform of the Lebanese system," the Lebanese National Movement advocated, among other objectives, Lebanon's complete solidarity with the Palestinians, the adoption of a proportional system of elections, and the elimination of political and administrative confessionalism.[33]

The radical Islamic-Leftist coalition found in the PLO presence in Lebanon a golden opportunity to upset the sectarian equilibrium of the country. Nevertheless, the LNM aims were thwarted by the pervasive confessional nature of the Lebanese body politic, the policies followed by Syria, and the internal bickering that marred relationships between the various Muslim groups and between them and the Palestinians.[34]

Together with the Progressive Socialist Party (PSP), the Muslim-Leftist coalition, which drew most of its fighters from the Sunni, Shiite, and Druze communities, included the following organizations: the Lebanese Communist Party, the Organization for Communist Action in Lebanon, the Movement of Independent Nasserites — al-Murabitun, the Syrian National Social Party, the Socialist Action Party, the Iraqi-supported Arab Socialist Baath Party, and the Lebanese section of the Syrian Baath Party.

Between the Lebanese Front and the Lebanese National Movement there exists a group of independent and sectarian politicians. On the Christian side, there is Raymond Edde, leader of the National Bloc and now in exile in Paris. Edde has been a champion of rapprochement between Christians and Muslims and has called for the withdrawal of all foreign armies from Lebanon. On the Muslim side, there are such traditional leaders as Saeb Salam and Rashid Karame, both Sunnis and former Lebanese prime ministers. Finally, in the Shiite community, there is the speaker of the parliament, Kamel al-Assaad. All these politicians advocated a gradual reform of institutions and a greater power-sharing to the Muslims.

In the course of the Lebanese War, several atrocities were committed against innocent civilians. The Lebanese identity card, which mentions the citizen's sect, became a matter of life and death. Religious institutions and churches became the target of indiscriminate attacks, and civilians were massacred along sectarian lines. Attacks against Christian and Muslim individuals and institutions declined after the first two years of the war.

These events could not but lead to a deepening of hatreds between Christians and Muslims in Lebanon. After each massacre, a population exodus ensued from both Christian- and Muslim-dominated areas, a flood of refugees seeking asylum in monasteries and churches in the Christian sector. Muslims, mostly Shiite from southern Lebanon, sought refuge in the abandoned apartments and shantytowns of west Beirut. This problem required large amounts of humanitarian aid, to which the Holy See and the Catholic Church contributed heavily, whereas Saudi Arabia granted financial aid to Islamic humanitarian agencies in Lebanon.

Having set the Lebanese War in its local and domestic perspectives, my analysis will now delve into the role and preferences of regional and global powers during the conflict.

In light of the military and diplomatic changes that occurred in the Middle East following the fourth Arab-Israeli war (1973), the Syrian leadership feared that the United States, together with Egypt and Israel, was bent on isolating Damascus from any future settlement of the Arab-Israeli quarrel. Lebanon offered a fertile ground for Syria's president, Hafez al-Assad, to enhance his regional stature and prove to the United States and its Middle Eastern allies that Syria was an important factor in any future settlement in the area.

The outbreak of the Lebanese War was perceived in Damascus as a threat to Syria's military and political positions against Israel. During the War, the goals of the Syrian leadership were threefold: (1) to prevent a leftist-Palestinian takeover in Lebanon, which would have inevitably led to a conflict between Syria and Israel, (2) to thwart any attempt toward the partition of Lebanon that could threaten the integrity of Syria itself, and (3) to maintain the status quo between the Lebanese warring factions.[35]

Initially successful in their aims, the Syrians found themselves caught in the quagmire of Lebanese and regional politics. Locally, Damascus had intervened in Lebanon to save another minority (the Maronites) from total annihilation. The sympathy that the ruling Alawi minority in Syria felt toward its Lebanese Christian allies was not lost on the majority Sunni population in Lebanon and the Arab countries.

Regionally, Lebanon has provided Syria's Arab enemies with an excellent opportunity to undermine the Syrian regime. In 1976 Iraq extended direct military aid to the Palestinians resisting Syrian intervention. Libya also funneled large amounts of aid to the Lebanese National Movement and its Palestinian allies. Egypt's position was dictated by its fundamental dispute with Syria over the 1975 disengagement agreement with Israel. At the beginning of the Lebanese War, Egypt came to the aid of the PLO despite the latter's vehement condemnation of the unilateral efforts undertaken by Egyptian President Sadat to negotiate with Israel.[36]

Moreover, the Lebanese War was a blow to the Syrian intention to include Jordan and the PLO in constructing an "eastern front" as a counterbalance to the Egyptian-Israeli entente. Finally, the war in Lebanon led Syria to request further aid and military support from the Soviet Union in order to counter United States and Israeli schemes to isolate and then drag Syria into the peace process.

Israel's objectives in Lebanon were not too different from those of Syria in that both countries loathed any radical change in the Lebanese formula of 1943. For Tel Aviv, the PLO should not be allowed a free hand in southern Lebanon to disrupt the northern Israeli settlements. From that point of view, the Israelis used the tactic of increased but controlled tensions in the south of Lebanon. Following each guerrilla attack, an Israeli retaliation ensued, creating an exodus of local populations and increasing pressures on the Lebanese government to take an action similar to that of Jordanian King Hussein when in 1970 he quashed PLO presence in his kingdom. The weakness of the central government in Beirut led the Israeli authorities to work out some kind of a tacit modus vivendi with the Syrians.[37]

By the spring of 1976, the Israelis were praising the Syrian intervention in Lebanon given Damascus's heavy hand against the leftist-Palestinian alliance. In July 1976 Israeli Prime Minister Yitzhak Rabin stated: "I do not criticize the Syrians if they want to pursue their massacre against the Palestinians; as far as we are concerned, they can keep at it."[38]

In 1978 the balance of power in Lebanon had shifted in favor of the Syrian-PLO forces, and Israel found eager allies in the Christian militias. Israeli aid to the Maronite fighters was reported to have amounted to $100 million.[39] The Israeli-Maronite connection was used by Tel Aviv as a propaganda tool to discredit the PLO claim of creating a secular pluricommunitarian Palestinian state similar to Lebanon.

The breakup of Lebanon was a boon for some Israelis who would counter all those who favored a Palestinian state with the tragic example of the "land of cedars."[40] Following the Israeli invasion of Lebanon in March 1978 and the withdrawal of Israeli troops a few months later, a tacit but tense Syrian-Israeli tutelage was established in Lebanon.

With the Likud-dominated coalition in power in Jerusalem, Israeli objectives in Lebanon were given a new impetus, especially by Defense Minister Ariel Sharon. In the summer of 1982 the Israeli army again invaded Lebanon with two far-reaching objectives: (1) destroying PLO bases in Lebanon and (2) installing a friendly Phalangist-dominated regime in Beirut. By the fall of 1982, Sharon's grandiose schemes ended following the tragic killing of Palestinian civilians in the Palestinian camps of Sabra and Shatila.[41]

At the global level, the United States was concerned with preserving the diplomatic gains it had obtained following the October 1973 war. The conflict in Lebanon was viewed in Washington as a sideshow designed to distract those parties who opposed the United States–sponsored peace process. This situation led the late Malcolm Kerr to write that "[perhaps] the objective of American policy has already been achieved with the simultaneous neutralization of Egypt, Syria, and the Palestine Liberation Organization. Instead of fighting Israel, they are now fighting each other, and the PLO is struggling for its very existence."[42]

At the beginning of the Lebanese War and until the end of the Carter administration, the United States allowed regional powers ample discretion, mostly Syria and Israel. Washington attempted to establish a situation of controlled equilibrium in Lebanon itself by mediating between Syrians and Israelis in order to avoid a possible confrontation between their armies.[43]

Given its traditional ties to Lebanon, France attempted to play a moderating role in the war. The first French initiative centered on gaining support for a roundtable to be held in Paris between major Lebanese protagonists. The second aspect of the French mediation mission (November 1975) was to warn the conservative Christian leaders in Lebanon to "freeze" for a while their antagonism toward the PLO. The second French mission (April 1976) was aimed at assessing the possibility for the French government to dispatch troops to Lebanon. The idea was formally announced during a visit to the United States (May 20, 1976) by President Valéry Giscard d'Estaing.[44]

Having set the background to the Lebanese War and the preferences and role of local, regional, and global actors, the role of the Holy See will now be examined.

THE HOLY SEE AND THE LEBANESE WAR: POLICY OBJECTIVES AND IMPLEMENTATION

Since the establishment of diplomatic relations with the Holy See in 1947, Lebanon has always been considered by successive Sovereign Pontiffs as an example and model of coexistence between Christians and Muslims.[45]

The importance given by the Holy See to the Lebanese formula was stressed by Pope John Paul II when accepting the credentials of a newly appointed Lebanese ambassador to the Holy See (January 8, 1983). In that speech the Pontiff stated:

> The original and harmonious coexistence between mono-theist believers has known auspicious periods, even if some difficult moments have created some doubt about the permanent possibility of such pluralism. Lebanon has given and can still give, without being pretentious, this beautiful example in the Middle East.[46]

In fact, and especially after the Second Vatican Council, the Holy See initiated a dialogue with Islamic communities around the world. Lebanon was supposed to be the ideal place for the concrete application of the principles advocated during the council—namely, pluralism and respect for human rights.[47]

The Holy See wanted to demonstrate to Arabs and Muslims alike that the Papacy was a universal institution and did not want to be identified with a specific geographical or cultural area. This explains why the Holy See "does not favor the westernization of Lebanon, which would seem like neocolonialism and would place Lebanese Christians in an extremely difficult situation."[48]

Since the beginning of the Lebanese War in 1975, the Holy See has followed a policy based on advocating the territorial integrity of Lebanon and the preservation of the Lebanese formula of coexistence with the required amendments. This meant that Rome was aware that the 1943 National Covenant had to be adapted to the changing realities of Lebanese society. Moreover, in their addresses and written statements both Paul VI and John Paul II have underlined their total support for the legitimate authorities represented by the president of the republic. The Holy See reiterated its prescription that the Lebanese were alone capable of solving their problems, and expressed its willingness to use its influence with friendly governments to defuse the bloodshed.

The war in Lebanon was a challenge to Holy See diplomacy. In fact, it had to operate at three interrelated levels of feuds: inter-Christian, inter-Lebanese, and Lebanese-Palestinian. In a sense, this challenge also faced other powers trying to mediate and find a solution to the strife. But for the Papacy the problem was compounded by the deep misunderstanding that developed between the Holy See and the Christian Maronite community.

The Maronites, or more precisely some influential Maronite politicians and clergymen, did not share the equidistant and conciliatory attitude that the Papacy adopted in the clash between Lebanese and Palestinian nationalism. The main Maronite contention was that Lebanese Christians were being sacrificed on the altar of Christian-Islamic dialogue. Rome did not seem to them to be taking the necessary steps to soothe the fears of Christian minorities in the Levant in order to allow the Maronites to pursue dialogue with their Muslim counterparts. To this contention, a Vatican official retorted that the "Holy See does not sacrifice anybody. Each human being has value, especially as regards the Maronite Church or other churches present in Lebanon [Armenian, Greek Catholic, Greek Orthodox, etc.], even non-Christians."[49] A careful analysis of papal statements and addresses delivered to Lebanese leaders and government officials throughout the war reveals the particular solicitude that the Papacy nurtured toward the Maronites and their Church because of its special and historical ties with the Holy See.

Maronites in Lebanon thought that they could count on the total and unswerving support of the Holy See in their struggle against the Palestinians and their Muslim allies. It is, however, the welfare of Christianity in the Middle East in general that dictates the Holy See's approach to Lebanese Christians—that is, to *save Lebanon as a sovereign entity in order to save the Christians*. This policy explains the Pope's consistent opposition to the partition or other similar schemes (federation, cantonization, etc.) proposed for Lebanon. If Lebanon were to be carved up into small ethno-religious entities, the creation of a Christian mini-state would have negative repercussions on other Christian communities living in Arab and Islamic countries. These groups would be exposed to hostility, oppression, and isolation. What mostly worried the Holy See was that, living in an autonomous Christian entity, Lebanese Christians "would cut themselves from the people with whom they are intimately linked by tradition and language, and would render their mission a dead letter."[50]

The militant stand adopted by some Maronite clergymen during the war led Vatican officials to talk about Christians in Lebanon as being "islamized." "The problem with Christians in Lebanon is that religious values are superseded by the fight for survival. Religion is used in an ethnic sense."[51] Maronite monks have always played a fundamental role in their community and the Holy See could not but acknowledge the importance of this factor in its approach toward Lebanon. Professor Edmond Rabbath has described the monks as:

> Incontestably an obstacle to Vatican diplomacy. The Vatican would never like to alienate the Maronites and confront directly the Maronite clergy. We cannot forget that in the past, in the late Middle Ages, the Maronites were at a certain moment separated from the Church. And that in the eighteenth and nineteenth centuries there were factions inside the Maronite clergy who were against Rome.[52]

Relations between the Holy See and Lebanese Christians were compared by Father René Chamussy to Moscow's strategy toward communist parties in the Middle East: interstate relations were more important than the fate of communist parties in the area. The difference is, according to this Jesuit scholar, that the Soviet Union "justifies its behavior to the eyes of its followers. Rome did not have the same reflex; it praised the formula of coexistence but remained silent on the concrete problems facing the Christians."[53] Disagreements between the Holy See and some Lebanese Christians were reflected in several important instances during the Lebanese War. Some of these instances will now be detailed.

In a message sent on August 1, 1976, to the International Eucharistic Congress in Philadelphia, Pope Paul VI deplored the "civil war" that ravaged Lebanon's "constitutional formula of peace."[54] In his message the Pontiff stated that those who suffered from the strife were, in addition to the Lebanese people, "the refugees from Palestine, frustrated in their 30-year wait to gain a homeland."[55] Finally, the Pope launched an appeal in favor of those who had been besieged in the Tall-Zaatar camp and called on Catholic relief organizations to cooperate.

Paul VI's Philadelphia message provoked a negative reaction from Camille Chamoun, former president of Lebanon and member of the Lebanese Front. He accused the Pope of "having a heart that has often bled for the wounded of Tall-Zaatar, but never did so for those Lebanese who fall daily."[56] The Pontiff responded to the Maronite leader's statement when he said on August 15, 1976:

> Rather than resorting to denunciations and public condemnations—even if the Christian side had to suffer damages and massacres—we have chosen to adopt a discrete but permanent action in favor of justice and conciliation for all, without excluding any party.[57]

Here Paul VI restated the Holy See's well-known stand regarding the Lebanese War: the Papacy would never change its stated objective to place its conciliatory efforts above factional interests in the war. Moreover, the Pontiff pointed out that the Holy See would not alter its role of being a balanced moderator and conciliator between the Lebanese and the Palestinians.

Another instance was also a source of misunderstanding between the Holy See and the Maronites. It was highlighted by the decision taken by the Christian militias to ask for

Israeli help. Rome's attitude toward Israeli-Maronite relations was illustrated in an important article written by Salim
al-Laouzi. The Lebanese journalist wrote that France and
the Holy See were totally opposed to the Israeli-Maronite
connection because of the negative consequences it could
have on Christian-Islamic relations.[58] Laouzi claimed that in
the early 1970s some Maronite leaders, through the monks
of Kaslik, contacted the Holy See to ask for suggestions regarding possible training centers for Maronite militias in
Europe. "A secret military organization based in Rome sent
experts who had previous experiences in the wars of southern
Sudan and Biafra. . . . These experts in guerrilla warfare
picked the best among Christian militias and sent them to
the city of Anvers [Belgium] where they joined special training centers."[59] Moreover, the Lebanese journalist alleged that
the Holy See advised the Maronite monks to fund the training of the militias through the Phalangist Party.

   The deep distrust that characterized the relationship be-
tween the Papacy and the Lebanese Front was further il-
lustrated in a vehement diatribe against the Holy See that
Father Jean Aucagne launched in an editorial in 1978.[60]
Aucagne, who has a regular column in the daily newspaper
Le Réveil, which was founded by the president of Lebanon,
Amin Gemayel, reflects a point of view highly respected in
Lebanese Christian circles. The Jesuit scholar's editorial, en-
titled "Therefore, who informs the Pope?," was provoked
by an error in reporting by the French news agency, *Agence
France Presse*.

   In his welcoming statement to Monsignor Shukrallah Harb,
present at the customary public audience in Rome (April
11, 1978), Pope Paul VI addressed the Maronite prelate:

> For his country, for Syria . . . and all the Catholic peo-
> ple who are there assembled and suffering, we have a
> thought, a greeting, and a special blessing.[61]

Because of an error in wire service transmission, the
French news agency's cable reported the Pope's statement
as follows:

In you we greet here the passion of the people whom you represent. We address a thought, a greeting, and a blessing to your people, to Lebanon, to Syria and all these populations there assembled, who suffer.

In light of the above statement, Aucagne wrote that he was not aware that the Holy See had adopted the thesis that considers "Syria and Lebanon as one people. . . . Are we to interpret these words as the outline of a Vatican solution (or others) to the Middle East problem: a Syrian-Lebanese-Palestinian federation?"[62]

Aucagne went further and wondered who informed the Pope. It was not the apostolic nuncio in Beirut, "whose knowledge and action in favor of Lebanon, the Catholic Church in Lebanon, the Christians in Lebanon, and all Lebanese without distinction of rite or religion, had earned him the esteem, respect, and gratitude of all."[63] Was it then the so-called "Arab lobby" in Rome? In answering this question, the Jesuit priest did not mince his words about the efforts being undertaken by the Holy See for a rapprochement with Islam.[64]

Later in the article, Aucagne criticized papal policy toward human rights and its relationship with the Soviet Union ("there will always be in an international gathering a Monsignor Casaroli—the Holy See's secretary of state—to bless anything without protesting"). Aucagne concluded saying that "the Pope is infallible only when he speaks *ex cathedra* and not when he is dealing with politics."[65]

In reply to Father Aucagne's accusations, Father Joseph Vandrisse, Roman correspondent for the French daily *Le Figaro*, emphasized that Holy See diplomacy could not be suspected of any schemes toward Lebanon. In fact, it was "directly inspired by Paul VI, and implemented by such competent and courageous" men as Cardinal Agostino Casaroli and Cardinal Paolo Bertoli. How could the Holy See's diplomacy be suspect, "when, for three years now, everything has been done at the international level and with ambassadors friendly to Lebanon and accredited to the Holy See in order to foster its total independence"?[66]

Since the eruption of the Lebanese War, the Holy See has been in continual touch with France, the United States, and Syria in order to find a viable solution to the strife in Lebanon. In 1976, following a request from the Vatican, the French foreign minister visited Washington. After a meeting with Secretary of State Henry Kissinger, it was agreed that a bigger role in Lebanon should be assigned to Syria, provided its presence did not encroach on Israel's "security zone" in southern Lebanon. Moreover, Kissinger had asked the Holy See to exert pressures on the Christian leadership in Lebanon to give the Syrian option a chance of success.[67]

In his book dealing with the events in Lebanon between 1976 and 1982, Karim Pakradouni, a Phalangist politician, refers to two important instances in which the Holy See was especially active. The first occurred when the former Lebanese president, Elias Sarkis, who in 1978 was preparing to meet with French leaders in Paris, told Pakradouni that he believed that "France in coordination with the Vatican would be able to preach some wisdom to the Christians [in Lebanon], warning them not to be accomplices of Israel."[68]

The second instance, according to Pakradouni, dealt with a diplomatic dispatch that the Lebanese ambassador to the Holy See, Antoine Fattal, had sent to President Sarkis. In his report, the Lebanese diplomat mentioned the meeting in June 1980 between John Paul II and President Carter. The Pope was able to raise the Lebanese question because, "according to Vatican circles, the Americans are proving to be more Lebanese than we are." The Holy See's secretary of state, Cardinal Casaroli, had asked his American counterpart, Edmund Muskie, if the United States could exert pressures on Syria to alleviate tensions in Lebanon. Muskie replied that, given that Syria did not yet "choose between East and West, we find ourselves compelled to deal tactfully with the Syrians."[69]

THE HOLY SEE, THE AMERICAN HIERARCHY,
AND THE LEBANESE WAR

In addition to its intervention with successive United States' administrations, the Holy See coordinated its efforts toward Lebanon with the American Catholic hierarchy. In fact, the active involvement of the Catholic community in the United States may have had an impact on US policy toward Lebanon.

The role of the Catholic hierarchy in the United States has been of great value to the Holy See's policy in Lebanon. During the war, the US National Conference of Catholic Bishops (NCCB) issued several statements related to the Arab-Israeli dispute and the conflict in Lebanon.[70]

A key figure in the American Catholic hierarchy was the late Cardinal Terence Cooke of New York. Cardinal Cooke was president of the Catholic Near East Welfare Association (CNEWA) and member of the board and executive committee of Catholic Relief Services (CRS). These two agencies are closely linked to the Holy See through the Sacred Congregation for Oriental Churches. Together with the Pontifical Mission for Palestine, they provide funding and relief for refugees and religious institutions in the Middle East.[71]

Cardinal Cooke had known John Paul II personally and was present at the two papal enclaves of 1978 that elected Pope John Paul I and Pope John Paul II. This factor, in addition to the friendship that the late cardinal maintained with both Presidents Carter and Reagan, facilitated the Holy See's access to the US administration.

In this framework, it is important to recall that, until January 10, 1984, there were no formal diplomatic relations between the Holy See and the United States. An apostolic delegate represented the Pope in his relations with the Catholic bishops and a presidential envoy represented the United States to the Holy See.

Cardinal Cooke visited Lebanon twice. The first time he went at the invitation of the Maronite patriarch (December

29, 1979, to January 1, 1980). Maronite Cardinal Khoreish visited the United States in September 1981 at the invitation of the NCCB and was welcomed by President Reagan and Cardinal Cooke.[72] The second visit that Cooke made to Lebanon was Christmas 1982, as the vicar of US military forces.

Following his first trip to Lebanon, the American prelate issued a "Report on Visit to Lebanon." In it Cardinal Cooke wrote that the conflict in Lebanon was not a civil war and that a solution to the strife depended on "finding a homeland for the Palestinians." Cooke also called for the US administration "to persuade Syria to withdraw its forces" from Lebanon, and "to exert its utmost influence" on the Palestinian forces and Israel" for a mutual cessation of hostilities in the South of Lebanon."[73]

In some of his points related to a solution to the Lebanese crisis, Cooke seemed to stress what papal envoys had said following their missions to Lebanon—namely, that the Lebanese needed help to be freed from external pressures in order "to agree among themselves."[74]

A copy of the unpublished report was given to me by Monsignor John G. Meaney, regional director of the Pontifical Mission in Lebanon. Commenting on the report, the prelate stated that "it had great influence in getting the State Department perspective on the right track. It shaped their policy to a great extent and the policy of Congress."[75] In fact, with the Reagan administration, the United States abandoned its attitude of considering Lebanon a "sideshow" and adopted a more active posture toward the crisis in Lebanon.[76] Together with the Holy See and Saudi Arabia, the Reagan administration was trying to find a solution to the Lebanese quagmire with full awareness of the confessional nature of Lebanese politics. Moreover, the late Cardinal Cooke was held in high esteem both in the United States and by the Holy See.[77]

Corroborating the change in US policy toward Lebanon, William A. Wilson, the United States ambassador to the Holy See, wrote:

I think it can be said that the Vatican and the United States are both working in their ways to bring about peace in Lebanon which would include getting the Israeli troops, the Syrian troops and even the PLO out of the country. . . . The Vatican, which incidentally has a very capable Middle East desk, is trying to exert its influence in a spiritual way to bring about reconciliation and understanding. They are in constant contact with the Cardinal [Khoreish], the Patriarchs and Bishops there through the Papal Nuncio in Lebanon, Monsignor Luciano Angeloni.[78]

Having set the policy of the Holy See toward the Lebanese War and its preferences regarding the various alternatives offered by local, regional, and global actors, my analysis will now turn to the Papacy's concrete involvement in the crisis. This will be done by assessing the four missions (1975, 1976, 1978, 1980) that the Holy See dispatched in the course of the war, the Papacy's reaction to the Israeli invasion of Lebanon in 1982, and the three pastoral letters that Pope John Paul II issued in May 1984.

THE HOLY SEE'S FIRST MISSION TO LEBANON: CARDINAL PAOLO BERTOLI (1975)

Pope Paul VI's choice of Cardinal Bertoli as the head of a fact-finding mission was not accidental. Bertoli was considered to be a veteran of Vatican diplomacy and he had excellent knowledge of Lebanon gained while he was apostolic nuncio in Beirut from 1959 to 1960. He had previous direct experience with Lebanese politics, when sent to Lebanon on a mission during the 1958 civil war.[79] Two other experts in Middle Eastern affairs came with Cardinal Bertoli. They were Monsignor Francesco Monterisi and Monsignor Agostino di Baggio from the Congregation for Oriental Churches.

Cardinal Bertoli's mission, November 9–16, 1975, was inspired by a message written by Paul VI to the Lebanese president, Suleiman Franjieh. In his appeal, the Pope called on the parties in Lebanon "to lay down definitively their weapons and solve their differences in a reciprocal understanding and brotherly dialogue."[80] The Pontiff reiterated the Holy See's position that, "while it supports all efforts by the leaders of interested parties to bring justice to the Palestinian people, [the Holy See] expresses its wishes for the safeguard of Lebanon in respect of its sovereignty and independence from any external involvement."[81]

An important point emerged from the papal message: the Holy See, although acknowledging the legitimacy of Palestinian rights, did not accept any tampering with Lebanese sovereignty. Lebanon, the last citadel of Christianity in the Levant, should not be reduced to a revolutionary quagmire. Moreover, the Holy Father's letter fell in line with the policy adopted by other Western powers, such as France and the United States, which warned against any outside meddling in internal Lebanese affairs.

Cardinal Bertoli's mission centered on establishing a dialogue between the conflicting parties, in order to find a formula to revive the pattern of Christian-Islamic coexistence in Lebanon. The papal emissary had to confront the claims and counterclaims of each side. The Lebanese, however, had different expectations for the Bertoli mission. The Maronites thought that Paul VI, through his envoy, was going to back their fight for survival against the Muslim-leftist coalition. The evenhanded approach that the Holy See decided to take in Lebanon served to mar its relationship with the Maronite community, reducing its margin of maneuverability in the quicksands of Lebanese politics.

The Muslims and their leftist allies thought that Bertoli had come to "disarm the Christians" and convince them to renounce their threat to partition Lebanon. René Chamussy, a Beirut-based Jesuit scholar, attributed to the papal envoy's persuasion the change in attitude in some Maronite quarters. "While the situation on the ground pointed increasingly towards the breakup of the country, some of them began to insist that partition was unthinkable."[82] Cardinal Bertoli stated that "a small Lebanon, a utopian idea, can never exist. If Lebanon cannot be reconstituted, Christians would suffer."[83]

His statement expressed clearly the declared aim of the Holy See to save Lebanon as a sovereign entity in order to preserve a safe presence for the Christians. But this goal was very difficult to achieve given the wide gap that existed between the perceptions of the Maronites and the Holy See regarding the future status of Lebanon. Furthermore, the position adopted by the Holy See to link the conflict in Lebanon to the resolution of the Israeli-Palestinian dispute clashed with the stated aims of the Lebanese Front to isolate the Lebanese crisis from an overall settlement of the Palestinian question.

Cardinal Bertoli began his meetings with the head of state, the leaders of religious hierarchies, and the heads of the various Lebanese parties. To each of them, Paul VI's emissary handed a copy of the letter that the Pope had sent to the Lebanese president on November 5. The papal message was intended to be a platform for discussion for an eventual intercommunitarian summit in Lebanon.

The most relevant meetings that Bertoli had in Lebanon were, besides those with the patriarch and the Maronite political leaders, those with the leaders of the Muslim communities (Sunni, Shiite, and Druze), and his encounter with the Palestinian leader, Yasser Arafat. Throughout these meetings, the Holy See's envoy repeated Paul VI's readiness to contribute toward narrowing the differences among the Lebanese factions. However, Monsignor Bruniera, the apostolic nuncio who accompanied Cardinal Bertoli in most of his meetings, continued to point out that it was up to the Lebanese to find a solution suitable to their problems.[84]

During Bertoli's meeting with the Muslim hierarchy (November 11), the spiritual leader of the Shiite community complained that the coexistence between Christians and Muslims was endangered by "those who are advocating the use of weapons, giving to the conflict a confessional aspect and claiming that Christianity in Lebanon was threatened."[85] Bertoli replied that the Lebanese formula of coexistence "is a universal model" and that the solution to the Lebanese conflict lies "in Lebanese hands."[86]

The pontifical delegation heard the same complaint from the religious leaders of the other two major Islamic communities in Lebanon (Sunni and Druze). The mufti, who is the spiritual head of Sunni Muslims, told Bertoli that there were two categories of Lebanese: "The first consists of Christians and Muslims who yearn for justice; the second category includes Maronite politicians who advocate religious and sectarian discrimination."[87]

In light of the Holy See's posture of fair moderator and conciliator in the Lebanese War, Cardinal Bertoli tried to get some precise clarifications from his Muslim interlocutors regarding their attitude toward the Palestinian presence in Lebanon. The Lebanese Front had accused the Muslims of hiding behind the PLO to gain leverage in their quest for more power in the Lebanese body politic.

The meeting between Arafat and the papal envoy took place on November 15, in the Church of the Capuchins in west Beirut. It is important to recall that this was the first high-level meeting between a representative of the Holy See and the chairman of the PLO. It also amounted to a semi-official recognition by the Holy See of the Palestinian guerrilla movement.

Arafat emphasized that his organization "is devoted to the sovereignty and independence of Lebanon,"[88] and that the Palestinians had adopted the Lebanese pluricommunitarian model of coexistence in their struggle against Israel.[89] Finally, the Palestinian leader thanked the Pope "for all his stands in favor of the Palestinian people."[90]

After one week in Lebanon, the Holy See's delegation left for Rome, leaving behind it a trail of mixed reactions. Two French authors, Albert Bourgi and Pierre Weiss, wrote that Bertoli's mission had failed because "of the uncompromising stand of the Lebanese right."[91] Nevertheless, the papal envoy's success was reflected by the decision of Lebanese President Franjieh and his prime minister, Rashid Karame, to discuss certain institutional reforms, which, according to Lebanese Muslims, were long overdue.

On November 27, 1975, Cardinal Bertoli was received in audience by Pope Paul VI. Following the meeting the papal emissary explained that his mission in Lebanon had a dual aspect: Lebanese and international. At the Lebanese level, the papal envoy stated that he felt a willingness among Lebanese to stop the bloodshed and preserve the unity and identity of Lebanon. Bertoli also stressed "the Holy See's firm intention to pursue its efforts for the good of Lebanon, a country that is an example of human and spiritual coexistence."[92] Regarding the international aspect, the cardinal said that the world community "did not clearly understand the importance of the Lebanese formula of coexistence and that it was the duty of all to reflect on its meaning and take a concrete step to restore peace in Lebanon."[93] Bertoli went on to say that international public opinion did not have an "objective" view of the Lebanese War. "This situation cannot but harm the Lebanese cause and render difficult the formulation of a solution that would be in the real interest of the country and to the benefit of the Middle East as a whole."[94]

The papal envoy wanted to put the Lebanese War in its proper perspective and demonstrate that the Holy See was well aware of the true nature of the Lebanese conflict. In fact, since the war began, some in the Western media characterized the war as a battle between Christians and Muslims, privileged versus dispossessed. A few days before Bertoli's arrival in Lebanon, the Holy See expressed its views in an editorial published by *L'Osservatore della Domenica*. In it the late Vatican spokesman, Professor Federico Alessandrini, wrote:

> Religion is only a pretext for this civil war. This was presented to us as the culminating stage of a class strug-

gle between a poor, proletarian, and underprivileged Muslim left, and a privileged Christian right whose interests are expressed by the Phalangist faction. These remarks are too schematic and simplistic to be true. Because Muslims in Lebanon do not all belong to the proletariat, poor and economically oppressed, neither are all the Christians oppressors and privileged.[95]

In assessing the impact of the Bertoli mission, a Lebanese diplomat wrote that the papal envoy's mediation efforts "were practically without effect. The crisis in Lebanon required something more than a mission of good offices. The Holy See, which has a great international influence, could have changed the course of events in Lebanon if it wanted to."[96] What this assessment overlooked was that Cardinal Bertoli did not come to Lebanon to "change the course of events." The Holy See, through its emissary, wanted to gather first-hand information about the situation in Lebanon. It also wanted to use its good offices to moderate the militancy adopted by some Christian groups and foster a dialogue between them and the Muslims. Moreover, the Papacy wanted to use its influence with the Palestinians to help the Lebanese solve their problems without external interference in their affairs. Finally, the Bertoli mission signaled the great importance that Lebanon occupied in the Pope's mind and the solidarity that the Holy See felt with the Maronite patriarch.[97]

THE HOLY SEE'S SECOND MISSION TO LEBANON: MONSIGNOR MARIO BRINI (1976)

Pastoral and humanitarian considerations dominated the second pontifical mission to Lebanon. In fact, since the eruption of the war, the Holy See had dispatched several delegations formed of representatives from Catholic relief organizations, such as Cor Unum, Caritas Internationalis, and Catholic Relief Services, to assess how much aid was needed by the victims of the strife.

The papal mission, which lasted ten days, April 16–25, 1976, was headed by Monsignor Mario Brini, secretary of the Congregation for Oriental Churches. Monsignor Brini had lived in Lebanon for five years, from 1947 to 1952. The delegation also included a Swiss Dominican, Father Henri de Riedmatten, secretary general of the Holy See's relief agency Cor Unum, Monsignor Francesco Monterisi of the Council for the Public Affairs of the Church, who had already visited Lebanon with Cardinal Bertoli, and Father Marco Brogi. The members of the second pontifical delegation symbolized the religious and humanitarian nature of the mission. Monsignor Brini reached Beirut on the eve of Easter. Given the importance of the feast for Christians, it is easy to see that the Pope wanted to express, through the timing of his delegation's arrival, his solidarity with the suffering Lebanese. Secondly, in an interview with *L'Orient-Le Jour*, Father de Riedmatten stated that "the choice of the secretary of the Congregation for Oriental Churches as the head of the mission is enough to demonstrate the ecclesiastical concern that motivates this mission. The presence of the universal Church and its support of its children must be felt, particularly in the current circumstances in Lebanon."[98] Finally, the importance of the pontifical initiative was underscored by the fact that the Lebanese ambassador to the Holy See, Butros Dib, had to return to Beirut to welcome the Brini delegation.[99]

The Holy See's delegation met with major Lebanese political leaders and PLO chief, Yasser Arafat. As in the preceding papal mission, the report after each meeting emphasized the Holy See's opposition to partition and the importance of the formula of Christian-Islamic coexistence in Lebanon.

Regarding the results of his mission, Monsignor Brini stated that he found all the parties in Lebanon anxious to find a solution to their plight and they "trust that the Holy See's action is contributing towards that goal in conformity with its nature and means."[100] In resorting to these words, Brini wanted to protect the Holy See from any accusation that its concern toward Lebanon did not translate into any positive change in the course of the Lebanese War. In fact, one of the major criticisms that some Lebanese circles formulated against Rome was that the Holy See did not mobilize all its resources to save Lebanon from its internal and external foes.

Two days after his return to Rome, *L'Osservatore Romano* published an interview with Monsignor Brini. In it the prelate said that "only the Lebanese could reestablish coexistence in the framework of the original formula inspired by tradition . . . provided it is modified to adapt to the needs of the current conditions."[101] This statement referred to the fact that the Holy See had acknowledged the Muslims' demands for constitutional reforms in the Lebanese body politic. It also reaffirmed the consistent pattern in papal diplomacy, highlighted by the choice of the members of the second pontifical delegation and the message delivered to all parties concerned.

Moreover, the visit of Monsignor Brini coincided with the preparations for presidential elections in Lebanon. Given the importance of the president in Lebanese politics, it was obvious that the Holy See wanted to inquire about the candidates and their policies.

The global dimensions of the second pontifical initiative were signaled by the meeting that Monsignor Brini had with the American mediator, Dean Brown. In fact, together with the American and Holy See delegations, there was also a French mediator in Lebanon at that time. The same situation had occurred immediately after the departure of Cardinal Bertoli from Lebanon in November 1975, when a French envoy reached Beirut for a fact-finding mission.

The Brini delegation was welcomed by Paul VI on May 3, 1976. After the audience, the Pontiff painted a grim picture of the destruction wrought by the war. "More than 300,000 refugees have been rendered homeless as a result of destruction, looting, or massacres." The Pope launched an appeal to the "universal church and the whole world to provide the necessary help needed by the victims of the strife."[102]

THE HOLY SEE'S THIRD MISSION TO LEBANON: CARDINAL PAOLO BERTOLI (1978)

The election of John Paul II (October 16, 1978) raised hopes among Lebanese that the new Pontiff, because of his Polish background, would be more sympathetic to the plight of their country. In fact, in an important address delivered to the General Assembly of the United Nations (October 2, 1979), the Pope reasserted his aim to work unrelentlessly for the "cause of peace." To illustrate his commitment to peace, the Pontiff used the opportunity of his UN speech to make specific reference to the conflict in the Middle East. John Paul II stated that a solution to the ongoing Lebanese War was linked to the "just settlement of the Palestinian question."[103] He also expressed his wish that the formula of coexistence be maintained in Lebanon "with the adjustments required by the development of the situation."[104] John Paul II's call for modifications in the 1943 covenant has been a constant theme of the Holy See. In fact, Pope Paul VI's envoy to Lebanon, Monsignor Mario Brini, had already stressed this same point after his visit to Lebanon in 1976.

The third pontifical delegation to reach Lebanon was headed by Cardinal Paolo Bertoli. This was the second time that the Holy See's veteran diplomat was sent to Lebanon and another major proof of the consistency and continuity of papal diplomacy. In addition to Cardinal Bertoli, the delegation included Monsignor Francesco Monterisi and Father Marco Brogi from the Congregation for Oriental Churches.

In light of this third papal initiative, it is important to consider how the evolution of the Lebanese War had an impact on the nature of the missions. The first delegation came to Lebanon on a fact-finding, exploratory trip. It reached

Beirut seven months after the beginning of fighting. The second mission was mostly pastoral and humanitarian in nature. In a sense it came to complete the task initiated by Cardinal Bertoli five months earlier.

A communiqué issued by the secretariat of the Maronite patriarch defined Bertoli's second visit as "an information mission and an effort at narrowing points of view towards the realization of national understanding."[105] In fact, Bertoli came to Lebanon on a conciliation mission. The papal envoy had three purposes in mind: (1) to unite and reconcile the Maronite community, (2) to seek a common denominator between all the parties in Lebanon for the revival of the formula of coexistence between Christians and Muslims, and (3) to create a united Lebanese stand toward the possibility of a permanent settlement of Palestinians in Lebanon.[106]

The Holy See's decision to send a delegation to Lebanon was taken in coordination and agreement with international powers. Two weeks before dispatching Cardinal Bertoli, the Holy See sent letters to President Carter, French President Valéry Giscard d'Estaing, British Prime Minister James Callaghan, and West German Chancellor Helmut Schmidt. All of them approved of the papal initiative, given the prestige the Papacy enjoyed.[107]

During his stay in Lebanon, December 6–19, 1978, Cardinal Bertoli met with the president of the republic and important government officials; then he conferred with the heads of the religious communities (Christian and Muslim). Finally, the papal emissary had a series of meetings with several party leaders. The purpose of these encounters was to inquire about the possibility of convening a summit of religious leaders, and to reconcile the Maronite community as a step toward national reconciliation.

An important incident occurred that underscored the sensitive nature of the pontifical mission. In the course of his talks (December 14), with members of an Islamic group (Rassemblement Islamique), two leftist leaders in west Beirut, Assem Kanso, head of the Lebanese branch of the Syrian

Baath Party, and Ibrahim Koleilat, leader of the Murabitun, refused to meet with Cardinal Bertoli. The two politicians asserted that, given that the papal envoy had previously visited the headquarters of the Phalangist Party and its allies, Bertoli should have done the same with the leftist groups.[108] Moreover, Kanso accused the cardinal of being favorable to the arguments advanced by the Lebanese Front.[109] In this context, it is important to mention that by 1978 relations between Syria and the Lebanese Front were at their lowest level since the beginning of the conflict. The decision taken by the head of the Baath Party in Lebanon could be interpreted as a sign of displeasure by Damascus toward the papal initiative.

In his final statement before leaving Beirut, Cardinal Bertoli thanked his hosts and said:

> All the Lebanese . . . have expressed their attachment to the principles of unity and independence of Lebanon. Given this agreement, it is indispensable in view of the dialogue on the future of Lebanon, to work to re-create unity inside the communities, and entente between the communities themselves. . . . To reach this dialogue Lebanon needs to be helped to liberate itself from pressures, and implement a total disarming under the supervision of the head of state and his government.[110]

Bertoli's statement was not a departure from the official policy that the Holy See followed throughout the Lebanese War. During both the first and second pontifical mission, Vatican envoys had made it a point to emphasize that all Lebanese were in agreement regarding the fate of their country. Nevertheless, what differentiated Bertoli's declaration from the others was that the Holy See had taken stock of the fact that there were external "pressures" (Syrian, Palestinian, Israeli) that the Lebanese needed to be helped to overcome.

Bertoli's statement could not but please the members of

the Lebanese Front who, since the beginning of the fighting, stressed the importance of finding an international solution to the Lebanese War. Cardinal Bertoli had in fact recognized the fact that the conflict in Lebanon also had an external dimension, which had become an obstacle to reconciliation. Moreover, if in 1975, reconciliation would have been easier to achieve, in 1978 there was the need for both inter- and intracommunity peace to further the dialogue among Lebanese leaders around a common platform.

Finally, there was another important difference between Bertoli's first and second visit: the papal emissary did not meet with Yasser Arafat or any other Palestinian representative. This was considered another concession to the Lebanese Front, which accused the PLO of being the major cause of Lebanon's predicament.

In assessing the impact of the third pontifical mission, the Lebanese daily *L'Orient-Le Jour* wrote:

> On the short term, this mission of conciliation does not seem to have reached any concrete results. The papal emissary, as he had probably wished to, could not meet with the representatives of all the parties in Lebanon. Moreover [Bertoli] could not obtain a total consensus either in Christian ranks or in the Muslim and leftist camps.[111]

Cardinal Bertoli's own impression of his visit to Lebanon was less pessimistic. In fact, the Holy See's envoy stated that he had "succeeded in obtaining important information" from his interlocutors and "in exposing with serenity the Holy See's standpoint."[112]

As a diplomat, but especially as a churchman and representative of the Pope, Cardinal Bertoli wanted to inform the Catholic community in Lebanon that the time was ripe to put an end to internal fighting and to resume negotiations for a Christian-Islamic dialogue. However, the fact of the matter remains that the intricacies of the Lebanese conflict

and the misperceptions that had deepened considerably between Lebanese leaders since 1975 had rendered any attempt
at reconciliation an impossible task. Furthermore, regional
factors became more pronounced and relevant to any solution of the Lebanese War. In some US and Israeli circles,
the idea of settling some of the Palestinians already in Lebanon as an alternative to the occupied West Bank had gained
some support.[113] This prospect alone paralyzed the Lebanese
regardless of their party affiliation, and the Holy See could
not by itself pacify their fears without major guarantees from
regional and global powers.

THE HOLY SEE'S FOURTH MISSION TO LEBANON:
CARDINAL AGOSTINO CASAROLI (1980)

This mission of the Holy See's secretary of state, March
29-April 2, can be considered as symbolizing the climax in
papal solicitude toward Lebanon. The visit was pastoral in
nature and Cardinal Casaroli used his good offices to narrow the split inside the Maronite community. Indeed, the
feud between the Lebanese forces of Bashir Gemayel and
the Marada of northern Lebanon had reached bloody levels,
deepening the hatreds between the two groups. The Holy
See's top diplomat, however, was not successful in his endeavor to reconcile the Maronites and the Lebanese in
general.

Following a visit to Franjieh in the north, Cardinal
Casaroli asked the former president to allow an exchange
of prisoners between his and the Phalangist militias, to
reopen the road linking Beirut to Tripoli, and to facilitate
the deployment of the Lebanese army in northern Lebanon.

After his meeting with John Paul II's emissary, Franjieh
seemed to have acquiesced to the cardinal's demands. But,
eight days later (April 8, 1980), at a press conference, the
northern Lebanese leader stated that "he was disappointed

that the number two man in the Vatican had undertaken
such a long journey to Lebanon to raise such futile issues,
which did not constitute the crux of the Lebanese crisis."[114]
Franjieh's attitude stemmed from his total disagreement with
the Lebanese Front's policy of collaboration with the Israelis.
Moreover, Father Jean Aucagne in an interview commented
on the surprise that Casaroli's visit evoked in the Maronite
community. In fact, the secretary of state's meeting occurred
at the time when the bishop of Tripoli, Monsignor Antoine
Jubair, had only recently been expelled from his see under
the pressures of the Marada, Franjieh's militia.[115]

If Cardinal Casaroli's encounter in northern Lebanon was
not encouraging, the papal emissary's meeting with the two
key leaders of the Lebanese Front, Camille Chamoun and
Pierre Gemayel, revealed that differences existed even between them and the Holy See.

During his talks with the Maronite leaders, Casaroli was
handed a memorandum. It called on the Holy See "to play
a greater role at the international level and at the United
Nations to save Lebanon."[116] Furthermore, the Lebanese
Front document asked the Papacy to use its influence to convince the Lebanese government to separate the Lebanese
crisis from the Arab-Israeli quarrel. The memorandum also
emphasized that "the Syrian and Palestinian armed presence
was not conducive to reconciliation and the consolidation
of security."[117]

The Lebanese Front's line of thinking was not compatible with the message that the Holy See had tried to enunciate throughout the Lebanese War. In an important speech
at the presidential palace (March 31, 1980), given in the
course of a luncheon that brought together Lebanon's spiritual leaders, Cardinal Casaroli said that the Holy See "has
been and will continue to be discreet in its judgments, pru-
dent in its suggestions or advice."[118] Given "the limit of
its possibilities and in conformity with its nature as a spiritual and religious force," the Holy See is ready to offer its

help to defend Lebanon's territorial integrity and specific identity."[119]

Moreover, the secretary of state emphasized that the Holy See's concern was not limited only to Lebanon and does not prevent Rome from opening its "heart to the problems of other peoples in this troubled area" to whom the Holy See "wants to give its modest help, which arises from a positive sign of good will."[120]

Two important points emerged from this statement. First, the secretary of state stressed once again the spiritual nature of the Holy See. Consequently, unrealistic hopes held by the parties in Lebanon that the Papacy alone could effectively resolve their country's problems should be put in perspective. In fact, back in Rome, Cardinal Casaroli said that "sometimes the magnitude of the hope has been a little worrisome to me. It is as if everything rested on the action of the Holy See and the Holy Father."[121]

Secondly, as an answer to the Lebanese Front's memorandum, Cardinal Casaroli pointed out that (1) the Holy See was "discreet in its judgments" — in a sense, given the paramount nature of its principles of openness and understanding, the Holy See believes that it cannot alienate certain groups and nations in the Middle East and (2) the Holy See sees a definitive link between the Lebanese War and the conflict between Arabs and Israelis. Thus, to the Holy See a resolution of the Palestinian question was of fundamental importance to attain peace in Lebanon.

The difficulties that both Cardinal Casaroli and before him Cardinal Bertoli faced in their attempts to reconcile the Maronite community were multifaceted. Religious leaders in Lebanon lost a major part of their influence within their communities. The Maronite patriarch, the symbol of his community's unity, was himself unable to control the animosities that had developed for personal and political reasons between former President Franjieh and the Lebanese Front.

For the Holy See this situation became a source of great concern. How could Rome call for dialogue with Muslims, when Christians themselves were bickering and resorting to violence to settle their disputes? On the other hand, the resurgence of Islamic fundamentalism in the region and the growing strength of the Muslim community in Lebanon, did not lay to rest the long-held, but justifiable fears, of the Christian minority. Finally, and at the inter-Christian level, the Maronites were, and still are, the most militant in their nationalism. The Greek Catholics, Armenians, Greek Orthodox, and other Christian communities in Lebanon did not have the same stakes in maintaining power in Lebanon.

All in all, what Casaroli had come to do in Lebanon was achieved. In a way, he indirectly and diplomatically warned the Lebanese not to pin too much hope on the actions of the Holy See. The Pope was willing to offer his help as a facilitator, but if the parties themselves could not find grounds for agreement, the Holy See would not be able to force a solution on them.

THE HOLY SEE AND THE ISRAELI INVASION OF LEBANON

Following the Israeli invasion of Lebanon in the summer of 1982, the Holy See issued several statements calling on the international community to do all it could to stop the bloodshed. In fact, the Pontiff dispatched Mother Theresa on a humanitarian mission to Lebanon to assess the extent of relief needed by civilian victims. Furthermore, the day after the invasion (June 7, 1982), John Paul II told President Reagan, on an official visit to the Vatican, that the crisis in Lebanon "merits the attention of the world because of the dangers it contains of further provocation in the Middle East with immense consequences for world peace."[122]

The Israeli invasion did not ease the tensions between the

Holy See and the Maronite community in Lebanon. The election of Bashir Gemayel and the meeting between John Paul II and Yasser Arafat challenged the diplomatic skills of the Holy See.

On August 23, 1982, Bashir Gemayel, commander of the Christian-dominated Lebanese forces was elected president of Lebanon. Prior to his election, Bashir Gemayel wrote in the official organ of the Phalangist Party, *Al-'Amal*, that "the Vatican should understand that Christians in Lebanon are not guinea pigs for the Christian-Islamic dialogue in the world. Lebanon's mission as a bridge [between the West and the Arab world] was over."[123] In these few words, the Maronite leader highlighted the cause of the differences between the Holy See and the Lebanese Front since the war began in 1975. In order to survive in a Muslim environment, the Christians in Lebanon had no other choice but to resort to arms and defend themselves. Dialogue with Muslims was impossible unless from a position of strength.

Nevertheless, in his last speech as president-elect, refining his previous statements on relations with the Holy See, Bashir Gemayel said that the Maronite community still holds "respect and profound attachment to the Holy See." He also expressed the hope that his community "could always rely on the paternal support that the Vatican has always given us."[124]

Two important incidents epitomized the attitude of the Holy See toward the newly elected president in Lebanon. These episodes occurred before and after the election of Bashir Gemayel. In a confidential dispatch to the foreign ministry, a Lebanese diplomat in Rome underlined the haste of Vatican authorities in transferring the apostolic nuncio in Beirut (Monsignor Carlo Furno) and replacing him with Monsignor Luciano Angeloni. The Holy See's desire to act quickly became more pronounced as the chances for a possible electoral victory by Bashir Gemayel became brighter. It appears that the Holy See was concerned by Gemayel's election and by the fact that Monsignor Furno had become a political "liability." The explanation given by the secretariat of state was that the appointment of a new nuncio in Beirut was strictly an administrative matter. Nevertheless, the author of the diplomatic report gave his own interpretation when he wrote:

> The only plausible hypothesis would be that, in its desire to appoint a new papal nuncio, the Holy see's secretariat of state wanted to demonstrate a change in style and cancel some small misunderstandings that had occurred in the past.[125]

In the course of the Lebanese War, the Holy See's apostolic nuncios were forced to play an active role in the internal political process. The involvement led inevitably to misunderstandings between papal representatives and some of the Lebanese protagonists. A Vatican official stated that the apostolic nunciature in Lebanon "was the most political nunciature in the world." By that he meant that Vatican diplomats had to infringe on the purely spiritual nature of their charges and get more and more involved in the political matters affecting local Catholic communities.

The second incident happened after Bashir Gemayel's election. Pope John Paul II sent a personal telegram congratulating the new Lebanese president. However, the Holy See's secretariat of state refrained from publishing the text of the Pope's cable in the Vatican daily newspaper, *L'Osservatore Romano*. In the same confidential report mentioned earlier, the Lebanese diplomat speculated that the Holy See was waiting for Arab heads of state to send their compliments to Bashir Gemayel. The same report stated that the muted attitude adopted by the Holy See stemmed from its desire not to show any manifest enthusiasm toward the new president of Lebanon. The Holy See, faithful to its role as a mediator, moderator, and conciliator, wanted to maintain its bridges to the Muslim communities in Lebanon.[126]

On September 15, 1982, John Paul II granted an audience to Yasser Arafat. This meeting, coming one day after the assassination of Bashir Gemayel, caused a further deterioration in the Holy See's relations with several personalities in the Maronite community. One of these leaders, Sheikh Najib Dahdah, said that Arafat's meeting with the Pope "was a plot against John Paul II mounted by pro-Palestinian sympathizers in the Roman Curia." The same diplomat went on to assert that Arafat's followers "had killed Bashir Gemayel."[127]

To these heavy-handed accusations, a Vatican official replied:

> The pope does not have the responsibility of the Lebanese leadership who agreed to the Palestinian presence in Lebanon and allowed their guerrillas to carry their weapons.
> . . . Why should they criticize the Pope who represents Christ on earth and has the duty to welcome everybody?[128]

One day after the meeting between John Paul II and Arafat, Israeli-sponsored Christian militias perpetrated a massacre against Palestinian civilians in the camps of Sabra and Shatila (September 16–18, 1982). Some of the militias were natives of the Christian coastal town of Damour, which had once known a massacre itself organized by some Palestinian and other elements fighting in the Lebanese War.

Pope John Paul II reacted by saying that there were "no sufficient words to condemn such crimes, which are repulsive to the human and Christian conscience."[129]

This episode of the Lebanese War was the most dramatic illustration of the degree of hatred in some Lebanese Christian circles toward the Palestinians. The PLO in its attempt to create a state within a state in Lebanon had alienated large sectors of the Lebanese population. The bloodbath in the two Palestinian camps was a warning to the Papacy that something more radical had to be done in order to develop some sort of understanding among Lebanese, and between them and the Palestinians. However, a more radical approach could lead the Holy See to take sides in the war between Lebanese and Palestinian nationalism, which has always been regarded as against the long-term interests of the Catholic Church.

JOHN PAUL II'S THREE LETTERS ON LEBANON (1984)

The Israeli invasion of Lebanon had led to a reshuffling of the cards on the Lebanese scene. In fact, several tragic events occurred between 1982 and 1984 that warranted the close attention of the Holy See. Of fundamental importance to this analysis is the further fragmentation and divisions that occurred inside the Christian community in Lebanon already suffering from the massacres and exodus from the Druze-controlled areas in the Shouf Mountains (1983). Moreover, the split between some leaders of the Maronite community and the Holy See deepened, involving the papal nuncio, Monsignor Luciano Angeloni.

Between 1983 and 1984, Angeloni became the target of bitter criticisms from the more militant Maronite leaders. The papal nuncio's explanation was that the Christian leadership was deeply frustrated by its abandonment by Israel, the United States, and Europe. In fact, following the massacres of Sabra and Shatila, a multinational force of US Marines, French, Italian, and British troops reached Lebanon for peacekeeping purposes. By early 1984, following a series of attacks against US and French troops, the MNF withdrew from Lebanon. In defending his position, Monsignor Angeloni stated that "the Holy See cannot adopt or take political stands; it can only advance suggestions and proposals."[130]

According to an article published in a reliable Lebanese newsweekly, diplomatic dispatches sent to Rome from the apostolic nunciature in Lebanon always contained accusations against the Lebanese Front, the late President Bashir Gemayel, the Phalangist and the National Liberal Party, and

the head of the Permanent Congress of the Lebanese Order
of Monks, Abbot Bulos Naaman.[131] The clash between the
Holy See and the Maronites evolved around Rome's view
of Lebanon as a small part of the Church's global policy
and that of the Maronite leadership, for whom the war in
Lebanon was a matter of survival, a much more parochial
stance to be sure, but for the Maronites the only realistic one.

An example of the gap between the perceptions of the
Vatican and those of the Maronites is the incident involving Abbot Naaman.

Abbot Naaman, an important figure in the Maronite community and a staunch supporter of Israeli policies in southern
Lebanon, came out in favor of the May 17, 1983, Lebanese
Israeli Agreement. By November 1983, Monsignor Angeloni
ordered Naaman to stop attending the meetings of the Lebanese Front and told him that the Maronite patriarch was
the only spokesman for the Maronite community. The patriarch, then in Rome, expressed his belief that the policy
followed by the Lebanese Forces had led to the massacre
and subsequent exodus of the Christians from the Shouf
Mountains. The patriarch's stand was in complete agreement
with the one adopted by the papal nuncio. More importantly, Abbot Naaman's position was in complete contradiction to President Amin Gemayel's policy of reconciliation
and rapprochement with Syria. In fact, since Gemayel came
to power in 1982 he had visited Pope John Paul II three
times to ask support for his action in Lebanon.[132]

The misunderstanding between the Holy See and Abbot
Naaman led the Pope to take two important initiatives. The
first was to dispatch in early March 1984 a delegation
headed by Monsignor Mario Brini. Monsignor Brini, who
had already visited Lebanon in 1976, came to reassert the
Holy See's stand advocating the sovereignty and territorial
integrity of Lebanon and the Papacy's concern for the Christians in Lebanon and the Middle East. The second papal
initiative was to summon Abbot Naaman to Rome. During his first visit (December 1983) the Maronite clergyman

was told to heed the Holy See's call for moderation, an order which he ignored, insisting on the soundness of his political and religious stands. The second time (April 1984) Abbot Naaman was invited to a meeting with the Pope that also included the four Catholic patriarchs of Lebanon: Cardinal Antonios Butros Khoreish (Maronite), Monsignor Maximos V Hakim (Greek Catholic), Monsignor Antoun II Hayek (Syrian Catholic), and Monsignor Jean-Pierre XIV Kasparian (Armenian Catholic).

John Paul II initiated the meeting by expressing the need for an immediate plan "to stop the Lebanese crisis," which was affecting to a great extent Holy See's concerns.[133] The relationship between Lebanon and Israel was the second item on the agenda. A heated debate ensued between the Greek Catholic and Maronite patriarchs. Cardinal Khoreish expressed his apprehension toward the policy followed by Abbot Naaman. The latter's sympathy toward Israel went against the policy set by the Maronite patriarchate since the inception of the Lebanese War. Greek Catholic Patriarch Hakim, in defending Abbot Naaman to the Pontiff, stated:

> The overwhelming majority of Lebanese Christians are attached to Israel as if it were a life preserver because they perceive the steps taken by the Vatican as limited only to prayers and blessings. . . . The Vatican must be fully aware of the fact that the gravity of the situation in Lebanon had reached a climax. Imminent and rapid action must be taken.[134]

The altercation between the two Lebanese prelates degenerated and John Paul II had to intervene to calm spirits. In the meanwhile, the Holy See's secretary of state, Cardinal Casaroli, who also attended the meeting, reiterated the Vatican's fears regarding both the pro-Israeli attitude adopted by some Christians in Lebanon—they firmly believed that the Jewish state was the only one capable of protecting them—and Christian disobedience to religious authority. Moreover, Casaroli expressed his concern that Israel was taking advantage of this situation to discredit both the Vatican and the United States—that is, to "use this card on the one hand in the American presidential elections . . . and on the other hand as a way to pressure the Vatican."[135]

This painful episode in the relationship between Lebanese Catholics and Rome, together with the important role played by Catholics in the American electoral process, led Pope John Paul II to issue three important messages in the spring of 1984. The first message was addressed to the Maronite patriarch; the second was a message to the Lebanese; and the third was an apostolic letter to all the bishops of the Catholic Church.[136] This last document was unique in that it was the first time that a Sovereign Pontiff addressed Catholic bishops on a subject that was not related to doctrinal or disciplinary matters, but dealt with a country—Lebanon—and the cause it represents.

John Paul II repeated the Holy See's constant theme since the Lebanese War erupted in 1975. "The Lebanon of 1984 must take up the challenge of moral improvement and the advent of a society faithful to its prestigious heritage of civilization, and clear with regard to its future."[137]

Christians in Lebanon are summoned to the special task of maintaining the example of Christian-Islamic coexistence that prevailed in Lebanon before the strife. The Pope, in addressing the bishops about Lebanese Christians, wrote:

> We are not forgetting them. More, rather: we are counting on them and on their presence in a democratic Lebanon, open to others, in dialogue with cultures and religions, which only in this way is capable of surviving and guaranteeing their existence in freedom and dignity. In addition, *the development of Christianity in Lebanon is a condition for the presence of Christian minorities in the Middle East: of this, the Pope and the universal Church are aware.*[138]

For John Paul II the fate of the Eastern Christian communities is directly and vitally linked to the fate of Christians in Lebanon. In a sense, the Pope was telling Lebanese Christians that they should first think and behave as Christians, then worry about their own national problems. Their responsibilities went beyond the borders of tiny Lebanon: all over the Middle East, the followers of Christ have their eyes and hopes pointed toward the "land of cedars." Implicitly John Paul II had singled out Lebanon as a symbol of the democratic harboring of minorities, a land where the human rights of all citizens were respected without discrimination. Considering the role of Christians in an Islamic (*dhimmi*) or Jewish (*goyim*) society, the papal call can be considered a symbolic and sublime message.

Furthermore, John Paul II acknowledged the difficult struggle facing Christians in Lebanon. He in fact called on them not to be "ever timid when it comes to defending your freedoms and particularly the freedom to proclaim and to live together the gospel values."[139] Nevertheless, this call for Christians to defend their religious values does not represent an aggressive attitude toward non-Christian Lebanese. On the contrary, John Paul II in his message to the bishops wrote:

> Let us also pray for our non-Christian Lebanese brothers and sisters who, together with their fellow citizens who profess faith in Christ have contributed to writing the history of Lebanon, a land of meeting and dialogue.[140]

The papal messages did not have the expected impact. John Paul II wanted to make the Holy See's role and perceptions in the Lebanese conflict clear once and for all. Moreover, the Pope wanted to enunciate to all concerned in Lebanon and to the universal church that Lebanon should stay a land of religious and democratic coexistence and that Lebanese Christians had a very important place in papal priorities.

The most noticeable change after the Pope's three messages occurred when the Maronite leadership in Lebanon ceased its criticisms of the Holy See and its representatives.

In a political environment characterized by the total disintegration of the state and by the increasing strength of Islamic fundamentalist groups, Christians in Lebanon understood finally that Rome had become their last beacon of hope in the area.

CONCLUSIONS

There has been an incremental but steady evolution in the Holy See's attitude during the Lebanese War. The nature and scope of each pontifical delegation were tailored to cope with the increasing tensions in Lebanon. The first delegation, headed by Cardinal Paolo Bertoli, a highly respected diplomat and veteran in Lebanese affairs, was defined as a fact-finding mission. The Holy See, seven months after the beginning of the strife, wanted to gather firsthand information from the Lebanese protagonists themselves.

The second delegation, headed by Monsignor Mario Brini, had pastoral and humanitarian aims. By sending it, the Pope intended to express his solicitude toward the Christian community in Lebanon and offer the necessary relief required by the victims of the war. It coincided with greater Syrian involvement in Lebanon and frequent disruptions in the daily lives of civilians.

The third pontifical delegation, headed once again by Cardinal Bertoli, denoted the continuity in the style of the Holy See's diplomacy. This mission went to Lebanon for conciliation purposes. However, by 1978 the Lebanese War had provoked further fragmentation in the Lebanese arena. In addition to inter-Lebanese and Lebanese-Palestinian feuds, the Maronite leadership was also split by internal wrangling. This factor alone warranted the return of Bertoli, with strong international support. The task facing the Holy See's trouble-shooter was almost impossible. The fate of Lebanon as a sovereign entity was threatened not only by prospects of a permanent settlement of the Palestinians in the country, but by the indirect war raging between Syrians and Israelis.

The fourth mission was mostly pastoral in nature and epitomized the deep concern that the Holy See had toward the Lebanese War. The second highest figure in the Holy See, Cardinal Agostino Casaroli, came himself to convince his Lebanese counterparts that the Papacy could not sacrifice its regional concerns—that is, the fate of Catholic communities in the Levant and the Palestinian issue, to the unwillingness of the Lebanese to reconcile and settle peacefully their differences. The Holy See was ready to contribute to narrow the gap internally and ask for intervention by other powers, but it could not offer solutions that were beyond its sphere of competence.

There are both parallels and differences that emerge from the Holy See's intervention in Lebanon and its involvement in both the Israeli-Palestinian dispute and the status of Jerusalem and the Holy Places.

The common thread that motivates the Holy See's interests in the Levant is the fate of Catholic minorities. But the way the Papacy approaches this issue varies. In the conflict between Israelis and Palestinians, the fundamental concern of the Holy See is to preserve a Christian presence in the Holy Land and muster all efforts to foster a just solution to the dispute through peaceful means. In Lebanon the Holy See has tried to preserve the integrity of the country with its pluricommunitarian formula in order to save the Catholic communities. Opposition to Holy See policy comes from those elements in the Maronite community who believe that Christians in the Middle East have no other recourse than armed self-defense against Muslims. This solution jeopardized what the Papacy was staunchly working for—a frank and sincere dialogue between the followers of Christ and the followers of Muhammad.

In the Israeli-Palestinian dispute and the Jerusalem issue, the basic obstacle to Holy See intervention stemmed from the deeply imbedded misperceptions that existed between the Holy See and the Israelis regarding, first, the issue of a Jewish homeland in Palestine and, secondly, the fate of the Palestinians.

In the final analysis, the victims of these contradictions are the ecumenical and interfaith concerns of the Holy See. Christian-Muslim and Christian-Jewish dialogue have to await better days, when the fears of minorities can be calmed in the framework of the respect of the legitimate rights—civil, political, and religious—of Christians, Jews, and Muslims.

4. Summary and Conclusions

SUMMARY

THIS BOOK HAS DEALT with the role of the Holy See in the Arab-Israeli conflict from 1962 to 1984. The three issue-areas included the role of the Holy See in the Israeli-Palestinian dispute, the issue of Jerusalem and the future of the Holy Places, and the Holy See's involvement in the Lebanese War.

Chapter 1, on the Holy See and the Israeli-Palestinian dispute, was framed by three propositions dealing with the religious-humanitarian involvement of the Holy See and its diplomatic intervention. The analysis traced the evolution of the attitude of the Catholic Church toward Judaism during Vatican II, and the resulting controversy with both Arabs and Israelis. What emerged from this controversy was a split between those Catholic clergymen in the West who were willing to acknowledge the historical and religious link of the Jewish state to Palestine, and those Eastern Catholic clergymen who were unhappy with the council's decision to confront the issue of Judaism, with the negative implications it could have for Christian-Islamic relations.

The issue of the absence of official diplomatic relations between the Holy See and Israel was discussed. Several reasons were mentioned and issues were divided into formal and substantial categories. The former included the fact that the Holy See has been reluctant to establish diplomatic relations with states that lack definitive and recognized borders. This was the case for both Israel and the Kingdom of Jordan. Among the substantial issues was the fact that the Pope had to take into consideration the feelings of Arab Christians in his approach toward the Jewish state, and the fact that formal diplomatic relations between the Holy See and Israel should entail guarantees regarding the regulation of the Catholic presence in Israel. Nevertheless, since 1967 and the occupation by Israel of Jerusalem, the Holy See has adopted a pragmatic attitude toward the Jewish state. Finally, there was the religious factor: some conservative elements in the Roman Curia were opposed to identifying a link between the Jews and the land of Israel.

The Holy See's attitude toward the Palestinians was dictated by the Church's concern to foster peace with justice, and to recognize the rights of the Palestinians to self-determination. Since the beginning of the conflict, the Holy See consistently expressed its distress at and condemnation of acts of terrorism and reprisal. Moreover, it has called on both Israelis and Palestinians to recognize the right of each other to security and statehood.

To express its solicitude toward the fate of Catholics and Palestinians, the Holy See instituted two organizations—Bethlehem University and the Pontifical Mission for Palestine—which have been an expression of the Papacy's awareness of the humanitarian nature of the dispute, and its commitment to the fostering of the right of peoples to self-determination. Both institutions have served as concrete examples of the Holy See's principles.

Two other test cases were utilized to explore the proposition that the Holy See has indeed made a choice between Israelis and Palestinians, but has conducted its affairs in a way that demonstrates that the Holy See is an impartial mediator. The first case dealt with the Israeli attack on the Beirut airport (1968) following a Palestinian commando action against an Israeli target. The fact that Pope Paul VI cabled the Lebanese president to express his commiseration elicited anger and polemic in Israel. The Israelis, in fact, accused the Holy See of being biased toward the Arabs and having forgotten the "passive" role that the Catholic Church played during the Holocaust.

The second test case centered on the meetings between Paul VI and Israeli Prime Minister Golda Meir (1973) and the audience granted by Pope John Paul II to PLO Chairman Yasser Arafat. In both instances, the Holy See attempted to maintain an impartial attitude. What has emerged from my analysis is the difference in personality between Pope Paul VI and Pope John Paul II. The first kept the tenor of his meeting with Meir at the formal level of bilateral relations, without making overarching statements on the resolution of the Israeli-Palestinian dispute. In contrast, John Paul II decided to let the Jewish community and the Israelis become aware of what the Church had done for them during the Holocaust. Furthermore, he firmly urged Arafat to renounce the use of terrorism to regain the legitimate rights of his people.

The third proposition evolved around the Capucci affair, and the emotions that the arrest of the Greek Catholic patriarchal vicar had provoked in the ranks of Israelis and Arabs—both Muslims and Christians. The Holy See decided to put all its efforts into a call for Israeli clemency and the freeing of the bishop. The fundamental point was that there exists some kind of implicit interdependence between the Holy See and the Jewish state. In fact, the Pope had to recognize that, to protect the welfare of Catholics in the Holy Land, he had to acknowledge the reality of Israel. Israel, on the other hand has been eagerly looking for openings to obtain official recognition from the Holy See. Moreover, given Israel's ties to several countries with large Catholic populations, it has had no interest in alienating the Holy See.

Regarding the question of Jerusalem and the Holy Places, the Holy See was and is a party to the dispute, having opted to preserve both the interfaith dialogue with Jews and Muslims and to stem the tide of the exodus of Christians from

the Holy Land. Chapter 2 dealt with the religious significance of Jerusalem to Jews, Christians, and Muslims. It then
focused on the juridical status of Jerusalem from the Ottoman era to the Israeli annexation of the city in 1967. A detailed analysis was presented of the threats and contradictions facing the Christian communities living in the Holy
City. Four major sources of tension were found: the problem of emigration, inter-Christian, Christian-Islamic, and
Christian-Israeli tensions. Those tensions were an obstacle
to the Holy See's ecumenical concerns.

An interesting aspect came to light in the course of the
analysis of the Christian communities. This aspect was highlighted by the difference between some Christian groups in
Lebanon who had expressed their open hostility to the Palestinian presence in their country, and the common bonds
that united Christian and Muslim Palestinians in the Holy
Land. Another key problem was illustrated by the dichotomy
between international religious interests in Jerusalem and
the interests of indigenous Christian communities. Following this analysis, a brief account was given of the attitude
of Arab and non-Arab Islamic states, and the United States
and the Soviet Union, toward the status of Jerusalem.

My analysis of the role of the Holy See in Jerusalem was
predicated on one main premise: the Holy See was opposed
to the exclusive religious and political control by the followers of any one of the three monotheistic faiths. Test cases
covered Israeli attempts to "judaize" Jerusalem and the Holy
See's opposition to it, the meeting between Pope Paul VI
and some African leaders, and the statement subsequently
issued which provoked an uproar in Israel regarding the Holy
See's call for an internationally guaranteed special status for
Jerusalem. Other case studies included the Holy See's reactions to the Tripoli Seminar, which stated that Jerusalem
was an Arab city, the important article on Jerusalem published by *L'Osservatore Romano* (1980), and John Paul II's
apostolic letter *Redemptionis Anno* (1984).

The Holy See's intervention to protect the precarious

rights of Christian communities living in Jerusalem was tested by the case of the Notre Dame affair, a hostel owned by French priests and sold to the Israeli government without Rome's consent. In 1973 the Israelis sold back Notre Dame to the Holy See. Since then it has become the symbol of the Papacy's attitude toward non-Jewish communities living in the Holy Land.

The third major conflict in which the Holy See was involved was the Lebanese War. Chapter 3 assessed the preferences of local, regional, and global powers toward the strife in Lebanon. This served as the background to an analysis of the role of the Holy See.

During the Lebanese War, the fundamental objective of the Holy See was to save Lebanon as an independent state in order to protect the Christian presence not only in Lebanon but throughout the Middle East. The Holy See opted to act as a mediator and conciliator among the various groups, underlining the limits inherent in the spiritual nature of its mission.

The Holy See's stand clashed with that of the Christian militias who thought that Rome should back them in their fight against the Palestinians. Moreover, the Holy See stressed that only the Lebanese could solve their problems and that they should unite around legitimate authorities, such as the president of the republic. Also, the Holy See's perception that there was a definitive link between the war in Lebanon and the Israeli-Palestinian dispute did not correspond to the interpretation of important Maronite leaders. They advocated the decoupling of the Lebanese conflict from regional problems.

Chapter 3 attempted to prove that the greater the threat to Christian-Islamic coexistence in Lebanon, the greater the probability of Holy See involvement. Of particular relevance here were the controversies and polemics that erupted between the Pope and some Maronite political and religious leaders. The decision by Christian militias to establish contacts with Israel was viewed negatively in Rome in light of the harm it could do to other Christian communities living in the Arab countries.

The fact that ecumenism and peaceful coexistence had a high priority in papal diplomacy toward Lebanon was tested by the four mediation missions that the Holy See dispatched to Lebanon. The main characteristic of these missions was the consistent pattern in Holy See diplomacy. Cardinal Paolo Bertoli, a veteran diplomat who had had previous experience in Lebanon, was sent twice: in 1975 and 1978. Monsignor Mario Brini also had lived in Lebanon and had deep knowledge of Middle Eastern affairs. All these missions were tailored to cope with the increasing fragmentation of the Lebanese communities.

In order to counter the threats facing the Catholic community, Pope John Paul II in 1980 dispatched his own secretary of state to Lebanon. Cardinal Casaroli had come on a pastoral mission and tried to conciliate first the Maronites, then the Lebanese.

CONCLUSIONS

The Holy See is an important transnational actor and should not be disregarded, especially now in light of the activist policy adopted by Pope John Paul II. Papal diplomacy is unique in international relations. First and foremost, the Holy See intervenes in world affairs as a religious institution. In light of the fact that it does not have tangible means — political, economic, military — at its disposal, the Holy See is one of the few actors, if not the only one, in international affairs that must rely on the impact of an intangible factor — the moral prestige of the Pope — to contribute toward peace. For instance, the Holy See, unlike the United States and the Soviet Union, can welcome Arab and Israeli leaders on an equal footing. Both Arabs and Israelis hold a great degree of respect for the person of the Pontiff, who is a symbol of moderation. The drawback of this advantage is that participants in the Middle East conflict attempt to manipulate the symbolism inherent in papal pronouncements and actions in an effort to justify their own claims.

The uniqueness of papal diplomacy is also seen when the Holy See deals with Arabs and Israelis. Here the Holy See interacts with them as Christians, Muslims, and Jews; consequently, the spiritual intertwines with the temporal, rendering papal intervention more problematic. A temporal power such as the United States chooses to deal with Arabs and Israelis on the basis of enhancing its own interests; the religion of America's interlocutors is not of great relevance, even when religious sensitivities need to be considered. But when the Pope enters the fray, it is of necessity as the head of the Roman Catholic Church, and papal diplomacy always concentrates on concerns that are spiritual in nature.

For instance, with Muslims and Jews, the Holy See has a long way to go in order to form solid bonds that would overcome problems in the political situation. Since Vatican II, the Papacy has managed to emphasize the commonalities between itself and Arab and Islamic countries with regard to temporal matters. However, differences at the religious level have still to be ironed out. Moreover, the Holy See is well aware of the fact that disagreements, in both religious and diplomatic affairs, need to be settled before any frank and harmonious relationship can be developed between the Holy See, the Jewish community, and the state of Israel. This situation clearly demonstrates the unique nature of papal diplomacy and the intricacies of the issues with which the Holy See must contend.

The Holy See as a unique transnational actor develops its diplomacy at the macrolevel—that is, policy is formulated from a global perspective and reflects the universal character of the Church. Such a policy dictates that the Holy See refrain from adopting partisan stands. Consequently, the Papacy becomes deeply involved in conflicts only when the welfare of Catholic communities is in immediate jeopardy.

In the Arab-Israeli conflict the Holy See avoids giving concrete solutions to problems affecting the peoples of the area.
This neutrality, however, is sometimes violated by the Papacy's sympathy for the Palestinians, a people considered
deprived of their legitimate rights, and by the fact that a
minority among Palestinians are Catholic.

Consistency and pragmatism shape papal diplomacy in
the three issue-areas — the Israeli-Palestinian conflict, the
status of Jerusalem and the Holy Places, and the Lebanese
War. These two attributes characterize the evolution of
papal involvement since the mid-1960s. For instance, the
Holy See's attitude toward the Jewish state has evolved from
a feeling of reluctance and fear to that of a willingness to
accommodate Catholic interests with Israel's. Keeping always in mind the fundamental aim of the Holy See — the
preservation of Catholic presence and interests — the Papacy
came to the conclusion that, although bilateral relations have
still a long way to go, the Holy See and Israel could formulate and follow a set of implicit rules that protect their
respective interests.

The same evolutionary pattern can be discerned in papal
diplomacy toward Jerusalem. In fact, when assessing the
Holy See's attitude toward the Holy City, I found that papal
policy had undergone five stages of evolution. The first stage
emphasized the preeminence of Catholic rights over those
of "infidels" and other Christian groups. The second stage
illustrated the Holy See's support for internationalization.
In the third stage, the Holy See called for a special status
for both Jerusalem and the Holy Places, and the safeguard
of the religious and civil rights of all communities living in
the city. The fourth stage highlighted the pragmatism and
practical nature of papal diplomacy. Rome accepted the control of one power over Jerusalem, with the proviso that this
control be placed under international supervision. The fifth
stage is found in John Paul II's call for an immediate solution to the question of Jerusalem, for the Pope believes that

Jerusalem could become the catalyst for a settlement between Arabs and Israelis.

The Holy See's approach toward the Lebanese War is guided by its view of Lebanon as a microcosm of the various conflicts that mar interstate and transnational relations in the Middle East. The success of the Lebanese formula of Christian-Islamic coexistence is crucial in terms of the fate of Christian communities in the Levant.

Throughout the conflict the Holy See has often repeated that only through dialogue can the Lebanese hope to solve their problems. The Pope and his mediators have warned the Lebanese not to set high hopes on the concrete effects of papal diplomacy. The Holy See expressed its solidarity with Lebanon by the mobilization of all the resources available to the Papacy—diplomatic and humanitarian. Since the beginning of the war, the pleas launched by the Pope in favor of Lebanon were not unheeded by the leaders of temporal powers such as France and the United States. The content of papal appeals concentrated on helping the Lebanese free themselves from external pressures and interferences.

What is most painful for the Holy See is that unity among Christians in Lebanon is still unrealized and elusive. Given the independent and closely knit nature of their community, some Maronites in Lebanon have refused to see their country entirely absorbed in the Arab-Islamic environment. On the other hand, the Greek Orthodox feel that their church and traditions are part and parcel of the Arab world. They disapprove therefore of the relationship that has developed between Christian militias in Lebanon and Israel.

Lebanon and the preservation of its Christian communities constitute the most important lead regarding future trends in papal diplomacy toward the Arab-Israeli conflict. If the situation in Lebanon were to portend some kind of compromise among its major communities, then the fate of the Christians could be considered somewhat secure. If Lebanon were to break up as a result of precarious agreements and continuous turmoil, then the Holy See would be forced to muster all the resources available to its diplomacy to salvage what would be left of the Christian presence. In light of the intractable problems of the Lebanese situation, the Papacy may well have to strike painful compromises and resort to concrete actions in order to prevent the Church in Lebanon and the Middle East from being "fossilized" by history.

The final observation to emerge from this book is that papal diplomacy is effective only in religious issue–areas. This was exemplified in the release of Archbishop Capucci and in the Notre Dame affair. These two cases challenged directly the prestige of the Papacy where it had to demonstrate to the indigenous Christian and non-Christian communities that the Holy See would not flinch from preserving Christian interests in the Levant.

In conflicts having ethnic and nationalistic aspects, the Holy See's effectiveness is limited by the divisions — ideological, political, and religious — among the warring parties. In Lebanon, for example, the longer the conflict between the various factions was protracted, the harder it became for the Holy See to implement a frank and peaceful dialogue among the Lebanese. The same situation occurred in the Israeli-Palestinian dispute. These two conflicts are already difficult to solve from the perspective of regional and global powers, which have exerted their diplomatic skills in finding a solution. It is not surprising, then, that the Holy See is apparently not very effective in its attempt to have the parties lessen the damage they inflict on each other because of their frictions.

In the future, the Holy See will, in all probability, maintain and enhance its principal guidelines toward the Middle East: protection of the Catholic and Christian minorities, opposition to any unilateral control over Jerusalem, calling on both Israelis and Palestinians to recognize each other's rights while favoring the Palestinians, and preserving the Lebanese formula of Christian-Islamic coexistence.

This study was born of the paucity of literature available

on the role of the Holy See in the Arab-Israeli conflict and the Middle East in general. It is a first step for other scholars to follow. The fundamental difficulty in this kind of research is the unavailability of primary sources. Vatican archives are closed for years to come. So the investigation of the role of the Papacy has to rely on secondary sources, interviews, extrapolations, which could be negated by developments in the area. Nevertheless, the advantage in assessing pontifical diplomacy is that the Holy See does not abruptly shift policy. The Church, as Cardinal Gasparri once said, thinks in terms of "eternity."

As a suggestion for future studies there is a need for a thorough analysis of the role of the American Catholic Church toward the Arab-Israeli conflict. Since the mid-1960s the Church in the United States has replaced its European counterpart as a focus of influence and organization. A study of how the National Council of Catholic Bishops has approached the Middle East would be of great value.

Another important topic for investigation would be an assessment of how Western Catholic clergymen approach the Israeli-Palestinian quarrel and how they differ from their counterparts in the Middle East. Is there a possibility that a sincere dialogue among Catholics could bring about a rapprochement between Christians, Muslims, and Jews?

A related topic for research resides in the study of Catholic organizations and institutions that have been involved in the Middle East—for example, the Pontifical Mission for Palestine, or the Jesuit community through its schools in the Arab countries. It would be relevant, for instance, to assess the impact that foreign missionaries had in the formation of the political elites in the Levant.

Finally, and most importantly, it would be of great usefulness if a study were to be undertaken on a comparative level of papal diplomacy in conflict situations (Biafra, Vietnam, Cambodia) where the degree of Holy See involvement and its characteristics could be evaluated. From this perspective, it would also be interesting to compare papal involvement with secular powers—for instance, a comparative study of the various mediation missions sent to Lebanon during the war by Arab countries, France, and the United States, and how they differ from or are similar to missions dispatched by the Holy See.

It was the goal of this book to open new vistas on the analysis of the Papacy and its role in a tormented and vitally important area of the world. Even if the Catholic presence is not as relevant as in Latin America, the policy that the Holy See adopts to follow in the Middle East could be an indication of where the Catholic Church is oriented. In fact, there are no other locations where the three monotheistic religions—concentrated as they are in a small geographical area—can prove or disprove the validity of their message.

Notes

INTRODUCTION

1. In this study the following definition of the term "Holy See" has been adopted: "By *Holy See* we mean the supreme organ of the Church, as understood by Canon 7. . . . The Holy See is to the Church what the government is to the State, with the difference that the monarchical constitution of the Church, being of divine origin, is not subject to change" (Hyginus Eugene Cardinale, *The Holy See and the International Order* [England: Colin Smythe Ltd., 1976], p. 85). The terms "Holy See," "Papacy," and "Vatican" will be used interchangeably.

2. This is an assessment made by Daniel Rossing, director of the Christian Communities Department, a special unit of the Israeli Ministry of Religious Affairs. Quoted in Robert D. Kaplan, "Special Report: Israeli Policy towards Christian Churches," *The Christian Century*, 97 (12 Nov. 1980), 36.

3. Ivan Vallier, " The Roman Catholic Church: A Transnational Actor," in *Transnational Relations and World Politics*, Robert L. Keohane and Joseph S. Nye, eds. (Cambridge: Harvard Univ. Press, 1976), p. 150.

4. Ibid., p. 147.

5. Personal interview with Monsignor Richard Mathes, Jerusalem, 7 May 1983.

1. THE HOLY SEE AND THE ISRAELI-PALESTINIAN DISPUTE

1. Personal interview with Father Marcel Dubois, Jerusalem, 10 May 1983. See also his "The Catholic View," *Encyclopaedia Judaica Year Book, 1974* (Jerusalem: Keter Publishing House, 1974), pp. 167–73. Father Dubois is an Israeli Dominican priest

165

and an advisor to the Holy See's Commission for Religious Relations with Judaism.

2. The official text of the Balfour Declaration (2 Nov. 1917) stated: "H. M. Government, after considering the aims of the Zionist Organization, accepts the principle of recognising Palestine as the National Home of the Jewish people and the right of the Jewish people to build up its National life in Palestine under a protection to be established at the conclusion of Peace, following upon the successful issue of the war." For further details on the Balfour Declaration, see Leonard Stein, *The Balfour Declaration* (London: Vallentine, Mitchell, 1961).

3. In the vast literature available on the Arab-Israeli dispute, the most balanced account to date is that by Fred J. Khouri, *The Arab-Israeli Dilemma* (Syracuse, NY: Syracuse Univ. Press, 2nd ed., 1980).

4. See Edward W. Said, *The Question of Palestine* (New York: Times Books, 1979).

5. Khouri, *Dilemma*, p. 5.

6. Quoted in *The Pilot*, 6 May 1983, p. 4.

7. Regarding Vatican II and the debates on Christian-Jewish relations, see Arthur Gilbert, *The Vatican Council and the Jews* (Cleveland: World Publishing Company, 1968); Rabbi Emanuel Rose, "Jews and Judaism in Vatican II," Diss., Hebrew Union College, Jewish Institute of Religion, Los Angeles, May 1969. On the evolution of the Christian-Jewish dialogue since the council, see Marie-Thérèse Hoch and Bernard Dupuy, compilers, *Les Eglises devant le Judaisme: Documents officiels, 1948–1978* (Paris: Les Editions du Cerf, 1980); L. Sestrieri and G. Cereti, compilers, *Le Chiese Cristiane e l'Ebraismo, 1947–1982* (Casale Monferrato: Casa Editrice Marietti, 1983). See also Eugene J. Fisher, "A New Maturity in Christian-Jewish Dialogue: An Annotated Bibliography 1973–1983," in *Face to Face: An Interreligious Bulletin*, 11 (Spring 1984) 29–63.

8. The full text of *Nostra Aetate* can be found in Walter M. Abbott, S.J., gen. ed., *The Documents of Vatican II* (Piscataway, NJ: Association Press, New Century Publishers, 1966), pp. 660–68. Originally, the council debated a document that dealt exclusively with the Jews. Subsequently and in the aftermath of various arguments advanced during the debate, the council fathers decided to include the document on the Jews in the context of the Catholic Church's relations with non-Christians in general.

9. Ibid., pp. 666–67.

10. Ibid., p. 665.

11. Marcel Dubois, "The Catholic Church and the State of Israel—Thirty Years After," *Encounter Today*, 14/4 (Spring-Summer 1980) 170.

12. Rose, "Jews," p. 131.

13. F. E. Cartus, "Vatican II and the Jews," *Commentary*, 39/1 (Jan. 1965) 21–22.

14. Personal interview, Jerusalem, 26 April 1983. Dr. Wigoder is vice-chairman of the Council on Inter-Faith Relations in Israel and Israel's representative on the International Council for Inter-Religious Consultation (IJCIC).

15. Rose, "Jews," p. 151.

16. Personal interview, Beirut, 29 March 1983. See also Rose, "Jews," pp. 150–52.

17. Anis al-Kassem, *Nahnu wal Vatikan wa Israil* (Beirut: PLO Research Center, June 1966).

18. See Saul Friedlander, *Pius XII and the Third Reich: A Documentation* (New York: Alfred A. Knopf, 1966); John F. Morley, *Vatican Diplomacy and the Jews during the Holocaust, 1939–1943* (New York: KTAV Publishing House, 1980); Sister Charlotte Klein, "In the Mirror of *Civiltà Cattolica*: Vatican View of Jewry, 1939–1962," *Christian Attitudes on Jews and Judaism*, 43 (Aug. 1975) 12–16; see also a series of four articles, "Commentaries: The Papacy and the Holocaust," *Social Science and Modern Society*, 20/3 (March-April 1983) 4–31. In order to counter all the claims and allegations against Pope Pius XII's "silence" and the Catholic Church's stand towards Nazism, the Vatican decided to open and publish the documents available in its archives related to this subject. See Pierre Blet, Robert A. Graham, Angelo Martini, and Burkhart Schneider, eds., *Actes et Documents du Saint-Siège relatifs à la Seconde Guerre Mondiale* (Vatican City: Libreria Editrice Vaticana, 1965–1980). Until now there are ten volumes available. For a thorough review of this collection, see Victor Conzemius, "Le Saint-Siège et la Deuxième Guerre Mondiale, Deux éditions de sources," *Revue d'Histoire de la Deuxième Guerre Mondiale et des Conflits Contemporains*, 128 (Oct. 1982) 71–94.

19. Al-Kassem, *Nahnu*, p. 26.

20. During the second and third sessions of Vatican II, the PLO was at its early formation stage.

21. Al-Kassem, *Nahnu*, p. 162.

22. Ibid., pp. 103–4.

23. Personal interview with Dr. Yonathan Prato, Jerusalem, 4 May 1983. Dr. Prato was legal counsellor in the Israeli Embassy in Rome.

24. Personal interview with Dr. Zwi Werblowski, Jerusalem, 2 May 1983. Dr. Werblowski is professor of comparative religion at the Hebrew University and former chairman of the Israel Interfaith Committee.

25. The full text of the French bishops' statement can be found in Helga Croner, compiler, *Stepping Stones to Further Jewish-Christian Relations* (London, New York: Stimulus Books, 1977), pp. 63–64.

26. R. J. Zwi Werblowsky, "Jewish-Christian Relations with Patricular Reference to the Contribution of the State of Israel," *Christian News from Israel*, 24/2–3 (14–15) (Autumn-Winter 1973) 120.

27. *Proche-Orient Chrétien*, 23 (1973) 200.

28. Ibid., p. 213.

29. See *Statement Issued on May 2, 1973, in Which More than 40 Jesuits Reject the Declaration (Orientations Pastorales) of the French Bishops' Committee for Relations with Judaism*. Copy of the statement was given to me by Father Joseph L. Ryan, S.J. See also his "The Catholic Faith and the Problem of Israel and Jerusalem," in *Jerusalem: The Key to World Peace* (London: Islamic Council of Europe, 1980), pp. 49–50.

30. Yehoshua Rash, "L'état d'Israël interroge l'Eglise," *Cahiers Universitaires Catholiques*, 5 (May-June 1980) 18. See also his "Le Vatican et le conflit Israélo-Arabe," *Politique Internationale*, 13 (Fall 1981) 250–74, and *Déminer un champ fertile: Les Catholiques Français et l'Etat d'Israël* (Paris: Les Editions du Cerf, 1982).

31. Walter Laqueur, "Zionism and Its Liberal Critics, 1896–1948," *Journal of Contemporary History*, 6/4 (1971) 180.

32. *Journal of Ecumenical Studies*, 6/2 (Spring 1969) 184.

33. Joseph L. Ryan, S.J., "Anti-Zionism and Anti-Semitism," *Journal of Ecumenical Studies*, 7/2 (Spring 1970) 321.

34. On the relationship between the Holy See and the Zionist movement since its inception, see Charlotte Klein, "Vatican and Zionism, 1897–1967," *Christian Attitude on Jews and Judaism*,

36–37 (June-Aug. 1974) 11–16; Pinchas Lapide, *Three Popes and the Jews* (New York: Hawthorn Books, 1967); Raphael Patai, ed., *The Complete Diaries of Theodor Herzl*, 5 vols. (New York/London: Herzl Press/Thomas Yoseloff, 1960); Florian Sokolow, *Nahum Sokolow: Life and Legend* (London: Jewish Chronical Publications, 1975); Esther Yolles Feldblum, *The American Catholic Press and the Jewish State, 1917–1959* (New York: KTAV Publishing House, 1977); Maria Grazia Enardu, *Palestine in Anglo-Vatican Relations, 1936–1939* (Florence, Italy: Cooperativa Universitaria Firenze, 1980); Yehoshua Rash, "Herzl, Weizmann, leurs papes et leurs cardinaux," *Sens*, 12 (Dec. 1983) 283–303.

35. *L'Osservatore Romano*, 28 May 1948.

36. *The Pilot*, 6 May 1983.

37. Personal interview, Jerusalem, 10 May 1983.

38. On this subject, see Edmund Francis Konczakowski, "Vatican Policy toward the German Oder-Neisse Line: A Study of Foreign Policy Evolution, 1945–1972," Diss., Univ. of Pennsylvania, 1976. The Holy See also has no diplomatic relations with the Hashemite Kingdom of Jordan.

39. Personal interview with Dr. Meir Mendes, former liaison officer between the Israeli Embassy in Rome and the Holy See, Tel Aviv, 1 May 1983. Dr. Mendes is the author of *The Vatican and Israel* published (in Hebrew) by the Leonard Davis Institute for International Relations, Hebrew Univ. of Jerusalem, 1983.

40. *Proche-Orient Chrétien*, the French Greek-Catholic journal published by the White Fathers in Jerusalem, gives regular account of tensions between some Israeli religious groups and local Christian communities.

41. Personal interview, Jerusalem, 2 May 1983.

42. *The New York Times*, 26 Nov. 1984.

43. Liz S. Armstrong, "Catholic, Jewish House Members Urge Vatican to Recognize Israel," *NC News*, 26 Nov. 1984.

44. *The New York Times*, 22 Oct. 1984.

45. Personal communication, 12 Dec. 1984.

46. On the Christian-Islamic Dialogue, see Pietro Rossano, "Les grands documents de l'Eglise au sujet des Musulmans," *IslamoChristiana* [Rome], 8 (1982) 13–23. Also Youakim Moubarac, *Recherches sur la pensée Chrétienne et l'Islam dans les temps modernes et à l'époque contemporaine* (Beirut: Publications

de l'Université Libanaise, 1977); Gaston Zananiri, O.P., *L'Eglise et l'Islam* (Paris: Spes, 1969).

47. Abbott, *Documents*, p. 663.

48. See, e.g., Paul VI's speech in welcoming President Sadat, *Proche-Orient Chrétien*, 26 (1976) 132–34; the speech delivered by Paul VI in welcoming Moshe Dayan, *Proche-Orient Chrétien*, 27 (1977) 341; and the speech Paul VI delivered during the visit of King Hussein of Jordan, *L'Osservatore Romano*, 30 April 1978.

49. *The Pilot*, 6 May 1983.

50. For further details on the Palestinians and the PLO, see Hatem I. Husseini, *The Palestine Problem: An Annotated Bibliography* (Washington, DC: Palestine Information Office, 1980); William B. Quandt, Fuad Jabber, and Ann Mosley Lesch, *The Politics of Palestinian Nationalism* (Berkeley: Univ. of California Press, 1973).

51. Personal interview, Washington, DC, 7 July 1983.

52. *L'Osservatore Romano*, 23 Dec. 1975.

53. See Joseph L. Ryan, S.J., "Palestinian Rights: Resonances in the Life and Themes of Pope John Paul II." prepared for the Fifth United Nations Seminar on the Inalienable Rights of the Palestinian People, (15–19 March 1982) (mimeographed).

54. *The Washington Post*, 6 Oct. 1980.

55. *Jewish Telegraphic Agency*, 8 Oct. 1980.

56. "Israeli Settlements on the West Bank of the Jordan," *L'Osservatore Romano*, English ed., 10 Nov. 1977.

57. From a pamphlet distributed by the CNEWA office in New York; also personal interview with Brother Joe Lowenstein, in charge of the Pontifical Mission for Palestine, Jerusalem, 25 April 1983; and Monsignor John G. Meaney, regional director of the Pontifical Mission for the Near East, Jall-Eddib, 27 May 1983. Monsignor Meaney told me that former secretary of state Alexander Haig's father was among the founding members of CNEWA.

In November 1983, a Holy See representative, Monsignor Antonio Franco, stated at the United Nations that "the Pontifical Mission's contribution to the refugees and other Palestinians in need since 1948 has amounted . . . to more than 150,000,000 dollars" (*L'Osservatore Romano*, English ed., 19 Dec. 1983).

58. J.T. Ryan, "Catholic Near East Welfare Association," *New Catholic Encyclopedia* (Washington, DC: Catholic Univ. of America, 1967), vol. 3, pp. 271–72.

59. From *Insegnamenti di Paolo VI* (Vatican City: Tipografia Poliglotta Vaticana, 1974), vol. 12, pp. 682–83. Also Ed Maxwell, "Palestine Refugees Key to Peace: Msgr. Nolan," *The Troy Record*, 30 March 1970.

60. Personal interview with Brother Thomas Scanlan, Bethlehem, 27 April 1983.

61. Memorandum prepared by the apostolic delegate for Monsignor Nolan, 26 Dec. 1972. Given to me by Brother Gottwald at Bethlehem Univ.

62. Personal interview.

63. Personal interview.

64. See Chaim Weizmann, *Trial and Error* (New York: Harper and Brothers, 1949), p. 286.

65. *L'Osservatore Romano*, 30 Dec. 1968.

66. *The Jerusalem Post*, 3 Jan. 1969.

67. Regarding Pope Paul VI's visit to the Holy Land, see *Il pellegrinaggio di Paolo VI in Terra Santa (4–6 gennaio, 1964)* (Vatican City: Libreria Editrice Vaticana, 1964). Jewish and Israeli admiration for John XXIII originated from the Pontiff's activism during his stay in Turkey and Eastern Europe where he undertook efforts to save Jews from Nazi extermination. When the Pope's encyclical *Pacem in Terris* (1963) was issued, it was translated into Hebrew. For further details on John XXIII, see Paul Dreyfus, *Jean XXIII* (Paris: Librairie Arthème Fayard, 1979); Peter Hebblethwaite, *John XXIII: Pope of the Council* (London: Geoffrey Chapman, 1984).

68. Sefardim are Oriental Jews. Rabbi Nissim refused to meet with Paul VI during his visit to the Holy Land in 1964.

69. *Proche-Orient Chrétien*, 19 (1969) 89.

70. On 1 Jan. 1969, the Vatican newspaper wrote that circumcision "had lost its justification, given that it was substituted by baptism." This article was interpreted as an attack on the Jewish faith, in which circumcision is still practiced, contradicting the ecumenical spirit advocated by Vatican II. *Proche-Orient Chrétien*, ibid., p. 88.

71. *The Jerusalem Post*, 3 Jan. 1969.

72. *Proche-Orient Chrétien*, 19 (1969) 92.

73. Ibid.

74. Libanius, "Paul VI et le Liban," *Le Réveil*, 13 Aug. 1978.

75. Ibid.

76. *Proche-Orient Chrétien*, 19 (1969) 89.

77. *L'Osservatore Romano*, 15–16 Jan. 1973; *The Jerusalem Post*, 17 Jan. 1973.

78. *The Jerusalem Post*, 17 Jan. 1973.

79. Golda Meir, *My Life* (New York: Dell Publishing, 1975), p. 393.

80. *Proche-Orient Chrétien*, 23 (1973) 82.

81. *The Jerusalem Post,*, 18 Jan. 1973.

82. *Proche-Orient Chrétien*, 23 (1973) 83.

83. *The Jerusalem Post*, 21 Jan. 1973. See also Golda Meir, *Life*, pp. 391–94.

84. *The Jerusalem Post*, 21 Jan. 1973.

85. *Le Monde*, 17 Sept. 1982.

86. Personal interview with Vatican official, 13 June 1983.

87. Personal interview.

88. Personal interview with Dr. Geofrey Wigoder.

89. Personal interview.

90. *Origins*, 23 Sept. 1982, p. 240.

91. *Philadelphia Enquirer*, 19 Sept. 1982.

92. *Origins*, 23 Sept. 1982, p. 240.

93. *The Pilot*, 6 May 1983.

94. *Origins*, 30 Sept. 1982, p. 243; emphasis added.

95. Quoted in Joseph L. Ryan, "Palestinian Rights," p. 13.

96. I secured a copy of the dispatch from the Embassy of Lebanon to the Holy See.

97. In a personal interview with Father Ibrahim Iyad, a key contact person between the PLO and the Holy See, the clergyman stated that it was Giulio Andreotti, the Italian foreign minister, who actively convinced the Italian president, Sandro Pertini, to welcome Arafat, Los Angeles, 22 Nov. 1982.

98. Personal interview, Bir Zeit Univ., 3 May 1983.

99. Personal interview, Tantur, 2 May 1983.

100. Personal interview, Jerusalem, 17 May 1983.

101. *Proche-Orient Chrétien*, 24 (1974) 343.

102. This is the name given to members of the Greek Church in the Middle East.

103. *Proche-Orient Chrétien*, 24 (1974) 338.

104. Personal interview, Jerusalem, 17 May 1983.

105. Personal interview.

106. *Al-Fajr*, Jerusalem Palestinian weekly, 19 Aug. 1983.

107. Personal interview.
108. *Proche-Orient Chrétien*, 24 (1974) 242.
109. Ibid, p. 337.
110. Ibid., p. 346.
111. Ibid.
112. *Proche-Orient Chrétien*, 25 (1975) 308.
113. *The Jerusalem Post*, 7 Nov. 1977.
114. *The New York Times*, 7 Nov. 1977.
115. *The Jerusalem Post*, 2 Nov. 1977.
116. *The Jerusalem Post*, 29 March 1981. The Cohen Law approved the total annexation of Jerusalem.
117. *Proche-Orient Chrétien*, 30 (1980) 350–57.

2. THE HOLY SEE, THE HOLY PLACES, AND JERUSALEM

1. Major sources regarding the Jerusalem issue are the books of Bernardin Collin: *Les Lieux Saints*, Coll. Que-Sais-Je? (Paris: Presses Universitaires de France, 2nd ed., 1968); *Le problème juridique des Lieux-Saints* (Paris: Sirey, 1956); *Pour une solution au problème des Lieux-Saints* (Paris: G.-P. Maisonneuve et Larose, 1974); and *Recueil de documents concernant Jérusalem et les Lieux-Saints* (Jerusalem: Franciscan Printing Press, 1982). See also *Jerusalem: A Collection of United Nations Documents* (Beirut: Institute for Palestine Studies, 1970); Michel Lelong, *Guerre ou paix à Jérusalem?* (Paris: Albin Michel, 1982); Evan M. Wilson, *Jerusalem, Key to Peace* (Washington, DC: Middle East Institute, 1970); H. Eugene Bovis, *The Jerusalem Question, 1917–1968* (Stanford, CA: Hoover Institution Press, Stanford Univ., 1971); Elihu Lauterpacht, *Jerusalem and the Holy Places* (London: Anglo-Israel Association, Dec. 1980), pamphlet no. 19; Henry Cattan, *Jerusalem* (London: Croom Helm, 1981); Father Joseph L. Ryan, S.J., "Jerusalem in Roman Catholic Perspectives," in *Jerusalem: Key to Peace in the Middle East*, ed. O. Kelly Ingram (Durham, NC: Triangle Friends of the Middle East, 1978), and his "The Catholic Faith and the Problem of Israel and Jerusalem," in *Jerusalem: The Key to World Peace* (London, 1980); see also the two unpublished manuscripts of Father Edward H. Flannery, "The Controversy over Jerusalem: Elements of a Solution," and "A Second Report on Jerusalem," both issued by the Secretariat

for Catholic-Jewish Relations in the United States, Oct. 1971 and April 1972; also the unpublished paper of Archbishop Joseph T. Ryan, D.D., "Some Thoughts on Jerusalem." The most exhaustive assessment to date concerning Jerusalem can be found in Joelle Le Morzellec, *La question de Jérusalem devant l'Organisation des Nations-Unies* (Brussels: Etablissements Emile Bruylant, 1979).

2. For further details, see Dr. Norton Mezvinsky, "The Jewish Faith and the Problem of Israel and Jerusalem," in *Jerusalem: The Key*, pp. 21–37; and Rabbi Elmer Berger, "Jerusalem in Jewish Perspectives," in *Jerusalem: Key to Peace in the Middle East* ed. Ingram, pp. 10–24.

3. *The Pilot*, 7 Aug. 1971.

4. Joelle Le Morzellec, *Question*, p. 419. See also Youakim Moubarac, "La Question de Jérusalem," *Revue d'Etudes Palestiniennes*, 4 (Summer 1982) 44–47.

5. Personal interview with Noemi Teasdale, assistant to the Mayor of Jerusalem for Christian Affairs, Jerusalem, 12 May 1983.

6. Moubarac, "Question," p. 48.

7. Ibid.

8. Ibid.

9. See A. L. Tibawi, *Jerusalem: Its Place in Islam and Arab History*, Monograph Series no. 19 (Beirut: Intitute for Palestine Studies, 1969); Dr. Isma'il R. al-Faruqi, "The Islamic Faith and the Problem of Israel and Jerusalem," in *Jerusalem: The Key*, pp. 77–105; also Moubarac, "Question," pp. 51–55.

10. Peter Mansfield, "From British Mandate to the Present Day," in *Jerusalem: The Key*, p. 155.

11. For further details on this period, see Collin, *Lieux-Saints*, pp. 45–65.

12. See Bovis, *Question*, pp. 1–5.

13. For further details on the *Status Quo*, see Collin, *Recueil*, pp. 89–119. See also S. Sayegh, *Le Statu quo des Lieux-Saints, Nature juridique et portée internationale* (Rome: Libreria Editrice della Pontificia Università Lateranense, 1971).

14. Bovis, *Question*, pp. 6–20.

15. Fred J. Khoury, *The Arab-Israeli Dilemma* (Syracuse, NY: Syracuse Univ. Press, 1980), p. 102; Bovis, *Question*, chap. 2.

16. Bovis, *Question*, pp. 39–41.

17. See *Jerusalem: A Collection*, p. 3.

18. Khoury, *Dilemma*, pp. 107–8; Bovis, *Question*, pp. 81–91; the full text of the Statute for the City of Jerusalem can be found in *Jerusalem: A Collection*, pp. 19–35.

19. Khoury, *Dilemma*, pp. 108–10.

20. For further details, see Silvio Ferrari, "The Holy See and the Postwar Palestine Issue: The Internationalization of Jerusalem and the Protection of the Holy Places," *International Affairs*, 60/2 (Spring 1984) 261–83.

21. *Bulletin of the Christian Information Center*, Jerusalem, 15 Feb. 1974.

22. Latin Patriarchate of Jerusalem, "The Religious Situation in the Holy Land—The Specific Task of Catholics" (Jerusalem, 1977) (mimeographed), p. 2.

23. *Journal d'Israël*, 18 Dec. 1979.

24. Daphne Tsimhoni, "Demographic Trends of the Christian Population in Jerusalem and the West Bank, 1948–1978," *The Middle East Journal*, 37/1 (Winter 1983) 61. See also her "The Greek Orthodox Community in Jerusalem and the West Bank, 1948–1978: A Profile of a Religious Minority in a National State," *Orient*, 23/2 (June 1982) 281–98.

25. Saul P. Colbi, *The Christian Churches in the State of Israel* (Jerusalem: The Israel Economist, 3rd ed., March 1982), p. 2; see also his "The Christian Establishment in Jerusalem," in *Jerusalem: Problems and Prospects*, ed. Joel L. Kramer (New York: Praeger, 1980), pp. 153–77.

26. Michael C. Hudson, *Arab Politics: The Search for Legitimacy* (New Haven, CT: Yale Univ. Press, 1977), p. 58.

27. For further details on Arab Christians, see Youakim Moubarac, *Les Chrétiens et le Monde Arabe, Tome IV, Pentalogie Islamo-Chrétienne* (Beirut, Lebanon: Editions du Cénacle Libanais, 1972-73); Robert Brenton Betts, *Christians in the Arab East: A Political Study* (Atlanta, GA: John Knox Press, 1978). A very important source regarding the Christian communities from an ecumenical standpoint is *Christianity in the Holy Land: Papers Read at the 1979 Tantur Conference on Christianity in the Holy Land*, D.-M.A. Jaeger, ed. (Jerusalem: Franciscan Printing Press, 1981).

28. See Henri Fesquet in *Le Monde*, 7–8 April 1974.

29. Rafiq Khoury, *La catéchèse dans l'Eglise locale de Jérusalem: Histoire, situation actuelle et perspectives d'avenir* (Rome: Pontificia Università Lateranense, 1978), pp. 89–90.

30. Khoury, *Catéchèse*, p. 99.

31. Personal interview with Father Frans Bouwen, Jerusalem, 23 April 1983.

32. This statement is reported in an unpublished paper entitled "Qu'est-ce que l'Eglise de Jérusalem?" Monsignor Laham gave me a copy.

33. Khoury, *Catéchèse*, pp. 101–2.

34. *The Jerusalem Post*, 1 Feb. 1980.

35. Walter Zander, *Israel and the Holy Places of Christendom* (New York: Praeger Publishers, 1971), p. 136.

36. *Proche-Orient Chrétien*, 18 (1968) 86–87.

37. For further details on the Israeli position, see Collin, *Solution*, pp. 75–79.

38. See Collin, *Recueil*, p. 268.

39. Le Morzellec, *Question*, p. 324.

40. Collin, *Recueil*, p. 268.

41. Ibid., p. 269.

42. Flannery, "Controversy," p. 18.

43. Regarding the issue of the "judaization" of Jerusalem, see Hazem Zaki Nuseibeh, *Palestine and the United Nations* (New York: Quartet Books, 1981), pp. 91–108; see also the articles of Father Giovanni Rulli, S.J., in *La Civiltà Cattolica*, 1971, II, pp. 429–39; 538–49; III, pp. 281–83, all published in one monograph entitled *Il problema di Gerusalemme* (Rome: La Civiltà Cattolica, n.d.).

44. Le Morzellec, *Question*, p. 421.

45. Collin, *Solution*, p. 97.

46. See Bovis, *Question*, p. 79.

47. Lelong, *Guerre*, p. 93. See also Youakim Moubarac, "La Question de Jérusalem (2)," *Revue d'Etudes Palestiniennes*, 6 (Winter 1983) 64–67.

48. For a full text of the Fahd Plan, see *A Compassionate Peace: A Future for the Middle East*, a report prepared for the American Friends Service Committee (New York: Hill and Wang, 1982), p. 226.

49. "The City of Peace," *The Tablet*, 28 July 1979, pp. 720–21.

50. *Statement of Lawrence S. Eagleburger, Under Secretary for Political Affairs, Department of State, before the Senate Foreign Relations Committee, US Senate*, 23 Feb. 1984, on S.2031, p. 3.

51. Khoury, *Catéchèse*, p. 107.

52. Regarding the Holy See and the issue of Jerusalem, see the article published by Pietro Pastorelli, "La Santa Sede e il problema di Gerusalemme," *Storia e Politica*, 1 (1982) 57–98. This document is considered to express the semi-official stand of the Holy See. J. D. Montoisy, *Le Vatican et le problème des Lieux Saints* (Jerusalem: Franciscan Printing Press, 1984); see also Silvio Ferrari, "Il Vaticano e la questione di Gerusalemme nel carteggio Spellman-Truman," *Storia Contemporanea*, 13/2 (April 1982) 285–319. This article is part of ongoing joint Italian-Israeli research on the Vatican and the Middle East, 1920–1976. Also, Anna Beccali, "Gerusalemme e la posizione della Santa Sede," *Il Politico*, 30/10 (March 1974); Bernardin Collin, *Rome, Jérusalem, et les Lieux Saints* (Paris: Editions Franciscaines, 1981).

53. Quoted in Bovis, *Question*, p. 7.

54. Collin, *Rome, Jérusalem*, p. 67.

55. Claudia Carlen, I.H.M., *The Papal Encyclicals, 1939–1958* (Raleigh, NC: McGrath Publishing, 1981), p. 162.

56. Ibid., p. 164.

57. Bovis, *Question*, p. 71.

58. Silvio Ferrari, "La Sante Sede e il problema della Palestina nel Secondo Dopoguerra," *Communità*, 185 (n.d.) 414–15. The Vatican strongly backed the 1947 partition resolution because it included provisions for *corpus separatum* for the Holy City and the Vatican pressed Catholic members of the UN to vote for this resolution. The Holy See continued to back internationalization up to and several months after the 1967 war. By late 1967, it began to drop the demand for a *corpus separatum* and rather to press for a legal statute internationally guaranteed because (1) one resolution in the UN General Assembly providing for *corpus separatum* failed to get the required two-thirds vote; (2) some Catholic countries began to move their embassies from Tel Aviv to Jerusalem; (3) the UN and the Big Powers did nothing to alter the situation; and (4) Israel was making it clear that she would not leave Jerusalem under any circumstances.

59. Quoted in Collin, *Recueil*, p. 36.

60. Middle East Council of Churches, *Jerusalem, Dossier III* (Beirut, 1979), p. 16.

61. *L'Osservatore Romano*, 25 March 1971.

62. Ibid.

63. *Proche-Orient Chrétien*, 24 (1974), 70–71.

64. Ibid.

65. Ibid., p. 72.

66. Ibid., p. 71.

67. "L'Esortazione Apostolica del Santo Padre sulle accresciute necessità della chiesa in Terra Santa," *L'Osservatore Romano*, 6 April 1976. See also Ryan, "Catholic Faith," p. 62.

68. *L'Osservatore Romano*, 6 April 1976.

69. Father Tucci, the head of Vatican Radio, elaborated on the Pope's mention of "citizens" in his address and stated that "people living in the Holy Land should be fully endowed morally and juridically with the rights of liberty and the full exercise of rights without hindrance." See *The Link*, May/June 1974, pp. 1–3.

70. *Proche-Orient Chrétien*, 24 (1974) 181.

71. Khoury, *Catéchèse*, pp. 111–12.

72. For a detailed account of the Tripoli Seminar, see Maurice Borrmans, "Le séminaire du dialogue Islamo-Chrétien de Tripoli (Libye), 1–6 fevrier, 1976," *IslamoChristiana*, 2 (1976) 135–70.

73. Ibid., p. 158.

74. Ibid.

75. See Yehoshua Rash, *Déminer un champ fertile: Les Catholiques Français et l'Etat d'Israël* (Paris: Les Editions du Cerf, 1982), pp. 161-64.

76. *L'Osservatore Romano*, 12 Feb. 1976.

77. *L'Osservatore Romano*, English ed., 1 July 1980.

78. Ibid.

79. Ibid.

80. *The Tablet*, 28 July 1979.

81. A copy of this letter was obtained from the office of the ambassador of the United States to the Holy See, June 1983.

82. Ibid.

83. Ibid.

84. *L'Osservatore Romano*, 30 April 1984, weekly edition, p. 6.

85. See Eugene J. Fischer, "The Pope and Israel," *Commonweal* (11 Jan. 1985), pp. 16–17.

86. *L'Osservatore Romano*, (n.84, above), p. 7.

87. Ibid.

88. Ibid.

89. *The Times*, 21 April 1984.

90. Personal interview with Monsignor Richard Mathes and Father Norman Metsy, Jerusalem, 7 May 1983. See also the supplement to the *Bulletin Diocésain* published by the Latin Patriarchate in Jerusalem, April 1971.

91. Jean-Dominique Montoisy, "Israël-Vatican: Le Nouveau Dialogue," *Studia Diplomatica*, 34/6 (1981) 761–62.

92. J. Gelin, "Notre Dame de France," *Le Bulletin Diocésain* (n.90, above), p. 4.

93. Zander, *Israel* (n.35, above), p. 159.

3. THE HOLY SEE AND THE LEBANESE WAR

1. This point is raised by David C. Gordon in his *The Republic of Lebanon: Nation in Jeopardy* (Boulder, CO: Westview Press, 1983). For a learned, detailed, and well-researched account on the formation of modern Lebanon and its Constitution, see Edmond Rabbath, *La formation historique du Liban politique et constitutionnel: Essai de synthèse* (Beirut: Publications de l'Université Libanaise, 1973); see also his *La constitution libanaise: Origines, textes et commentaires* (Beirut: Publications de l'Université Libanaise, 1982). These two works, especially the first, have seldom been quoted in books on Lebanon published in the United States. See also Nagib Dahdah, *Evolution historique du Liban* (Beirut: Librairie du Liban, 1968).

2. Antoine Jabre, *La guerre du Liban: Moscou et la crise du Proche-Orient* (Paris: Pierre Belfond, 1980), p. 246.

3. From all standpoints, the most comprehensive chronology of the conflict in Lebanon from 1975 onwards, with special attention to the Holy See's involvement and the role of local Christian hierarchies, is printed in *Proche-Orient Chrétien*, a quarterly journal published in French by the White Fathers in Jerusalem. Another important documented chronology of the war, published in Arabic, is the work by Antoine Khuwayri, *Mausu'at al-Harb fi Lubnan, 1975–1981*, 12 vols., published by the author's own Dar al-Abjadiyya lil Sahafa wal Tiba'a wal Nashr, Sarba, Lebanon. An objective French assessment of the first two years of the war (1975–1977) can be found in Albert Bourgi and Pierre Weiss, *Les complots libanais* (Paris: Berger-Levrault, 1978), and their more recent work, which covers the war from 1978 to the Israeli invasion, summer 1982, *Liban: La cinquième guerre du Proche-*

Orient (Paris: Editions Publisud, 1983). Primary sources written by two major protagonists of the Lebanese War include Kamal Joumblatt, *Pour le Liban* (Paris: Editions Stock, 1978) and Camille Chamoun, *Crise au Liban* (Beirut: n.p., 1977). There is already a huge amount of books and pamphlets on the Lebanese War written by Lebanese. Among other titles, see Benassar, *Anatomie d'une guerre et d'une occupation: Evènements du Liban de 1975 a 1978* (Paris: Editions Galilee, 1978) and his *Paix d'Israël au Liban* (Beirut: Les Editions L'Orient-Le Jour, May 1983). A Phalangist perspective of the first two years of the war can be found in Nicolas Nasr, *Harb Lubnan wa Madaha* (Beirut: Dar al-Amal, 1977), and J.A. Nasr, *Mihnat Lubnan fi Thawrat al-Yasar* (Beirut: Dar al'Amal, 1977). A Lebanese Marxist perspective can be found in Mahdi Amel, *Al-Qadiyya al-Filistiniyya fi Idiolojiat al-Burjuaziyya al-Lubnaniyya* (Beirut: Research Center, Palestine Liberation Organization, 1980) and his *Bahs fi Ashab al-Harb al-Ahliyya fi Lubnan*, vol. 1 (Beirut: Dar al-Fara'bi, 1979). In the United States, the most valid scholarly assessment of the war is found in Walid Khalidi, *Conflict and Violence in Lebanon, Confrontation in the Middle East* (Cambridge, MA: Harvard Center for International Affairs, 1979). An Italian Evangelical perspective is found in Sergio Ribet, *Il nodo del conflitto Libanese: Tra resistenza Palestinese e destra Maronita* (Turin: Claudiana, 1977). A German analysis of Christian groups in Lebanon and their involvement in the war can be found in Michael Kuderna, *Christliche Gruppen in Libanon* (Wiesbaden: Franz Steiner Verlag, 1983). Finally, a useful tool for research is Linda Sadaka and Nawaf Salam, compilers, *The Civil War in Lebanon: 1975–1976: A Bibliographical Guide* (Beirut: Center for Middle East Studies, America Univ. of Beirut, 1982.)

    4. For an interesting and in-depth analysis of Arab politics after 1967, see Fouad Ajami, *The Arab Predicament: Arab Political Thought and Practice since 1967* (Cambridge, MA: Cambridge Univ. Press, 1981).

    5. *Osservatore della Domenica*, 2 Oct. 1975.

    6. The use of the term "mosaic" to define Lebanon is used by Michael W. Suleiman, *Political Parties in Lebanon: A Challenge of a Fragmented Political Culture* (Ithaca, NY: Cornell Univ. Press, 1967); see also Edmond Rabbath, "Du regime com-

munautaire au confessionalisme," *Esprit*, 5–6 (May-June 1983) 74–82.

7. On the National Covenant and its implications, see Edmond Rabbath, *Formation historique*, pp. 515–70. See also Bassim al-Jisr, *Mitha'k 1943* (Beirut: An-Nahar, 1978).

8. George Naccache, as quoted in "Liban: Mort et Résurrection," *Le Monde: Dossiers et Documents*, Oct. 1982, p. 7.

9. For further details on the communities in Lebanon, see Rabbath, *Formation historique*, pp. 1–144; see also A. J. Arberry, ed., *Religion in the Middle East: Three Religions in Concord and Conflict*. Vol. 1, *Judaism and Christianity*; vol. 2, *Islam* (London: Cambridge Univ. Press, 1969). A reliable and important statistical source regarding Christian communities in the Near East is *Oriente Cattolico: Cenni storici e statistiche*, (Vatican City: Sacra Congregazione per le Chiese Orientali, 4th ed., 1974); see also Luc-Henri de Bar, *Les communautés confessionnelles du Liban* (Paris: Editions Recherches sur les Civilisations, 1983).

10. For an exhaustive history of the role of the Maronite patriarch in Lebanese history, see David A. Kerr, "The Temporal Authority of the Maronite Patriarchate, 1920–1958: A Study in the Relationship of Religious and Secular Power," Diss., Oxford Univ., 1973; see also Rev. Seely Joseph Beggiani, "The Relations of the Holy See and the Maronites from the Papacy of Pope Gregory XIII (1572–1585) to the Synod of Mount Lebanon in 1736," Diss., Catholic Univ. of America, 1963; see also Philippe Rondot, "Antoine Pierre Khoraiche, Patriarche Maronite d'Antioche et de tout l'Orient," *Maghreb-Machrek*, 78 (Oct.-Dec. 1977) 21–25.

11. See interviews with the former and current superiors of the Permanent Congress of the Lebanese Orders of Monks, Father Sharbel Kassis and Father Bulos Naaman, in *Al-Fusul al-Lubnaniyya*, 2 (Spring 1980) 58–62, and *Al-Fusul al-Lubnaniyya*, 3 (Summer 1980) 82–86.

12. See *Lumières franches sur la crise libanaise*, in the collection "Question Libanaise" (Kaslik: Publications de l'Université Saint-Esprit, 1975), pp. 49–51. (pamphlet no. 3)

13. Regarding the legal status of non-Muslim minorities, see Antoine Fattal, *le Statut Légal des non-Musulmans en pays d'Islam* (Beirut: Imprimerie Catholique, 1958); Benjamin Braude and Ber-

nard Lewis, eds., *Christians and Jews in the Ottoman Empire.*
Vol. I, *The Central Lands*; vol. 2, *The Arab-Speaking Lands* (New
York: Holmes & Meier, 1982).

14. *Lumières franches*, pp. 50–51.

15. Father Kassis has played a crucial role in the Lebanese conflict. He advocated a militant line in opposing the Palestinian-
Leftist alliance in Lebanon. Justifying the active role played by
the Maronite monks in the War, Father Kassis said: "Monks are
existentially and organically linked to the people. . . . In order
to defend himself, every Christian has the right to be trained to
handle weapons." (*Proche-Orient Chrétien*, 26 [1976] 145).

16. Personal interview with Father Kassis, Jbail, 11 April
1983. See also his interview with *Le Réveil*, 5 April 1977. In this
interview the Maronite monk stated that Muslims have demonstrated, in their psychological and military attitude during the war,
their "being capable of tolerance, not coexistence."

17. Camille Chamoun had proposed the creation of a Swisslike
system of cantons, political decentralization, or a federal system
for Lebanon. Pierre Gemayel, the leader of the Phalangist Party,
did not share Chamoun's proposed solutions. For further details,
see *Proche-Orient Chrétien*, 28 (1978) 357.

18. For an official history of the Phalangist (Kata'ib) Party,
see *Tarikh Hizb al-Kata'ib al-Lubnaniyya, 1936–1946*, 2 vols.,
put out by the party's publishing house (Beirut: Dar al-'Amal lil
Nashr, 1979, 1981), See also Suleiman, *Political Parties*, pp.
232–49.

19. See Al-Montada Reports, *The Lebanese Conflict, 1975–
1979, Dossier 2* (Beirut: Middle East Council of Churches Documentation and Information, 1979), p. 34; and Elizabeth Picard,
"Rôle et evolution du Front Libanais dans la guerre civile," *Maghreb-
Machrek*, 90 (Oct.-Dec. 1980) 16–39.

20. Regarding the events and the issues surrounding the Palestinian camp of Tall-Zaatar, see Antoine Khuwayri, *Al-Harb fi
Lubnan, 1976*, vol. 2 (Jounieh: Al-Bulusiya Press, 1977), pp.
784–86, 801, 809–10. For the Tall-Zaatar events as seen from
a PLO perspective, see *Tall-Zaatar: The Fight against Fascism*
(Beirut: PLO, Unified Information, Foreign Information Department, 1976) (pamphlet).

21. See David Kerr's thesis, "Temporal Authority," pp. 248–59.

22. See Yaacov Sharett, "L'état juif et l'intégrité du Liban,"

Le Monde Diplomatique, Dec. 1983, pp. 16–17. Also Livia Rokach, *Israel's Sacred Terrorism. A Study Based on Moshe Sharett's Personal Diary and Other Documents* (Belmont, MA: Association of Arab-American Univ. Graduates, 2nd ed., 1982). An Israeli assessment of Maronite-Israeli relationships can be found in Yossef Olmert, *Lebanon's Christians and Israel*, Research Report no. 15 (London: Institute for Jewish Affairs, Oct. 1982).

23. See *Proche-Orient Chrétien*, 28 (1978) 171–72; and Antoine Khuwayri, *Hawadith Lubnan, 1977–1978*, vol. 6, *Wa Akhiran Harakuh* (Jounieh: Manshurat Dar al-Abjadiyya, 1978), pp. 296–302.

24. Testimony of Daniel Le Gac, as quoted in *Proche-Orient Chrétien*, 27 (1977) 362.

25. Regarding both the Greek Orthodox and the Greek Catholic communities' role in Lebanese politics, see de Bar, pp. 39–73; and Robert Brenton Betts, *Christians in the Arab East: A Political Study* (Atlanta, GA: John Knox Press, 1978), pp. 188–210.

26. *Proche-Orient Chrétien*, 26 (1976) 163-65.

27. Ibid., 28 (1978) 329.

28. Regarding the Shiite community in Lebanon, see de Bar, *Communautés*, pp. 17–24.

29. For further details on "Harakat Amal," see Augustus Richard Norton, "Harakat Amal (The Movement of Hope)," in *Religion and Politics, Political Anthropology*, vol. 3, Myron Aronoff, ed. (New Brunswick, NJ: Transaction Books, 1984), pp. 105–31.

30. Regarding the Druze community, see de Bar, *Communautés*, pp. 119–37.

31. These Muslim objectives were presented to Cardinal Bertoli in 1978 by the mufti. For further details, see Khuwayri, *Hawadith Lubnan, 1977-1978*, vol 6, pp. 664–66.

32. On the debate in Lebanon regarding laicism and secularism, see P.T., "Débat autour de la laicité au Liban," *Proche-Orient Chrétien*, 27 (1977) 145–56.

33. For a detailed account of the Lebanese National Movement and its program of reforms, see Sami Zhibian, *Al-Haraka al-Wataniyya al-Lubnaniyya* (Beirut: Dar al-Masirat, 1977).

34. For further details, see Khalidi, *Conflict* (n.3, above), pp. 75–79.

35. Regarding Syrian policy in Lebanon, see Adeed Dawisha, *Syria and the Lebanese Crisis* (New York: St. Martin's Press, 1980); Daniel Tschirgi with George Irani, *The United States, Syria, and the Lebanese Crisis*, Research Note no. 8 (Los Angeles: UCLA, Center for International and Strategic Affairs, Jan. 1982); also Itamar Rabinovich, "The Limits of Military Power: Syria's Role," in *Lebanon in Crisis: Participants and Issues*, P. Edward Haley and Lewis W. Snider, eds. (Syracuse, NY: Syracuse Univ. Press, 1979), pp. 55–73.

36. Khalidi, *Conflict*, pp. 84–86.

37. Regarding Israel's policy in the Lebanese War, see Lewis W. Snider, P. Edward Haley, Abraham R. Wagner, and Nicki J. Cohen, "Israel," in Haley and Snider, *Lebanon in Crisis*, pp. 91–112.

38. Quoted in Bourgi and Weiss, *Complots*, p. 117.

39. Khalidi, *Conflict*, p. 91.

40. Takieddine Solh, a former Lebanese prime minister said, when assessing the causes of the Lebanese conflict: "The Palestinians proposed that Israel become like Lebanon, a pluricommunitarian, democratic society; Israel's response was that it did all it could to render Lebanon to its image. This was at the origin of the drama that Lebanon has known in the last eight years." (*An Nahar Arab and International*, 329 [22–28 Aug. 1983] 6)

41. Regarding Sharon's policy in Lebanon, see Amos Perlmutter, "Begin's Rhetoric and Sharon's Tactics," *Foreign Affairs* (Fall 1982), pp. 67–83. For further details on the Israeli invasion, see Giovanni Rulli, "L'invasione Israeliana nel Libano," *La Civiltà Cattolica*, 3169 (3 July 1982), 84–91. Also, "The War in Lebanon," special issue of the *Journal of Palestine Studies*, vol. 11, no. 4; vol. 12, no 1, 44/45 (Summer/Fall 1982). On the massacres of Sabra and Shatila, see Amnon Kapeliouk, *Sabra et Chatila: Enquête sur un massacre* (Paris: Editions du Seuil, 1982).

42. U.S. Congress, Senate, 94th Cong., 2nd sess., "Prospects for Peace in the Middle East," *Hearings before the Subcommittee on Near Eastern and South Asian Affairs of the Committee on Foreign Relations* (Washington, DC: U.S. Government Printing Office, 1976), p. 247.

43. Regarding US policy towards the Lebanese War, see Robert W. Stookey, "The United States," in Haley and Snider, *Lebanon in Crisis*, pp. 225–48. In the spring of 1976, Ambassador

L. Dean Brown was dispatched to Lebanon by Secretary of State Henry Kissinger. The underlying motive behind the US initiative had an internal American political aspect. According to Jonathan Randall, "Kissinger had dispatched Brown largely to deprive Ronald Reagan, Ford's serious challenger for the Republican presidential nomination that summer (1976), of the argument that the administration had been derelict in attending to the festering Lebanese mess." See his controversial book, *Going all the Way: Christian Warlords, Israeli Adventurers, and the War in Lebanon* (New York: Viking Press, 1983), p. 178.

44. For further details on the French initiatives, see "Les mediations étrangères," *Problèmes Politiques et Sociaux* (20 Aug. 1976), pp. 51–55.

45. For the historical background on the relations between the Holy See and Lebanon, see Lahd Khater, *Al-Vatikan wa Lubnan* (Sidon, Lebanon: Manshurat Majallat al-Risala al-Mukhlisiyya, 1966).

46. *La Documentation Catholique*, 80/6 (20 March 1983) n. 1848, p. 300.

47. Personal interview with Vatican official, Rome, 8 June 1983.

48. Personal interview with Father Jean Aucagne, S.J., Beirut, 4 April 1983.

49. Personal interview with Vatican official, Rome, 8 June 1983.

50. Personal interview with Monsignor John G. Meaney, Jal-Eddib, 27 May 1983.

51. Personal interview with Vatican official, Beirut, 27 May 1983.

52. Personal interview, Beirut, 29 March 1983.

53. René Chamussy, *Chronique d'une guerre: Le Liban, 1975–1977* (Paris: Desclée, 1978), 123–24.

54. *Proche-Orient Chrétien*, 26 (1976) 275. The frequent mention by Paul VI that the conflict in Lebanon was a "civil war" did not please the Maronites. Even the patriarch disagreed with this qualification in a message he sent on 2 May 1976 to the heads and members of the conferences of bishops around the world. See *Proche-Orient Chrétien*, 26 (1976) 250–58.

55. Ibid.

56. *Proche-Orient Chrétien*, 26 (1976) 276.

57. Ibid.

58. Salim al-Laouzi, ["Is all hope lost to see the Maronites back in the Arab fold?"] *Al-Hawadess*, 15 Dec. 1978, pp. 17–24.

59. Ibid.

60. Jean Aucagne, S.J., "Qui donc informe le Pape?" *Le Réveil*, 15 April 1978.

61. *Le Réveil*, 18 April 1978.

62. Aucagne, "Informe le Pape."

63. Ibid.

64. In addition to the so-called Arab lobby, some observers alleged that there also exists a Lebanese lobby inside the Holy See. The presence of this lobby was also raised by Father René Chamussy (personal interview, Beirut, 19 March 1983). This issue is further emphasized in a Lebanese diplomatic cable. Writing about Lebanese clergymen and prelates working in the Roman Curia, the author of the cable mentions that among them "we find sympathizers of former president Franjieh; of Raymond Edde, leader of the National Bloc; and sympathizers of the Maronite patriarch."

65. Aucagne, "Informe le Pape."

66. Joseph Vandrisse, "Réponse à Jean Aucagne, S.J.," *Le Réveil*, 18 April 1978.

67. *Al-Hawadess*, editorial, 25 Aug. 1978, and *An Nahar Arab and International*, 13–19 Aug. 1984, pp. 11–12.

68. Karim Pakradouni, *La paix manquée: Le mandat d'Elias Sarkis, 1976–1982* (Beirut: Editions Fiches du Monde Arabe, 1983), p. 186.

69. Ibid., p. 224.

70. See the statement by Cardinal Joseph Bernardin on 23 Jan. 1976, as quoted in *Proche-Orient Chrétien*, 26 (1976) 157; see also the statement by Archbishop John R. Quinn in *L'Osservatore Romano*, 20 Sept. 1978, p. 2; also National Conference of Catholic Bishops, "Statement on the Middle East: The Pursuit of Peace with Justice" (Washington, DC: US Catholic Conference, 16 Nov. 1978).

71. For a biography on the late Cardinal Cooke, see *L'Osservatore Romano*, English weekly ed., 10 Oct. 1983, pp. 2, 16.

72. *Proche-Orient Chrétien*, 31 (1981) 287–88.

73. Cardinal Terence Cooke, "Report on Visit to Lebanon," 29 Dec. 1979 to 3 Jan. 1980 (mimeographed), p. 9.

74. Ibid.

75. Personal interview, Jall-Eddib, May 1983.

76. For further details on the debate inside the Reagan administration regarding Lebanon policy, see Michael G. Fry, "United States Policy in the Middle East: Lebanon and the Palestinian Question," *Arab Studies Quarterly*, 7/1 (Winter 1985) 27–35.

77. Joseph Kossaifi, "The Role of the Vatican in the Arab World," *At-Tadamon*, 12 (2 July 1983) 10.

78. Personal communication, 24 Oct. 1983.

79. See the special issue on "The Papacy, Lebanon, and the Arabs," *Al-Hawadess*, Beirut, 25 Aug. 1978, pp. 73–77.

80. *Proche-Orient Chrétien*, 25 (1975) 365.

81. Ibid.

82. Chamussy, *Chronique* (n. 53, above), pp. 117–18.

83. Personal interview, Rome, 14 June 1983.

84. Fuad Matar, *Suqut al-Imbraturiyya el-Lubnaniyya*, vol. 1, *As-Sharara* (Beirut: Dar al-Qadaya, 1976), p. 199.

85. Ibid., pp. 201–2.

86. Ibid., p. 201.

87. Ibid.

88. Ibid., p. 210.

89. It seemed that Cardinal Bertoli had asked the PLO chairman to work actively to help promote reconciliation in Lebanon (personal interview with Father Ibrahim Iyad, who helped in arranging the meeting between the two, Los Angeles, 22 Nov. 1982).

90. Matar, *Suqut*, p. 210.

91. Bourgi and Weiss, *Complots*, p. 111.

92. Quoted in *Le livre blanc libanais: Documents diplomatiques, 1975–1976* (Beirut: République Libanaise, Ministère des Affaires Etrangères et des Libanais d'Outre-Mer, 1976), pp. 23–24.

93. Ibid.

94. Ibid.

95. *L'Orient-Le Jour*, 8 Nov. 1975.

96. Jabre, *Guerre* (n. 2, above), p. 246.

97. Personal interview with Butros Dib, Beirut, 5 April 1983. Dib told the researcher that Bertoli's visit was interpreted as a reconciliation between the cardinal and Pope Paul VI. In 1973 Cardinal Bertoli resigned as head of the Sacred Congregation for

the Causes of Saints. For further details on this episode, see Paul
Hofmann, *O Vatican!* (New York: Congdon and Weed, 1984),
pp. 117–18.

98. *L'Orient-Le Jour*, 18 April 1976.

99. Ibid., 17 April 1976.

100. *Proche-Orient Chrétien*, 26 (1976) 159.

101. *L'Orient-Le Jour*, 28 April 1976.

102. *Proche-Orient Chrétien*, 26 (1976) 164.

103. "Address of His Holiness Pope John Paul II to the XXXIV
General Assembly of the United Nations Organization," *Pilgrim
of Peace: The Homilies and Addresses of His Holiness Pope John
Paul II on the Occasion of His Visit to the United States of Amer-
ica, October 1979* (Washington, DC: Publications Office, United
States Catholic Conference, 1979), p. 21.

104. Ibid.

105. *Proche-Orient Chrétien*, 28 (1978) 360.

106. *L'Orient-Le Jour*, 8 Dec. 1978.

107. *An Nahar Arab and International*, 18 Dec. 1978, p. 3.

108. *L'Orient-Le Jour*, 20 Dec. 1978.

109. *Proche-Orient Chrétien*, 28 (1978) 362.

110. Ibid., p. 363.

111. *L'Orient-Le Jour*, 20 Dec. 1978.

112. *Proche-Orient Chrétien*, 28 (1978) 360.

113. A former US ambassador to Lebanon, Richard Parker,
is reported to have told Camille Chamoun that the solution was
"for the Palestinians to stay in Lebanon and repatriate 100,000
to the West Bank and Gaza." There are more than 400,000
Palestinian refugees in Lebanon. See Khuwayri, *Hawadith*, p. 654.

114. *Proche-Orient Chrétien*, 30 (1980) 303.

115. Personal interview, Beirut, 4 April 1983.

116. Antoine Khuwayri, *Hawadith Lubnan, 1980*, vol. 9,
Lubnan Bayna al-Shariat wal Ihtilal (Jounieh: Dar al-Abjadiyya
lil Sahafa wal Tibaa wal Nashr, 1982), p. 289.

117. Ibid.

118. *Proche-Orient Chrétien*, 30 (1980) 301.

119. Khuwayri, *Hawadith Lubnan*, p. 287, and *Proche-Orient
Chrétien*, 30 (1980) 299–303.

120. Ibid.

121. *Proche-Orient Chrétien*, 30 (1980) 302.

122. *L'Osservatore Romano*, 7–8 June 1982.

123. Quoted in *Al-Masira*, issued by the Lebanese Forces, 1 Nov. 1982, p. 12.

124. *La Documentation Catholique*, 1848 (20 March 1983) 305–7.

125. A copy of this report was obtained from the embassy of Lebanon to the Holy See.

126. Following the tragic assassination of Bashir Gemayel and the election of his brother Amin (21 Sept. 1982), John Paul II's telegram of congratulations was published in *L'Osservatore Romano* (23 Sept. 1982).

127. Sheikh Najib Dahdah was former Lebanese ambassador to the Holy See. Personal interview, Beirut, April 1983.

128. Personal interview, Rome, June 1983.

129. *Proche-Orient Chrétien*, 32/3–4 (1982) 386.

130. Personal interview, Harissa, 17 Dec. 1984. For further details on the aftermath of the Israeli invasion and US intervention, see William B. Quandt, "Reagan's Lebanon Policy: Trial and Error," *The Middle East Journal*, 38/2 (Spring 1984) 237–54.

131. For further details see, *An Nahar Arab and International*, 367 (14–20 May 1984) 28–29.

132. Ibid.

133. *Magazine,* 12 May 1984, p. 30.

134. Ibid. The clash between the two Lebanese Catholic prelates was also reported to me by other sources. No official denial has been issued by either the Maronite or Greek Catholic patriarchates.

135. *Magazine*, 12 May 1984, p. 30.

136. *L'Osservatore Romano*, weekly edition, 14 May 1984, pp. 10–11. John Paul II's concern and solicitude towards Lebanon were once again reiterated in the clearest terms in a message he sent to the Maronite Patriarch Khoreish on 25 Jan. 1985.

137. *L'Osservatore Romano*, 14 May 1984, p. 11.

138. Ibid., p. 10.

139. Ibid., p. 11.

140. Ibid., p. 10.

Bibliography

PRIMARY SOURCES

Bibliographical Aids and Guides

Husseini, Hatem I. *The Palestine Problem: An Annotated Bibliography.* Washington, DC: Palestine Information Office, 1980.
Manns, Frederic. *Bibliographie du Judéo-Christianisme.* Jerusalem: Franciscan Printing Press, 1979.
Raymond, Jean. *Essai de Bibliographie Maronite.* Kaslik: Bibliothèque de l'Université Saint-Esprit, 1980.
Walsh, Michael J. *Vatican City State.* World Bibliographic Series, vol. 41. Oxford, England/Santa Barbara, CA: CLIO Press, 1983.

Unpublished

Correspondence

Cooke, Cardinal Terence, "Report on Visit to Lebanon, December 29, 1979, to January 3, 1980."
Letter from Zbigniew Brzezinski to Terence Cardinal Cooke. Washington, DC, 27 Feb. 1980.
Letter from Jimmy Carter to Terence Cardinal Cooke. Washington, DC, 14 Feb. 1980.
Letter from Rabbi Martin A. Cohen and Rabbi David H. Panitz to Agostino Cardinal Casaroli. Anti-Defamation League of B'nai B'rith, New York, 2 July 1980.
Letter from Kurt Waldheim to Terence Cardinal Cooke. New York, 19 Feb. 1980.
Letter from William A. Wilson to Monsignor John G. Nolan. Rome, 2 Feb. 1982.

Letters from William A. Wilson, Ambassador of the United States to the Holy See. Rome, 24 Oct. 1983 and 12 Dec. 1984.

Letter from Bishop Francis M. Zayek to Terence Cardinal Cooke. Brooklyn, 19 Feb. 1980.

Memorandum prepared by the Apostolic Delegate for Monsignor Nolan. Jerusalem, 26 Dec. 1972.

Interviews

Abi-Jaoude, Roland, Monsignor. Secretary, Maronite Patriarch. Bkerke, 26 March 1983.

Angeloni, Luciano, Monsignor. Apostolic Nuncio to Lebanon. Hazmieh, 11 April 1983.

Arnaud, Florent. Vatican Pilgrims Liaison Office. Jerusalem, 29 April 1983.

Aucagne, Jean, S.J. Editorialist. Beirut, 4 April 1983.

Ayad, Ibrahim, Rev. President, Latin Ecclesiastical Court of Lebanon; Official of the PLO. Los Angeles, 22 Nov. 1982.

Baramki, Gaby, Dr. Vice-President, Bir Zeit University. Bir Zeit-West Bank, 3 May 1983.

Ben Chorin, Nathan. Minister in Charge of Vatican Affairs, Israeli Embassy. Rome, 9 June 1983.

Bertoli, Paolo, Cardinal. Rome, 14 June 1983.

Bouwen, Frans, Rev. Editor, *Proche-Orient Chrétien*, 23 April 1983.

Capucci, Hilarion, Archbishop. Rome, 13 June 1983.

Colbi, Saul P. Former director, Christian Affairs Desk, Ministry for Religious Affairs. Jerusalem, 25 April 1983.

Dahdah, Najib, Sheikh. Former ambassador of Lebanon to the Holy See. Beirut, 7 April 1983.

Dakak, Ibrahim, Dr. President, Arab Thought Forum. Jerusalem, 4 May 1983.

Dib, Butros, Dr. Former ambassador of Lebanon to the Holy See. Beirut, 15 April 1983.

Doumit, Michel, Monsignor. Member, Sacred Congregation for Oriental Churches. Sarba, 13 April 1983.

Dubois, Marcel, Rev. Professor, Department of Philosophy, Hebrew Univ.; Consultant, Commission for Religious Relations with Judaism. Jerusalem, 10 May 1983.

Emanuel, Josef. Director, Israel Interfaith Association. Jerusalem, 4 May 1983.

Fattal, Antoine, Dr. Former ambassador of Lebanon to the Holy See. Beirut, 2 April 1983.

Flusser, David, Dr. Chairman, Department of Comparative Religions, Hebrew Univ. Jerusalem, 26 April 1983.

Gatti, Luigi, Monsignor. Vatican Secretariat of State. 13 June 1983.

El-Hashem, Munged, Monsignor. Vatican Secretariat of State. June 8, 1983.

Hélou, Charles, President. Former ambassador of Lebanon to the Holy See. Kaslik, 12 April 1983.

Hornblow, Michael. Former deputy assistant, U.S. Ambassador to the Holy See. Rome, 9 June 1983.

Hussar, Bruno, Rev. Founder, Center for Judaic Studies and Maison Saint-Isaïe. Jerusalem, 17 May 1983.

Kafiiti, Samir, Bishop. Anglican Bishopry. Jerusalem, 22 April 1983.

Kassis, Sharbel, Rev. Former superior of the Permanent Congress of the Lebanese Orders of Monks. Byblos, 11 April 1983.

Khodr, George, Monsignor. Bishop of Mount Lebanon for the Greek Orthodox. Beirut, 6 April 1983.

El-Khoury, Sami, Sheikh. Lawyer, Maronite Patriarchate. Antelias, 16 April 1983.

Kubaissi, Ahmad. Supreme Shiite Council of Lebanon. Beirut, 26 May 1983.

Laghi, Pio, Archbishop. Apostolic Nuncio in the United States. Washington, DC, 7 July 1983.

Laham, Lutfi, Monsignor. Greek Catholic Patriarchal Vicar. Jerusalem, 17 May 1983.

de Lavergnée, Fernand Brejon. First Counsellor, French Embassy to the Holy See. Rome, 22 June 1983.

Lazzarotto, Giuseppe, Monsignor. Apostolic Delegation. Jerusalem, 7 May 1983.

Lippel, Israel, Dr. Director, Jerusalem Institute for Interreligious Relations and Research. Jerusalem, 29 April 1983.

Lowenstein, Joe, Brother. Pontifical Mission for Palestine. Jerusalem, 25 April 1983.

Majaj, Amin, Dr. Director, Islamic Hospital Makased. Jerusalem, 12 May 1983.

Mathes, Richard, Monsignor. Cultural Attaché, Apostolic Delegation. Jerusalem, 7 May 1983.

Meaney, John G., Monsignor. Former regional director, Pontifical Mission-Middle East. Jall-Eddib, 27 May 1983.

Médebielle, Pierre, Rev. Secretary General, Conference of Latin Bishops in the Middle East. Jerusalem, 3 May 1983.

Mejia, Jorge, Monsignor. Secretary, Commission for Religious Relations with Judaism. Rome, 22 June 1983.

Mendes, Meir, Dr. Former minister, counsellor for Vatican Affairs, Israel Embassy, Italy. Tel Aviv, 1 May 1983.

Metsy, Norman G., Rev. Vice-Chargé of the Holy See. Jerusalem, 23 April 1983.

Nasr, Cesar, Dr. Director, Centre des Etudes Stratégiques pour la Paix, House of the Future. Beirut, 31 March 1983.

Nicholl, Donald, Dr. Ecumenical Institute for Theological Research. Tantur, 2 May 1983.

Pastorelli, Pietro. Professor, Univ. of Rome. Rome, 10 June 1983.

Prato, Jonathan, Dr. Former legal counsellor, Israeli Embassy in Italy. Jerusalem, 4 May 1983.

Rabbath, Edmond. Professor and Historian. Beirut, 29 March 1983.

Rahmé, Georges, Rev. Director, Catholic Information Center in Lebanon. Jall-Eddib, 15 April 1983.

Rash, Yehoshua. Former Israeli diplomat. Ramat-Gan, 22 April 1983.

Rock, Alberto, Rev. Director, Franciscans for Relations with Christian Communities and Muslim Waqfs. Jerusalem, 13 May 1983.

Rossing, Daniel, Dr. Director, Department for Christian Communities, Ministry of Religious Affairs. Jerusalem, 25 April 1983.

Sabanagh, Edouard Sami Martin, Rev. Commission for Religious Relations with Islam. Rome, 22 June 1983.

Safieh, Antoun. Former aide, Municipality of Jerusalem. Jerusalem, 5 May 1983.

Salhab, Nasri. Ambassador of Lebanon to the Holy See. Rome, 17 June 1983.

Scanlan, Thomas, Brother. Vice-Chancellor, Bethlehem Univ. Bethlehem, 27 April 1983.

Tauran, Jean-Louis, Monsignor. Apostolic Nunciature. Beirut, 27 May 1983.

Teasdale, Noemi. Assistant to the Mayor for Christian Affairs. Jerusalem, 12 May 1983.

Tournay, Raymond, Rev. *Caritas Internationalis.* Former director, Biblical School. Jerusalem, 12 May 1983.

Werblowski, Zwi, Dr. Professor of Comparative Religion, Hebrew Univ. Jerusalem, 2 May 1983.

Wigoder, Geofrey, Dr. Vice-Chairman of the Council on Interfaith Relations. Jerusalem, 26 April 1983.

Yunes, Manuel, Dr. Former member, Lebanese Parliament. Beirut, 1 June 1983.

Published

Official Documents (Great Britain)

Hachey, Thomas E., ed. *Anglo-Vatican Relations, 1914–1939: Confidential Annual Reports of the British Ministries to the Holy See. Her Majesty's Stationery Office, London, England.* Boston, MA: G. K. Hall, 1972.

The Holy See and the Catholic Church

Abbott, Walter M., S.J. Gen. ed. *The Documents of Vatican II.* Piscataway, NJ: Association Press, New Century Publishers, 1966.

Blet, Pierre; Graham, Robert A.; Martini, Angelo; and Schneider, Burkhart, eds. *Actes et Documents du Saint-Siège relatifs à la Seconde Guerre Mondiale.* Vatican City: Libreria Editrice Vaticana, 1965–1980.

Blet, Pierre; Martini, Angelo; and Schneider, Burkhart, eds. *The Holy See and the War in Europe, March 1939-August 1940. Records and Documents of the Holy See Relating to the Second World War,* vol. 1. Washington, DC: Corpus Books, 1965.

Carlen, Claudia, I. H. M., compiler. *The Papal Encyclicals, 1958–1981.* Raleigh, NC: McGrath Publishing, 1981.

Hoch, Marie Thérèse, and Dupuy, Bernard, compilers. *Les Eglises devant le Judaisme: Documents officiels, 1948–1978.* Paris: Les Editions du Cerf, 1980.

Insegnamenti di Paolo VI, vol. 12. Vatican City: Tipografia Poliglotta Vaticana, 1974.

National Conference of Catholic Bishops (USA). "Statement on the Middle East."

Oriente Cattolico. Cenni Storici e Statistiche. Vatican City: Sacra Congregazione per le Chiese Orientali, 4th ed., 1974.

Il Pellegrinaggio di Paolo VI in Terra Santa (4–6 Gennaio 1964). Vatican City: Libreria Editrice Vaticana, 1964.

Pilgrim of Peace: The Homilies and Addresses of His Holiness Pope John Paul II on the Occasion of His Visit to the United States of America, October 1979. Washington, DC: Publications Office, United States Catholic Conference, 1979.

The Pursuit of Peace with Justice. Washington, DC: US Catholic Conference, 16 Nov. 1978.

Segretariato per i Non-Cristiani. *Chiesa e Islam.* Vatican City: Tipografia Poliglotta Vaticana, 1981.

Sestrieri, L., and Cereti, G., compilers. *Le Chiese Cristiane e l'Ebraismo, 1947–1982.* Casale Monferrato: Casa Editrice Marietti, 1983.

Vian, Nello, compiler. *Anni e Opere di Paolo VI.* Rome: Istituto della Enciclopedia Italiana, 1978.

Jerusalem

Collin, Bernardin, compiler. *Recueil de Documents concernant Jérusalem et les Lieux Saints.* Jerusalem: Franciscan Printing Press, 1982.

Jerusalem: A Collection of United Nations Documents. Beirut: Institute for Palestine Studies, 1970.

Lebanon

Le livre blanc libanais: Documents diplomatiques, 1975–1976. Beirut: République Libanaise, Ministère des Affaires Etrangères et des Libanais d'Outre-Mer, 1976.

United States of America

Statement of Lawrence S. Eagleburger, Undersecretary for Political Affairs, Department of State, before the Senate Foreign Relations Committee. US Senate. 23 Feb 1984, on S. 2031.

U.S. Congress, Senate, 94th Cong., 2nd Session. "Prospects for Peace in the Middle East." *Hearings before the Subcommittee on Near Eastern and South Asian Affairs of the Committee on Foreign Relations.* Washington, DC: US Government Printing Office, 1976.

Private Papers (Israel)

Meir, Golda. *My Life.* New York: Dell Publishing, 1975.
Patai, Raphael, ed. *The Complete Diaries of Theodor Herzl,* 5
    vols. New York and London: Herzl Press and Thomas Yo-
    seloff, 1960.
Sokolow, Florian. *Nahum Sokolow: Life and Legend.* London:
    Jewish Chronicle Publications, 1975.
Weizmann, Chaim. *Trial and Error.* New York: Harper and
    Brothers, 1949.

Newspaper and Periodical Sources

Commonweal. 11 Jan. 1985.
La Documentation Catholique. 20 March 1983.
Al-Fajr. 19 Aug. 1983.
Al-Fusul al-Lubnaniyya. Spring 1980; Summer 1980.
Al-Hawadess. 25 Aug. 1978; 15 Dec. 1978.
The Jerusalem Post. 3 Jan. 1969; 15 Jan. 1973; 17 Jan. 1973,
    18 Jan. 1973; 21 Jan. 1973; 2 Nov. 1977; 7 Nov. 1977; 1
    Feb. 1980; 29 March 1981.
The Jerusalem Post Magazine. 17 May 1974.
Jeune Afrique. 19 Jan. 1971.
Jewish Telegraphic Agency. 8 Oct. 1980.
The Link. May-June 1974.
Magazine. 18 May 1984.
Al-Masirat. 1 Nov. 1982.
Le Monde. 7–8 April 1974; 17 Sep. 1982.
Le Monde: Dossiers et Documents. Oct. 1982.
An-Nahar. 10 Dec. 1978; 12 Dec. 1978.
An-Nahar Arab and International. 18 Dec. 1978; 22–28 Aug.
    1983; 14–20 May 1984; 13–19 Aug. 1984.
NC News. 26 Nov. 1984.
The New York Times. 22 Oct. 1984; 26 Nov. 1984.
L'Orient Le-Jour. 8 Nov. 1975; 17 April 1976; 18 April 1976;
    28 April 1976; 8 Aug. 1978; 8 Dec. 1978; 20 Dec. 1978; 23
    June 1981.
Origins. 23 Sep. 1982; 30 Sep. 1982; 24 May 1984.
L'Osservatore della Domenica. 5 Oct. 1975.
L'Osservatore Romano. 28 May 1948; 30 Dec. 1968; 25 March
    1971; 15-16 Jan. 1973; 23 Dec. 1975; 12 Feb. 1976; 6 April

1976; 30 April 1978; 29 Sep. 1978; 7–8 June 1982; 23 Sep. 1982.

L'Osservatore Romano, English ed. 10 Nov. 1977; 1 July 1980; 10 Oct. 1983; 19 Dec. 1983; 20 April 1984.

Philadelphia Enquirer. 19 Sept. 1982.

The Pilot. 7 Aug. 1971; 6 May 1983.

Proche-Orient Chrétien. 14 (1964); 18 (1968); 19 (1969); 23 (1973); 24 (1974); 25 (1975); 26 (1976); 27 (1977); 28 (1978); 30 (1980); 31 (1981); 32 (1982).

Le Réveil. 5 April 1977; 18 April 1978; 13 Aug. 1978; 6 Dec. 1978.

The Tablet. 28 July 1979.

At-Tadamon. 2 July 1983.

The Times. 21 Apr. 1984.

The Troy Record. 30 March, 1970.

The Washington Post. 6 Oct. 1980.

Secondary Sources

Books

Ajami, Fouad. *The Arab Predicament: Arab Political Thought and Practice since 1967.* Cambridge, MA: Cambridge Univ. Press, 1981.

Amel, Mahdi. *Bahs fi Asbab al-Harb al-Ahliyya fi Lubnan.* Vol. 1. Beirut: Dar al-Farabi, 1979.

————. *Al-Qadiyya al-Filistiniyya fi Idiolojiat al-Burjuazia al-Lubnaniyya.* Beirut: Research Center, Palestine Liberation Organization, 1980.

Arberry, A. J., ed., *Religion in the Middle East: Three Religions in Concord and Conflict.* Vol. 1, *Judaism and Christianity*; vol. 2, *Islam.* London: Cambridge Univ. Press, 1969.

Atallah, Daad Bou Malhab. *Le Liban: Guerre civile ou conflit international.* Beirut: Al-Hurriyat, 1980.

Aubert, Roger, ed. *The Church in a Secularised Society.* Vol. 5, *The Christian Centuries.* New York: Paulist Press, 1978.

Baz, Selim. *Pièces diplomatiques relatives aux événements de 1860 au Liban.* Beirut: Librairie Orientale, 1978.

Benassar. *Anatomie d'une guerre et d'une occupation. Evénements du Liban de 1975 à 1978.* Paris: Editions Galilée, 1978.

_____. *Paix d'Israël au Liban.* Beirut: Les Editions L'Orient-Le Jour, May 1983.

Berger, Elmer, Rabbi. "Jerusalem in Jewish Perspectives." In *Jerusalem: Key to Peace in the Middle East*, ed. O. Kelly Ingram. Durham, NC: Triangle Friends of the Middle East, 1978.

Betts, Robert Brenton. *Christians in the Arab East: A Political Study.* Atlanta, GA: John Knox Press, 1978.

Bourgi, Albert and Weiss, Pierre. *Les Complots Libanais.* Paris: Berger-Levrault, 1978.

_____. *Liban: La cinquième guerre du Proche-Orient.* Paris: Editions Publisud, 1983.

Bovis, H. Eugene. *The Jerusalem Question, 1917–1968.* Stanford, CA: Hoover Institution Press, 1971.

Braude, Benjamin, and Lewis, Bernard, eds. *Christians and Jews in the Ottoman Empire.* Vol. 1, *The Central Lands*; vol. 2, *The Arab-Speaking Lands.* New York: Holmes and Meir Publishers, 1982.

Cardinale, H. E. *The Holy See and the International Order.* England: Colin Smythe, 1976.

Casaroli, Agostino. *La Santa Sede fra tensioni e distensione.* Turin: Elle Di Ci, Collana "Vita della Chiesa," no. 22, 1978.

Cattan, Henry. *Jerusalem.* London: Croom Helm, 1981.

Chamoun, Camille. *Crise au Moyen-Orient.* Paris: Gallimard, 1963.

_____. *Crise au Liban.* Beirut: n.p., 1977.

Chamussy, René. *Chronique d'une guerre: Le Liban, 1975–1977.* Paris: Desclée, 1978.

Colbi, S. P. "The Christian Establishment in Jerusalem." In *Jerusalem: Problems and Prospects*, ed. Joel L. Kramer. New York: Praeger, 1980.

_____. *The Christian Churches in the State of Israel.* Jerusalem: The Israel Economist, 3rd rev. ed., March 1982.

Collin, Bernardin. *Le Problème Juridique des Lieux-Saints.* Paris: Sirey, 1956.

_____. *Les Lieux-Saints*, Coll., Que-Sais-Je? Paris: Presses Universitaires de France, 2nd ed., 1968.

_____. *Pour une Solution au Problème des Lieux-Saints.* Paris: Maisonneuve et Larose, 1974.

_____. *Rome, Jérusalem, et les Lieux Saints.* Paris: Editions Franciscaines, 1981.

A Compassionate Peace: A Future for the Middle East. A Report Prepared for the American Friends Service Committee. New York: Hill and Wang, 1982.

Corbon, Jean. *L'Eglise des Arabes*. Paris: Editions du Cerf, 1977.

Croner, Helga, compiler. *Stepping Stones to Further Jewish-Christian Relations*. London, New York: Stimulus Books, 1977.

Dahdah, Nagib. *Evolution historique du Liban*. Beirut: Librairie du Liban, 1968.

Dawisha, Adeed I. *Syria and the Lebanese Crisis*. New York: St. Martin's Press, 1980.

De Bar, Luc-Henri. *Les communautés confessionnelles du Liban*. Paris: Editions Recherches sur les Civilisations, 1983.

Dreyfus, Paul. *Jean XXIII*. Paris: Librairie Arthème Fayard, 1979.

Dubois, Marcel. "The Catholic View." *Encyclopaedia Judaica Yearbook, 1974*. Jerusalem: Keter Publishing House, 1974.

Dupuy, André. *La diplomatie du Saint-Siège*. Paris: Tequi, 1980.

Enardu, Maria Grazia. *Palestine in Anglo-Vatican Relations, 1936–1939*. Florence, Italy: Cooperativa Universitaria Firenze, 1980.

Al-Faruqi, Ismail R. "The Islamic Faith and the Problem of Israel and Jerusalem." *Jerusalem: The Key to World Peace*. London: Islamic Council of Europe, 1980.

Fattal, Antoine. *Le Statut Légal des non-Musulmans en pays d'Islam*. Beirut: Imprimerie Catholique, 1958.

Feldblum, Esther Yolles. *The American Catholic Press and the Jewish State, 1917–1959*. New York: KTAV Publishing House, 1977.

Flannery, Austin P., ed. *Documents of Vatican II*. Grand Rapids, MI: William B. Erdman's Publishing Company, 1975.

Friedlander, Saul. *Pius XII and the Third Reich: A Documentation*. New York: Alfred A. Knopf, 1966.

Gilbert, Arthur. *The Vatican Council and the Jews*. Cleveland, OH: World Publishing Company, 1968.

Gordon, David C. *The Republic of Lebanon: Nation in Jeopardy*. Boulder, CO: Westview Press, 1983.

Granfield, Patrick. *The Papacy in Transition*. Garden City, NY: Doubleday, 1980.

Hajjar, J. "The Eastern Churches," In *The Church in a Secularised Society*. Vol. 5, the Christian Centuries, ed. Rogert Aubert. New York: Paulist Press, 1st ed., 1978.

Hofmann, Paul. *O Vatican!* New York! Congdon and Weed, 1984.

Hudson, Michael C. *The Precarious Republic: Political Modernization in Lebanon.* New York: Random House, 1968.

———. *Arab Politics: The Search for Legitimacy.* New Haven, CT: Yale Univ. Press, 1977.

Institute of Palestine Studies. *Jerusalem: A Collection of United Nations Documents.* Beirut, 1970.

Jabre, Antoine. *La Guerre du Liban: Moscou et la crise du Proche-Orient.* Paris: Pierre Belfond, 1980.

Jaeger, D.-M.A., ed. *Christianity in the Holy Land: Papers Read at the 1979 Tantur Conference on Christianity in the Holy Land.* Jerusalem: Franciscan Printing Press, 1981.

Al-Jisr, Bassim. *Mitha'k 1943.* Beirut: An-Nahar, 1978.

Joumblatt, Kamal, *Pour le Liban.* Paris: Editions Stock, 1978.

Kapeliouk, Amnon. *Sabra et Chatila: Enquête sur un Massacre.* Paris: Editions du Seuil, 1982.

Al-Kassem, Anis. *Nahnu wal Vatikan wa Israil.* Beirut; PLO Research Center, June 1966.

Khalidi, Walid. *Conflict and Violence in Lebanon: Confrontation in the Middle East.* Cambridge, MA: Harvard Center for International Affairs, 1979.

Khater, Lahd. *Al-Vatikan wa Lubnan.* Sidon, Lebanon: Manshurat Majallat al-Risala al-Mukhlisiyya, 1966.

El-Khoury, Yussuf, Father, ed. *Bulus as-Sadis fi watan al-Masih.* Kaslik, Lebanon: Manshurat Ma'had al-Ruh al-Kuds, 1964.

Khouri, Fred J. *The Arab-Israeli Dilemma.* Syracuse, NY: Syracuse Univ. Press, 2nd ed., 1980.

Khoury, Rafiq. *La catéchèse dans l'Eglise locale de Jérusalem: Histoire, situation actuelle et perspectives d'avenir.* Rome: Pontificia Università Lateranense, 1978.

Khuwayri, Antoine. *Mausuat al-Harb fi Lubnan, 1975–1981,* 12 vols. Jounieh, Lebanon: Dar al-Abjadiyya lil Sahafa wal Tiba'a wal Nashr, 1975–1981.

———. *Hawadith Lubnan, 1975,* vol. 1. Jounieh: Al-Bulusiya Press, 1976.

———. *Al-Harb fi Lubnan, 1976,* vol. 2. Jounieh: Al-Bulusiya Press, 1977.

———. *Hawadith Lubnan, 1977–78,* vol. 6, *Wa Akhiran Harakuh.* Jounieh: Manshurat Dar al-Abjadiyya, 1978.

———. *Hawadith Lubnan, 1980,* vol. 9, *Lubnan bayn al-Shariat wal Ihtilal.* Jounieh: Dar al-Abjadiyya Lil Sahafa wal Tiba'a wal Nashr, 1982.

Kramer, Joel L., ed. *Jerusalem: Problems and Prospects.* New York: Praeger Publishers for CBS Education and Professional Publishing, 1980.

Kriegel, Annie. *Israël est-il Coupable?* Paris: Robert Laffont, 1982.

Kuderna, Michael. *Christliche Gruppen im Libanon.* Wiesbaden: Franz Steiner Verlag, 1983.

Lapide, Pinchas E. *Three Popes and the Jews.* New York: Hawthorn Books, 1967.

Latin Patriarchate of Jerusalem. *The Religious Situation in the Holy Land and the Specific Task of Catholics.* Jerusalem, 1977.

Lauterpacht, Elihu. *Jerusalem and the Holy Places.* London: Anglo-Israel Association, December 1980 (pamphlet no. 19).

Lelong, Michel. *Guerre ou paix à Jérusalem?* Paris: Albin Michel, 1982.

Le Morzellec, Joelle. *La question de Jérusalem devant l'Organisation des Nations-Unies.* Brussels: Establissements Emile Bruylant, 1979.

Lenormant, François. *Une persécution du Christianisme en 1860.* Jounieh: Dar al-Abjadyya, 1983.

Lumières franches sur la crise libanaise. Coll., "Question Libanaise." Kaslik: Publications de l'Université Saint-Esprit, 1975 (pamphlet no. 3).

Mansfield, Peter. "From British Mandate to the Present Day." In *Jerusalem: The Key to World Peace.* London: Islamic Council of Europe, 1980.

Matar, Fuad. *Suqut al-Imbraturiyya al-Lubnaniyya.* Vol. 1, *Al-Sharara.* Beirut: Dar al Qadaya, 1976.

_____. Vol. 3, *Al-Inquisam.* Beirut: Dar al Qadaya, 1976.

Mendes, Meir. *The Vatican and Israel.* Jerusalem: Leonard Davis Institute for International Relations, Hebrew Univ. of Jerusalem, 1983.

Mezvinsky, Norton. "The Jewish Faith and the Problem of Israel and Jerusalem," in *Jerusalem: The Key to World Peace.* London: Islamic Council of Europe, 1980.

Middle East Council of Churches. *Jerusalem, Dossier III.* Beirut, 1979.

Al-Montada Reports. *The Lebanese Conflict, 1975–1979: Dossier*

2. Beirut: Middle East Council of Churches Documentation and Information, 1979.

Montoisy, J. D. *Le Vatican et le problème des Lieux Saints.* Jerusalem: Franciscan Printing Press, 1984.

Morley, John F. *Vatican Diplomacy and the Jews during the Holocaust, 1939–1943.* New York: KTAV Publishing House, 1980.

Moubarac, Youakim. *Les Chrétiens et le monde Arabe. Vol. 4, Pentalogie Islamo-Chrétienne.* Beirut: Editions du Cénacle Libanais, 1972–73.

_____. *Recherches sur la pensée chrétienne et l'Islam dans les temps modernes et à l'époque contemporaine.* Beirut: Publications de l'Université Libanaise, 1977.

Nasr, J. A. *Mihnat Lubnan fi Thawrat al-Yasar.* Beirut: Dar-al-'Amal, 1977.

Nasr, Nicolas. *Harb Lubnan wa Madaha.* Beirut: Dar al-'Amal, 1977.

Norton, Augustus Richard. "Harakat Amal (The Movement of Hope)." In *Religion and Politics, Political Anthropology,* vol. 3, ed. Myron Aronoff, New Brunswick, NJ: Transaction Books, 1984.

Nuseibeh, Hazem Zaki. *Palestine and the United Nations.* New York: Quartet Books, 1981.

Olmert, Yossef. *Lebanon's Christians and Israel.* Research Report no. 15. London: Institute for Jewish Affairs, Oct. 1982.

Pakradouni, Karim. *La paix manquée: Le mandat d'Elias Sarkis, 1976–1982.* Beirut: Editions Fiches du Monde Arabe, 1983.

Palestine Liberation Organization. *Tall-al-Zaatar: The Fight Against Fascism.* Beirut: Unified Information, Foreign Information Department, 1976.

Quandt, William B., Jabber, Fuad, and Mosley-Lesch, Ann. *The Politics of Palestinian Nationalism.* Berkeley: Univ. of California Press, 1973.

Qubain, Fahim L. *Crisis in Lebanon.* Washington, DC: Middle East Institute, 1961.

Rabbath, Edmond. *La formation historique du Liban politique et constitutionnel: Essai de synthèse.* Beirut: Publications de l'Université Libanaise, Librairie Orientale, 1973.

_____. *La Constitution Libanaise: Origines, textes et commentaires.* Beirut: Publications de l'Université Libanaise, 1982.

Rabinovich, Itamar. "The Limits of Military Power: Syria's Role." In *Lebanon in Crisis: Participants and Issues*, ed. P. Edward Haley and Lewis W. Snider. Syracuse, NY: Syracuse Univ. Press, 1979.

Rahmé, Georges. *Coordonnées de la crise libanaise*. Lebanon: Centre de Documentation et de Recherches (CEDRE), June 1, 1979.

Randall, Jonathan. *Going All the Way: Christian Warlords, Israeli Adventurers and the War in Lebanon*. New York: Viking Press, 1983.

Rash, Yehoshua. *Déminer un champ fertile: Les Catholiques Français et l'état d'Israël*. Paris: Les Editions du Cerf, 1982.

Ribet, Sergio. *Il nodo del conflitto libanese: Tra resistenza palestinese e destra maronita*. Turin: Claudiana, 1977.

Rizk, Charles. *Entre l'Islam et l'Arabisme: Les Arabes jusqu'en 1945*. Paris: Albin Michel, 1983.

Rodinson, Maxime. *The Arabs*. Chicago: Univ. of Chicago Press, 1981.

Rokach, Livia. *Israel's Sacred Terrorism. A Study Based on Moshe Sharett's Personal Diary and Other Documents*. Belmont, MA: Association of Arab-American Univ. Graduates, 1982.

Rulli, Giovanni, S.J. *Il problema di Gerusalemme*. Rome: La Civiltà Cattolica, n.d.

Ryan, Joseph L. "Jerusalem in Roman Catholic Perspectives." In *Jerusalem: Key to Peace in the Middle East*, ed. O. Kelly Ingram. Durham, NC: Triangle Friends of the Middle East, 1978.

———. "The Catholic Faith and the Problem of Israel and Jerusalem." In *Jerusalem: The Key to World Peace*. London: Islamic Council of Europe, 1980.

———. "Religion and the United States Foreign Policy towards the Middle East: A Catholic Perspective." In *American Church Politics and the Middle East*, ed. Basheer K. Nijim. Belmont, MA: Association of Arab-American University Graduates, 1982.

Ryan, Joseph T., D. D., Archbishop. "Some Thoughts on Jerusalem." For private circulation, n.d.

Ryan, J. T. "Catholic Near East Welfare Association." *New Catholic Encyclopedia*, vol. 3. Washington, DC: Catholic Univ. of America, 1967.

Sadaka, Linda, and Salam, Nawaf, compilers. *The Civil War in Lebanon 1975–1976: A Bibliographical Guide.* Beirut: Center for Middle East Studies, American Univ. of Beirut, 1982.

Said, Edward. *The Question of Palestine.* New York: Times Books, 1979.

Sayegh, S. *Le statu quo des Lieux-Saints, Nature juridique et portée internationale.* Rome: Libreria Editrice della Pontificia Università Lateranense, 1971.

Setton, Kenneth M. *The Thirteenth and Fourteenth Centuries.* Vol. 1, *The Papacy and the Levant (1204–1511).* Philadelphia, PA: American Philosophical Society, 1976.

Snider, Lewis W., Haley, P. Edward, Wagner, Abraham R., and Cohen, Nicki J. "Israel." In *Lebanon in Crisis: Participants and Issues,* ed. P. Edward Haley and Lewis W. Snider. Syracuse, NY: Syracuse Univ. Press, 1979.

Sofer, Naim. "The Political Status of Jerusalem in the Hashemite Kingdom of Jordan, 1948–1967." In *Palestine and Israel in the 19th and 20th Centuries,* ed. Elie Kedourie and Sylvia Haim. London: Frank Cass, 1982.

Spiller, Roger J. *"Not War but Like War": The American Intervention in Lebanon.* Leavenworth Papers no. 3. Fort Leavenworth, KS: Combat Studies Institute, US Army Command and General Staff College, 1981.

"Statement Issued on May 2, 1973, in Which More than 40 Jesuits Reject the Declaration (Orientations Pastorales) of the French Bishop's Committee for Relations with Judaism" (mimeographed).

Stein, Leonard. *The Balfour Declaration.* London: Vallentine, Michell, 1961.

Stookey, Robert W. "The United States." In *Lebanon in Crisis: Participants and Issues,* ed. P. Edward Haley and Lewis W. Snider. Syracuse: Syracuse Univ. Press, 1979.

Suleiman, Michael W. *Political Parties in Lebanon: The Challenge of a Fragmented Political Culture.* Ithaca: Cornell Univ. Press, 1967.

Tarikh Hizb al-Kata'ib Al-Lubnaniyya, 1936–1946, 2 vols. Beirut: Dar al-'Amal lil Nashr, 1979, 1981.

Tibawi, A. L. *Jerusalem: Its Place in Islam and Arab History.* Monograph Series no. 19. Beirut: Institute for Palestine Studies, 1969.

Touval, Saadia. *The Peace Brokers: Mediators in the Arab-Israeli Conflict, 1948–1979.* Princeton: Princeton Univ. Press, 1982.

Tschirgi, Daniel, with Irani, George. *The United States, Syria, and the Lebanese Crisis.* Research Note no. 8. Los Angeles: UCLA, Center for International and Strategic Affairs, Jan. 1982.

Vallier, Ivan. *Catholicism, Social Control, and Modernization in Latin America.* Englewood Cliffs, NJ: Prentice-Hall, 1970.

———. "The Roman Catholic Church: A Transnational Actor." In *Transnational Relations in World Politics*, ed. R. O. Keohane and J. S. Nye. Cambridge, MA: Harvard Univ. Press, 1976.

Werblowski, R. J. Zwi. *Gerusalemme: Città Santa di tre religioni.* Jerusalem: Hebrew Univ., March 1976.

Williams, George H. *The Mind of John Paul II: Origins of His Thought and Action.* New York: Seabury Press, 1981.

———. *The Contours of Church and State in the Thoughts of John Paul II.* Monograph Series, Institute of Church-State Studies. Waco, TX: Baylor Univ. Press, 1983.

Wilson, Evan M. *Jerusalem, Key to Peace.* Washington, DC: Middle East Institute, 1970.

Zananiri, Gaston, O.P. *Pape et patriarches.* Paris: Nouvelles Editions Latines, 1962.

———. *L'Eglise et l'Islam.* Paris: Spes, 1969.

Zander, Walter. *Israel and the Holy Places of Christendom.* New York: Praeger Publishers, 1971.

Zhibian, Sami. *Al-Haraka al-Wataniyya al-Lubnaniyya.* Beirut: Dar al-Masirat, 1977.

Zizola, Giancarlo. *The Utopia of Pope John XXIII.* Maryknoll, NY: Orbis Books, 1978.

Articles

Al-Laouzi, Salim. ["Is all hope lost to see the Maronites back in the Arab fold?"] *Al-Hawadess* (15 Dec. 1978) 17–24.

Aucagne, Jean, S.J. "Qui donc informe le pape?" *Le Réveil* (15 April 1978).

Beccalli, Anna. "Gerusalemme e la posizione della Santa Sede." *Il Politico* (March 1974) 118–26.

Borrmans, Maurice. "Le Séminaire du Dialogue Islamo-Chrétien de Tripoli (Libye) (1–6 fev. 1946)." *IslamoChristiana*, 2 (1976) 135–70.

Bulletin of the Christian Information Center, Jerusalem, 15 Feb. 1974.

Cartus, F. E. "Vatican II and the Jews." *Commentary*, 30/1 (Jan. 1965) 19–29.

Chamussy, René. "Le Liban: La mise à mort." *Etudes* (March 1976), 344–48.

Cobban, Helena. "Lebanon's Chinese Puzzle." *Foreign Policy*, 53 (Winter 1983–84) 34–48.

"Commentaries: The Papacy and the Holocaust." *Social Science and Modern Society*, 20/3 (March-April 1983).

Conzemius, Victor. "Le Saint-Siège et la Deuxième Guerre Mondiale, Deux éditions de sources." *Revue d'histoire de la Deuxième Guerre Mondiale et des conflits contemporains*, 128 (Oct. 1982) 71–94.

Corm, Georges. "Du Libanisme a la Libanité: Réflexions sur les minorités chrétiennes." *Esprit* (May-June 1983) 91–100.

Donovan, Thomas A. "The Vatican Foreign Service." *Foreign Service Journal* (Feb. 1976) 19–21.

Dubois, Marcel. "The Catholic Church and the State of Israel Thirty Years After." *Encounter Today*, 14/4 (Spring-Summer 1980) 167–78.

Evans, Anita. "Bethlehem U: New Hope for West Bankers." *The Daily Star* (6 April 1975) no. 8394.

Ferrari, Silvio. "La Santa Sede e il problema della Palestina nel Secondo Dopoguerra." *Communità* (185) 400–46.

_____. "Il Vaticano e la questione di Gerusalemme nel carteggio Spellman-Truman," *Storia Contemporanea*, 13/2 (April 1982) 285–320.

_____. "The Holy See and the Postwar Palestine Issue: The Internationalization of Jerusalem and the Protection of the Holy Places." *International Affairs*, 60/2 (Spring 1984) 261–83.

Fisher, Eugene. "Catholics and Jews." *The Tablet*, 17 (Sept. 1983) 888–90.

_____. "A New Maturity in Christian-Jewish Dialogue: An Annotated Bibliography 1973–1983." *Face to Face: An Interreligious Bulletin*, 11 (Spring 1984) 29–63.

_____. "The Pope and Israel." *Commonweal* (11 Jan. 1985) 16–17.

Flannery, Edward H. "Anti-Zionism and the Christian Psyche." *Journal of Ecumenical Studies*, 6/2 (Spring 1969) 173–84.

————. "The Controversy over Jerusalem: Elements of a Solution." Secretariat for Catholic-Jewish Relations in the United States, Oct. 1971 (mimeographed).

————. "A Second Report on Jerusalem." Secretariat for Catholic-Jewish Relations in the United States, Apr. 1972 (mimeographed).

Fry, Michael G. "United States Policy in the Middle East: Lebanon and the Palestinian Question." *Arab Studies Quarterly*, 7/1 (Winter 1985) 27–35.

Journal of Palestine Studies. Special issue on the war in Lebanon, 11/4; 12/1 (Summer-Fall 1982), issue nos. 44/45.

Kassis, Sharbel. Interview in *Al-Fusul al-Lubnaniyya*, 2 (Spring 1980) 58–62.

Klein, Charlotte. "Vatican and Zionism, 1897–1967." *Christian Attitude on Jews and Judaism*, 36–37 (June-Aug. 1974) 11–16.

————. "In the Mirror of *Civiltà Cattolica*: Vatican View of Jewry, 1939–1962." *Christian Attitudes on Jews and Judaism*, 43 (Aug. 1975) 12–16.

Kossaifi, Joseph. "Dawr al-Vatikan fi al-Alam, al-Arabi." *At Tadamon*, 12 (2 July 1983) 8–10.

Laham, Lutfi. "Qu'est-ce que l'Eglise de Jérusalem?" (mimeographed paper).

Laqueur, Walter. "Zionism and its Liberal Critics, 1896–1948." *Journal of Contemporary History*, 6/4 (1971) 161–82.

Maxwell, Ed. "Palestine Refugees Key to Peace: Msgr. Nolan." *The Troy Record*, 30 March 1970.

"Les médiations étrangères." *Problèmes Politiques et Sociaux* (20 Aug. 1976) 51–55.

Mejia, Jorge Msgr. "Pope John Paul II and the Jews." Paper presented at the Institute for Judaeo-Christian Studies, Seton Hall Univ., Orange, NJ, 1 May 1983 (mimeographed).

Montoisy, Jean-Dominique. "Israel-Vatican: Le nouveau dialogue." *Studia Diplomatica*, 34/6 (1981) 753–70.

Moubarac, Youakim. "La question de Jérusalem." *Revue d'Etudes Palestiniennes*, 4 (Summer 1982) 3–55.

————. "La question de Jérusalem (2)." *Revue d'Etudes Palestiniennes* 6 (Winter 1983) 35–87.

Murphy, William F. "The Holy See and the Middle East." *The Pilot*, 29 April 1983; 6 May 1983.

Naaman, Boulos. Interview in *Al-Fusul al-Lubnaniyya*, 3 (Summer 1980) 82–86.

Nasrallah, Joseph. "Les Chrétiens et le Nationalisme Arabe." *France-Pays Arabes*, 105 (Jan.-Feb. 1983) 40–43.

"Notre Dame de France à Jérusalem." Latin Patriarchate [Jerusalem], special issue, *Bulletin Diocésain* (Apr. 1971), 2–16.

Novak, Michael. "Creation Theology—John Paul II and the American Experience." *This World*, 3 (Fall 1982) 71–88.

Pastorelli, Pietro. "La Santa Sede e il problema di Gerusalemme." *Storia e Politica*, 1 (1982) 57–98.

Perlmutter, Amos. "Begin's Rhetoric and Sharon's Tactics." *Foreign Affairs* (Fall 1982) 68–83.

Picard, Elizabeth. "Rôle et Evolution du Front Libanais dans la Guerre Civile." *Maghreb-Machrek*, 90 (Oct.-Dec. 1980) 16–39.

Quandt, William B. "Reagan's Lebanon Policy: Trial and Error." *The Middle East Journal*, 28/2 (Spring 1984) 237–54.

Rabbath, Edmond. "Du régime communautaire au confessionalisme." *Esprit*, 5–6 (May-June 1983) 74–82.

Rahman, F. "Islam's Attitude toward Judaism." *Muslim World*, 72/1 (Jan. 1982) 1–13.

Rash, Yehoshua. "L'état d'Israël interroge l'Eglise." *Cahiers Universitaires Catholiques*, 5 (May-June 1980) 13–21.

_____. "Le Vatican et le conflit Israélo-Arabe." *Politique Internationale*, 13 (Autumn 1981) 259–74.

_____. "Jean Paul II, Arafat et Israel." *Tenou'a*, 32 (Oct. 1982).

_____. "Herzl, Weizmann, leurs papes et leurs cardinaux." *Sens*, 12 (Dec. 1983) 283–303.

Robbins, John E. "The Vatican's Political Role in the International Sphere." *International Perspectives* (Jan.-Feb. 1974) 44–46.

Rock, Albert, O.F.M. "Kadiyyat Al-Quds." *As-Salam Ual Khair* [Jerusalem] (1982) 13–16.

Rokach, Livia. "Arabs Worried by Vatican Shift on Middle East." *Middle East International*, 11 (April 1980) 3.

Rondot, Philippe. "Antoine Pierre Khoraiche, Patriarche Maronite d'Antioche et de tout l'Orient." *Maghreb-Machrek*, 78 (Oct.-Dec. 1977) 21–25.

Rossano, Pietro, "Les grands documents de L'Eglise au sujet des Musulmans." *IslamoChristiana* [Rome], 8 (1982) 13–23.

Rulli, Giovanni. "L'invasione Israeliana nel Libano." *La Civiltà Cattolica*, 3169 (3 July 1982) 84–91.

Ryan, Joseph L. "Anti-Zionism and Anti-Semitism." *Journal of Ecumenical Studies*, 7/2 (Spring 1970) 321–24.

———. "Vatican II and Muslims: Five Years Later." *Homiletic and Pastoral Review*, 71 (May 1971) 60–65.

———. "Palestinian Rights: Resonances in the Life and Times of Pope John Paul II." Paper presented at the Fifth UN Seminar on the Inalienable Rights of the Palestinian People, 15–19 March 1982, UN Headquarters, New York (mimeographed).

Sharett, Yaacov. "L'état juif et l'intégrité du Liban." *Le Monde Diplomatique* (Dec. 1983) 16–17.

Tsimhoni, Daphne. "The Greek Orthodox Community in Jerusalem and the West Bank, 1948–1978: A Profile of a Religious Minority in a National State." *Orient*, 23/2 (June 1982) 281–98.

———. "Demographic Trends of the Christian Population in Jerusalem and the West Bank, 1948–1978." *The Middle East Journal*, 37/1 (Winter 1983) 54–64.

Werblowski, R. J. Zwi. "Jewish-Christian Relations with Particular Reference to the Contribution of the State of Israel." *Christian News from Israel*, 24/2–3 (14–15) (Autumn-Winter 1973) 116–21.

Williams, George Huntston, "John Paul II's Concepts of Church, State, and Society." *Journal of Church and State*, 24/3 (Autumn 1982) 463–96.

———. "The Ecumenism of John Paul II." *Journal of Ecumenical Studies*, 19/4 (Fall 1982) 681–718.

Unpublished Dissertations

Beggiani, Seely Joseph, Rev. "The Relations of the Holy See and the Maronites from the Papacy of Pope Gregory XIII (1572–1585) to the Synod of Mount Lebanon in 1736." Catholic Univ. of America, 1963.

Garber, George. "The Impact of the Establishment of the State of Israel on the Attitude of the Catholic Church towards Israel during the Years 1943–1975, as Reflected in American Catholic Periodicals." New York Univ., 1976.

Kerr, David. "The Temporal Authority of the Maronite Patriarchate, 1920–1958: A Study in the Relationship of Religious and Secular Power." Oxford Univ., 1973.

Konczakowski, Edmund Francis. "Vatican Policy toward the German-Polish Oder-Neisse Line: A Study of Foreign Policy Evolution, 1945–1972." Univ. of Pennsylvania, 1976.

Rose, Emanuel. "Jews and Judaism in Vatican II." Hebrew Union College, Jewish Institute of Religion, May 1969.

Index